MURDER
IN THE
GRAVEYARD

DON HALE

MURDER
IN THE
GRAVEYARD

A BRUTAL MURDER. A WRONGFUL CONVICTION.
A 27-YEAR FIGHT FOR JUSTICE.

HARPER
element

HarperElement
An imprint of HarperCollins*Publishers*
1 London Bridge Street
London SE1 9GF

www.harpercollins.co.uk

First published as *Town Without Pity* by Century,
an imprint of Random House 2002
This revised and updated edition published HarperElement 2019

3 5 7 9 10 8 6 4 2

© Don Hale 2019

A catalogue record of this book is
available from the British Library

ISBN 978-0-00-833162-7

Printed and bound in Great Britain by
CPI Group (UK) Ltd, Croydon

MIX
Paper from
responsible sources
FSC™ C007454

This book is dedicated to my wife Kath,
to my family and to everyone else who supported
my campaign for justice in any way

CONTENTS

CAST OF CHARACTERS

THE VICTIM AND HER FAMILY

Wendy Sewell
David Sewell
John Marshall

THE MAIN SUSPECT AND HIS FAMILY

Stephen Downing
Ray Downing
Juanita Downing
Christine Downing

PERSONS OF INTEREST

Mr Orange
Syd Oulsnam
Mr Red
Mr Blue (the running man)
The businessman

PRIVATE INVESTIGATOR AND INFORMANTS

Robert Ervin
Port Vale
Chelsea
Spurs

DERBYSHIRE POLICE

PC Ernie Charlesworth
PC Ball
Detective Younger
Detective Johnson
Detective Rodney Jones
Detective Superintendent Tom Naylor
Chief Constable John Newing
Deputy Chief Constable Don Dovaston

MATLOCK MERCURY STAFF

Sam Fay
Jackie Dunn
Norman Taylor
Marcus Edwards
Matt Barlow

OTHER JOURNALISTS

Nick Pryer (*Mail on Sunday*)
Frank Curran (*Daily Star*)
Matthew Parris (*The Times*)

Rob Hollingsworth (*Sheffield Star*)
Allan Taylor (Central Television)

OFFICIALS

Patrick McLoughlin MP
CCRC Commissioner Barry Capon

WITNESSES

Charlie Carman
Wilf Walker
Peter Moran
Mr Watts
Mr Dawson
Louisa Hadfield
George Paling
Marie Bright
Jayne Atkins
Margaret Beebe
Ian Beebe
Lucy Beebe
John Osmaston
Rita
Ms Yellow
Cynthia Smithurst
Yvonne Spencer
Crabby
Steven Martin

MAP OF BAKEWELL CEMETERY

A: Anthony Naylor's grave on the lower path where Wendy was attacked, and where Stephen found her.

B: Sarah Bradbury's grave where Wendy had moved to after Stephen returned with Wilf Walker, and where she was seen by the workmen.

C: The consecrated chapel. Jayne Atkins saw Wendy on the path behind here embracing a man.

D: The spot where little Ian Beebe saw Wendy as he cycled up the middle path.

E: The unconsecrated chapel used as the workmen's store.

F: The Garden of Remembrance.

G: The Kissing Gate

H: The Gatekeeper's Lodge, home of Wilf Walker.

I: The main cemetery gates.

J: The phone box.

K: The back gate to the cemetery through which Jayne Atkins entered and left.

L: Syd Oulsnam's van was seen parked here.

M: Bakewell Methodist Junior School.

N: The spot where Louisa Hadfield saw the running man going towards Lady Manners School.

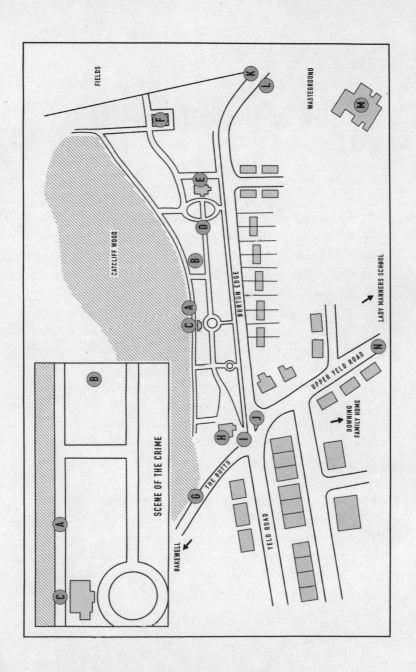

INTRODUCTION

It was a cold, drizzly night in March 1995, and I was working late at the *Matlock Mercury* office, with no one but my dog Jess for company, when the phone rang. It was a young woman on the other end of the line. She said there was a large fire at a nearby farm, which sounded serious and newsworthy to me.

I quickly grabbed my gear, cameras and all, and jumped in my car with Jess, who snuggled in her blanket on the back seat as we travelled through the bleak Derbyshire hills in the direction of the fire.

It was a challenging road at times, snaking its way through a barren landscape and miles upon miles of desperately bleak moorland. The road seemed totally deserted, and I was in an almost dream-like state navigating the deep dips of this roller-coaster track, when suddenly out of nowhere an enormous truck appeared right behind me, with its powerful headlights and a top searchlight burning into my rear-view mirror.

Dazzled by the lights, I slowed to let it pass, but the truck driver also slackened his speed, and remained directly behind me.

As I reached the location of the fire, all was calm and there wasn't even a whiff of smoke. I realised I had been the victim of a hoax. It was time to turn the car round and head for home. I swung into a lay-by, steering in a wide arc, and almost clipped the lorry as it clattered past.

That's the last I'll see of him, I thought, as I changed up into third gear. But then, to my surprise and shock, I saw this monster in my mirror, with its roaring engine, hissing air brakes and screeching tyres, also perform a spectacular U-turn in my wake.

The darkened cab was now illuminated. The driver appeared to be talking into a CB radio. I pressed down on the accelerator but the lorry was still gaining speed on me, and very rapidly. Jess whimpered softly, so I reached back and patted her head, taking my eyes off the road for a split second – and we almost took off on one of the major dips I subsequently misjudged.

It took a second or two to adjust my vision as the headlight beams bounced back off the dark, shiny road surface. There were no other vehicles on the road; it was just me and my pursuer. I turned off onto the narrow road which led back to Cromford and Matlock, and home – but still he followed.

I put my foot down, but I was now sweating with fear, my hands and legs trembling. It was pitch black apart from the dim lights of some distant farmhouse, and I knew I would have to slow down soon.

I decided to cut off the main road to the left, which would take me back down the valley towards the picturesque villages of Winster and Elton, on an even narrower road. If I could reach there, I'd surely be safe.

The lorry was so close it was almost in the back seat with Jess, and again its bright lights blazed into my mirrors.

I jumped out of my skin when its horn, a deep and very loud siren, blared repeatedly into my ears ... and then came the impact. A juddering bump in the rear, jolting my car forward.

The horn sounded again and again, and then another sickening bump. I had to think quickly. In a minute or so the junction down to Elton would appear on my left. Suddenly, I had an idea.

As the fork approached I signalled right then, at the very last moment, jerked the wheel and turned hard left. But the lorry driver copied my actions, clipping a signpost and ploughing over the grass verge in the process.

My head was throbbing, my blood pumping, and, as I wiped the sweat from my face, I knew the road would come to another T-junction in less than two miles. I was pushing 55 mph, as fast as I dared – it was too dark and the road too narrow to go any faster.

The horn sounded again, then another bang. As I was pushed away from each shunt, I noticed the driver was back on his CB radio again. It dawned on me that someone else must be involved.

The junction was now fast approaching, less than half a mile away. I could see a signpost in the distance and noticed a large, dark shape in the middle of the road, which seemed to be growing in size rapidly.

What the hell is it? I wondered, peering into the blackness. Five hundred yards and closing, three hundred and fifty yards and closing quickly.

Two hundred and fifty yards – and I was still travelling fast.

Christ, it's another truck!

A tipper truck was parked sideways across the road, totally blocking the way. There was a shadowy outline of someone standing near the front of the vehicle. He had some kind of large object in his hand. One hundred yards and my heart was racing. *Where could I go?*

As if in answer to my desperate plea, my headlights picked out a reflector on a small gatepost about fifty yards ahead. *Maybe there was an open gateway into a field.* It was too late for anything else. I touched the accelerator then immediately hit the brake and yanked the wheel hard left, ramming the car through the open gateway into a rain-sodden field. There was a terrific bang as the lorry hurtled past. Its airbrakes hissed, screeched and locked, but it was too late for it to stop. It skidded on the wet surface and slid hard into the side of the other truck.

The field sloped downwards slightly and away from the gate. It was a sea of wet grass and mud. I gripped the steering wheel with all my might in a desperate attempt to keep control and somehow managed to turn the car round in a large horseshoe to face the gate again. The rear wheels spun wildly, but I kept up the revs, spun back up the field and hastily drove back out of the same gate.

I didn't bother to look either way as I pulled out and roared back down the road. I was soaked with sweat, and through my rear-view mirror I could see white smoke and steam pouring from one of the lorries. Jess barked in defiance and, as I turned to offer a comforting hand, I noticed the driver-side mirror now hanging by a thread – just as my life had been.

All the way home I kept checking the rear-view mirror, any headlights causing my mind to whirl in a frenzy of paranoia and anxiety. The adrenaline continued to pour through my body.

Someone was definitely trying to kill me. I knew they had tried before, and it seemed certain that they would try again.

Yet I kept asking myself, if Stephen Downing had killed Wendy Sewell, why would anyone want to get rid of me?

CHAPTER 1

'STEPHEN WHO?'

There was nothing auspicious about that particular Monday, 14 March 1994. Certainly nothing to suggest that it would put in motion events that would help to change so many lives, and make an indelible mark on both British and European law.

In fact, the day started in domestic chaos, as I forgot to set the alarm following a late-night return from Amsterdam. My wife, Kath, had no choice but to dash off for work, while I did the school run, dropping off my youngest boy at Highfields School, and on the way back admired the spectacular panoramic view across Matlock and the Derbyshire Dales.

After a few days of luxury in Amsterdam it felt good to be home, and I was relieved to be heading back to reality at the *Matlock Mercury*. I was termed a 'foreigner' by many of the locals when I first moved to Matlock from Manchester. I was an outsider. But it was home for me now, the latest stop in a career in journalism that had seen me work for the likes of the BBC, the *Manchester Evening News*, and most recently the *Bury Messenger*, before the opportunity to head up the Mercury came along.

I parked up at the side of the office, and said hello to our stray tabby cat, who would often perch precariously on the upper window ledge, looking at us with a mischievous grin and probably thanking his lucky stars he didn't have to work in our building, a former print works that had definitely seen better days.

As I entered via the back door, I could hear the old typewriters clattering away and see my reporters going about their business.

'Good morning, everyone,' I said cheerfully, hoping they hadn't noticed that I was ten minutes late. 'Anything special happened since I've been away?'

Jackie Dunn, one of my young journalists, cheekily asked if my flight had been delayed, before she gave me a brief summary of events from the previous week.

My sports editor Norman Taylor, a retired train driver, said Matlock Town had still not scored – but had won a corner, a comment that earned a glare from Sam Fay, my deputy editor. A war veteran in his late sixties, he worked on a part-time basis, covering match reports and local politics.

I took my jacket off, settled down and began to plough my way through all the paperwork, while I asked Sam for a meeting to discuss stories for the next edition.

The small sliding window in the frosted glass partition, which divided editorial from the advertising department, suddenly slid open with a loud bang.

The receptionist announced, 'Don, there's a man wanting to make an appointment with you. He says it's something about a murder.'

She cupped her hand over the receiver. 'Do you want to take the call?' she asked. 'It's something to do with his son, Stephen.'

I beckoned to her to put the call through.

When I answered, the man chatted away at ten to the dozen. It was like trying to decipher a verbal machine gun. 'Stephen who?' I asked.

'Stephen Downing,' came the reply, sounding rather agitated, as if I should know all about him. The man explained that he was his father, Ray, and claimed his son was still in jail after 20-something years for a murder he didn't commit.

He said the murder had occurred in the cemetery at Bakewell, a pretty, picture-postcard market town in the Peak District, about eight miles away. I let him continue for a while before I interrupted, saying, 'It's all right, Mr Downing ...'

'Call me Ray,' he quickly replied.

'Okay then, Ray. You don't have to make an appointment to see me. I'm usually here from dawn till dusk.' I found it very difficult to take in half of what he'd said to me over the phone. 'Yes, Ray, 2.30 p.m. today is fine. And bring some paperwork with you if you wish. I'm not sure what I can do but I'll have a look.'

I looked round to see that some of my team were also listening. I told them, 'It's a Mr Downing, who says it's something to do with an old murder involving his son. I think he said it was in 1973. He's a local taxi driver, and both he and his wife want to see me today. This afternoon, in fact.'

Sam pulled out a cigarette and lit it. He frowned at me, and half spluttered, 'Don, I will have to go out for a short while but I'll speak with you later. We must have a chat about this Stephen Downing.' With that he disappeared in a trail of smoke.

*   *   *

At precisely 2.30 p.m. there was a knock on my office door. 'A Mr and Mrs Downing to see you, Don. They have an appointment?' said Susan, one of our advertising reps.

'Yes, of course, show them in, please,' I replied, and ushered the pair into my private office. Ray Downing was struggling to hold a large pile of documents, which he then dumped firmly on my desk. I had to move them aside slightly so I could see their faces.

Ray was a fairly small man with a bald head and a worried expression. I guessed he was probably in his late fifties or early sixties. His wife, whom he introduced as Juanita, was about the same age. She looked quite frail and had sharp, almost bird-like features. She was very nervous and extremely thin. Both wore their Sunday best.

Ray outlined his reasons for contacting me. He claimed his son Stephen had been jailed in 1974 for the murder of a woman in the town cemetery the previous year. Ray kept saying he was innocent, and that everyone in Bakewell knew he was innocent. He kept stressing that word.

'What's more,' said Ray, 'I can probably tell you who was responsible. Nearly everyone in Bakewell seems to know who did it.'

I was taken aback by his comments. Ray didn't mention any name, but I was puzzled by his claim and wondered, *If it was all so obvious, why was his lad still in jail?*

Ray alleged that Stephen had been framed for the murder as part of a conspiracy because the town needed someone else to blame. He claimed the police forced Stephen to wrongfully confess to an assault on a young, married woman, who later died from her injuries.

Ray claimed the woman, Wendy Sewell, was promiscuous, and had taken several prominent local businessmen as lovers. He suggested a long list of individuals, and said they were all well known in the Bakewell area. He believed the powers that be in the town had conspired to protect the victim's secret life, and perhaps themselves, from a massive scandal.

He explained that several other characters had been seen in or around the cemetery on the day of the attack, and that potential witnesses had either been ignored by the police or deliberately warned off.

He strongly believed that one particular officer, who 'had it in for Stephen', went flat-out to get a quick confession. Ray said that although his son quickly retracted it, the confession still formed the main plank of the prosecution evidence from which he was convicted.

Ray said there had been some previous attempts to obtain an appeal against conviction, the first being in October 1974, a few months after his trial, and the second some 13 years before, in 1981. Both failed. He then admitted to hiring a private investigator, Robert Ervin, a former army investigator, who worked on the case for about ten years but died some time ago.

Juanita let Ray do most of the talking. She looked uncomfortable and agitated, and began fumbling through the paperwork, before extracting some old cuttings that reported the previous attempts to appeal. She explained that the rest of the paperwork included court papers, copies of some old witness statements from years ago and various other official reports she thought I might find of interest.

Ray was anxious to continue, and he confirmed that the reason they wanted to see me that day was because a woman had telephoned them anonymously to say she had sent both me and the editor of the *Star* some fresh evidence that could help clear their son's name.

'The *Star*?' I asked. 'Do you mean the *Sheffield Star* or the *Daily Star*?'

'Don't know, she just said the *Star*.'

'Look, I've just returned from a short break,' I said. 'I don't think anything's arrived here, nobody has mentioned anything, but I'll go and check.' I brushed past them and made my way to the main office.

'Does anyone know anything about a letter concerning Stephen Downing?' I asked. 'His parents think some fresh evidence may have been sent here.' Everyone shook their heads.

Jackie said, 'Whatever came in that we couldn't deal with is on your desk. I don't recall anything about a Stephen Downing, though.'

'What's this all about?' asked Norman.

'I'm not quite sure at this stage, but their son Stephen has been in jail for murder for over 20 years. They are desperate and need a lifeline. I'll ask Sam when he comes back,' I replied.

I returned to my office and told the Downings that nothing had been received so far, but that I had contacts at both newspapers and would get back to them as soon as I could. We made arrangements to meet a day or two later at their home in Bakewell.

I was intrigued by what they had said. They were obviously biased, but it seemed worthy of investigation – particularly if some fresh evidence had come to light.

The Downings seemed a likeable couple, who genuinely believed in their son's innocence. Ray had spoken of numerous conspiracy theories, while Juanita had maintained a more dignified stance, sitting there patiently listening to her husband's defiant explanations.

I was apprehensive about getting involved, but my youngest son was now about the same age as Stephen was when he was convicted of murder.

Sam returned with another cigarette in his mouth. The ash was hovering precariously. 'Did Ray Downing come in?' he asked.

'Yes, Sam. So what do you know about the case?'

Sam grabbed my arm and led me back into my office. 'Ray's well known around here,' he explained, closing the door. 'He drives people crazy with this tale about his son's innocence. He has spent years trying to solve the crime and clear his lad. Poor sod. I really can't blame him, though. Stephen was only a kid, and a bit simple too, from memory.'

In his hat and coat, Sam looked like a detective from a 1950s movie. I explained about the family's current claim of an anonymous caller and some potential fresh evidence. He wasn't too impressed. He had two or three more drags on his cigarette, then started to talk about the case through a haze.

'It was all a long time ago, but I was on the story leading up to the trial. As far as I can recall, there was a slight feeling of surprise when he was convicted. He was only 16 or 17, I think?'

'Seventeen, Sam,' I confirmed.

'Yes, whatever. I know other names were bandied about and the murdered woman was well known in the area, if you see what I mean?'

'No, not really, Sam.'

'She'd left her husband and I think there was some sort of scandal. You know what Bakewell is like. I think Stephen admitted something, then retracted it.'

'I'm going to their house on Thursday. They want to show me a few other things of interest.'

Sam stared at me. 'Be careful, be very careful,' he said. 'It's a minefield. Don't get sucked into it.'

CHAPTER 2

THE DOWNINGS

I contacted my friend Frank Curran at the *Daily Star* and Rob Hollingworth at the *Sheffield Star*. Neither had seen any letters relating to the Downing case, but said they would call if anything turned up.

My reporters were keen to become involved with something out of the ordinary and willingly helped with my investigations. Jackie spent a lot of time collating information from old newspaper cuttings from the early 1970s, trying to build up a true picture of the Wendy Sewell murder. She also contacted all the official channels for copies of any important paperwork. I tried to track down any relevant forensic or medical reports, and between us we soon built a substantial portfolio about the case.

Over the next few weeks we held several case conferences to discuss updates or developments. Following my initial review, I wrote to the Chief Constable at Ripley, asking for the release of some paperwork and any other relevant information regarding the murder.

It appeared the murder had naturally made quite an impact locally, but not necessarily nationally. And most of the press reports were fairly consistent.

On Friday 14 September 1973, the *Derbyshire Times* declared:

MURDER BID CHARGE

Critically ill in Chesterfield Royal Hospital with serious head injuries is an attractive 32-year-old housewife, who was found unconscious in a Bakewell cemetery just after lunchtime on Wednesday.

Yesterday morning, Derbyshire police said that a young man had been charged with attempted murder and would appear at a special court in Bakewell later that day. The accused is understood to be 17-year-old Stephen Downing, a gardener from a Bakewell council estate.

The woman, Mrs Wendy Sewell of Middleton-by-Youlgreave, was found just after 1.15 p.m. She was rushed to Chesterfield Royal Hospital but early yesterday morning had still not regained consciousness. Police are waiting at her bedside.

She was discovered lying face downwards between gravestones in an old part of the churchyard, close to dense woodland. The cemetery was sealed off as police began their investigations.

Fifty CID and uniformed officers were drafted into the quiet market town and the area surrounding the cemetery was combed by tracker-dogs. Detective Supt Peter Bayliss announced that a 17-year-old youth had been formally charged with attempted murder.

Mrs Sewell worked for the Forestry Commission. She left the office just after midday and was seen walking along the 'Butts' in the direction of the cemetery shortly after 12.30 pm. Neighbours said on Wednesday night that Mrs Sewell often visited her mother at Haddon Road, Bakewell, after finishing work.

A slightly later cutting, dated Friday 21 September, explained:

WOMAN DIES AFTER ATTACK IN CEMETERY

Stephen Downing (17), a gardener, is due to appear in court following an eight-day remand in custody.

The papers for the case have been forwarded to the Director of Public Prosecutions, but no information was available this week as to whether the charge would be increased to one of murder. Downing made a two-minute appearance before a special court in Bakewell last Thursday and was charged that he did attempt to murder Mrs Wendy Sewell.

On 22 February 1974, following the trial at Nottingham Crown Court, the same paper reported:

YOUTH ON MURDER CHARGE IS FOUND GUILTY

Stephen Downing, aged 17, was found guilty of murdering 32-year-old typist Mrs Wendy Sewell in a cemetery in Bakewell, Derbyshire, by a unanimous verdict.

Downing, who was alleged to have bludgeoned his victim with a pickaxe shaft and sexually assaulted her before leaving the body among the tombstones, was ordered to be detained at the Queen's pleasure. They took only an hour to reach their unanimous verdict last Friday.

Passing sentence, Mr Justice Nield told Downing, who worked in the cemetery as a gardener, 'You have been convicted on the clearest evidence of this very serious offence.'

Mr Patrick Bennett QC, prosecuting, had described how Downing had followed Mrs Sewell in the cemetery before carrying out the savage attack with a pickaxe handle. Downing claimed that he had found Mrs Sewell's half-naked body and then sexually assaulted her.

Mrs Sewell, who lived at Green Farm, Middleton-by-Youlgreave, died in hospital two days after the attack from skull and brain injuries. Downing was alleged to have admitted the assault late at night after spending several hours in the police station. He was alleged to have described how he struck Mrs Sewell with the pick shaft on the back of the head and undressed her.

Police officers denied that Downing had been shaken to keep him awake after spending hours at Bakewell police station. His mother, Mrs Juanita Downing, told the jury that her son had never gone out with girls and only had one good friend.

Downing said that bloodspots on his clothing got there when Mrs Sewell raised herself on the ground and shook her head violently. He had told the jury that he found the victim lying semi-conscious in the graveyard after going home during his lunch hour, but the prosecution said that his lunchtime walk was only an alibi after he had carried out the attack. Downing had pleaded not guilty to the murder.

Other regional papers carried similar copy, stating, 'A savage assault by a teenager with a pickaxe handle. She sustained repeated blows as many as seven or eight to the head – and had then fallen against tombstones.'

Many papers made a reference to Judge Nield, who kept referring to Downing's statement, which was 'signed over and over again' and formed the main plank of evidence for the prosecution.

To all intents and purposes, it seemed like a fairly straightforward conviction. A confession had been obtained on the day the attack took place, and although Downing retracted it before trial the prosecution case still relied very heavily on this admission.

The trial lasted three days. The jury heard just one day of evidence and took less than an hour to reach their unanimous verdict of guilty. It all seemed so quick, clean and convenient. This alone made me consider it curious and worthy of initial investigation.

*　　*　　*

A few days later, I set out on the short but pleasant drive along the A6 to Bakewell. The Downings lived at Stanton View, just a few hundred yards from the cemetery – the scene of the crime. They lived in a small semi-detached house on the council estate. It was the same property that Ray, Juanita, Stephen and his sister Christine had all lived in together until that fateful day in 1973.

Despite the fact that Stephen had remained in custody ever since his arrest, his mother kept his room just as it was. The family had campaigned for his freedom ever since his conviction. Ray never looked well, and at first he probably thought I was just another journalist who would write a brief update and then disappear into oblivion.

Ray told me about his work as a taxi driver and, over a cup of tea, explained how he and Juanita first met in a Blackpool ballroom in 1952, when he was completing his national service in the RAF.

Juanita, who had been watching me like a hawk, told me to call her Nita, and explained how she had been adopted from the age of three and never really knew her parents. Born Juanita Williams, she was brought up near Liverpool. She and Ray later married and moved to Burton Edge in Ray's home town of Bakewell.

Following national service Ray obtained a job at Cintride, as a first-aid attendant, before he left to drive ambulances and coaches. Stephen was born at their home in March 1956, with their daughter Christine born exactly three years later.

Ray said Stephen had a quiet, reserved nature, just like his mother, and was good with his hands but struggled academically. He confirmed that Stephen had the reading ability of an 11-year-old at the time of the murder, and said he believed himself to be a failure at school, with few friends, and preferred his own company.

Nita, though, explained how Stephen loved animals, and said that on the day of the attack he returned home to change his boots and to feed some baby hedgehogs found abandoned just a few days earlier.

She also said Stephen was a bit lazy and a poor time-keeper – a worrying problem that had cost him several jobs. On the day of the cemetery attack Stephen was employed there as a gardener for Bakewell Urban District Council.

I knew that if I were to have any hope of understanding this case and the Downings' allegations, I would need to examine the crime scene myself. Ray agreed to give me a tour of the cemetery, and we walked across the road to it. It was hard to imagine how such a gruesome murder could have been committed in broad daylight, and so close to a busy housing estate, with much of the area overlooked by dozens of houses. Ray was somewhat disappointed that I had not read much of his paperwork, and at first seemed quite abrupt. I told him that I needed to keep an open mind.

The cemetery was situated at the top of a steep hill overlooking Bakewell. The main access was via two large iron gates. Just inside was a gatekeeper's lodge. It was quite a compact area, probably about 450 yards in length, with two main tarmacked pathways running parallel, one adjacent to Catcliff Wood and the other close to a large beech hedge. The woodland area included a dark, secluded section. The main path ran directly towards the old chapel, and a bit further on and to the rear was the unconsecrated chapel, where Stephen worked at the time of the murder.

Ray showed me where Wendy Sewell was attacked. He then indicated where Stephen said he found her, lying on the path next to an old grave. The headstone bore the inscription 'In the Midst of Life We Are in Death'. It was the grave of Anthony Naylor, who died in 1872.

Immediately behind the grave was a low drystone wall, and a few feet below was Catcliff Wood. I could see how someone could easily escape if they had attacked Wendy, disappearing into thick undergrowth.

As we wandered further along, Ray pointed out another spot across some displaced gravestones, back towards the centre path. 'Now here is where Wendy moved to,' he explained.

'Moved to?' I asked, as we carefully negotiated our way around a number of ancient and broken graves.

'Yes. After Stephen found her he went to get help, but when he returned she'd moved,' he said. Ray then stopped next to the grave of Sarah Bradbury. 'Wendy was found just here.'

I was surprised. 'So how did she move, Ray?' I asked, wondering how a seriously injured woman could drag herself 25 yards or so along the path, and across several gravestones.

'Well, there's the mystery,' said Ray. 'No one has been able to answer that one. It didn't come up at trial either, and the police never queried it.'

Ray then showed me Stephen's former workplace inside the unconsecrated chapel. He explained that this was where the council workers stored their tools, and that it had been used by quite a few men at the time of the murder.

We turned and headed back out towards the main gates, and I tried to put the case into some sort of perspective as I listened to Ray. He kept mentioning the names of several individuals who had supposedly been identified near the cemetery at that time. I realised I would need to read his papers for any of this to make sense.

As we headed part way down the Butts, a very steep walkway heading back into town, Ray showed me the Kissing Gate, an old two-way iron contraption that led back into Catcliff Wood.

It was the reverse route to that taken by the victim as she approached the cemetery during her lunch break. It was also the path taken by a number of key witnesses, who could perhaps have helped confirm Stephen's alibi and his movements on the day.

As I tried to consider all the probabilities and possibilities offered by Ray, I thought this so-called remote location appeared more like Piccadilly Circus immediately prior to and just after the attack, with people coming and going back to work after lunch. It seemed to be a simple routine, and yet, according to Ray, everyone reported different timings and information within their statements.

We returned to the Downings' home, where the kettle was already whistling on the stove. Nita had seen us both walking back, and as we walked in she said, 'I thought you would have been back before now.'

'There's a lot to see,' Ray replied. 'And Mr Hale wanted to see everything.'

'It's Don, Ray. Call me Don. This Mr Hale sounds more like a bailiff.'

Ray laughed. 'Don't mention bailiffs. There's one round here that we don't care for at all, isn't that right, Nita?'

She laughed too. It was obviously some in-joke. Nita handed me a hot mug of tea. It was a family home full of personal mementoes and treasured photographs, yet Stephen's face was always missing, apart from a few childhood snaps. Their only contact with him now was on infrequent visits to a distant prison several hours' drive away.

This thought of Stephen suddenly reminded Ray of something, and he scurried away into the lounge before returning with a large basket. He said excitedly, 'This is Stephen's clothing from the day of the attack,' and tipped out the contents on to the table.

I was shocked to see Stephen's old jeans, T-shirt and work boots, together with rings, a watch and a leather wrist strap.

I couldn't understand why the police had returned these items, and why the family still retained his clothes after all these years. Incredibly, as I looked much closer, I could just about see some very tiny spots of blood on his T-shirt, but only because they were highlighted by a yellow forensic marker.

Ray pointed out a particular dark stain on the left knee of these discoloured and dirty jeans, which he said was congealed blood. No other stains were obvious to the naked eye. 'Look at all these clothes,' he said. 'They are not drenched in blood. And yet our Stephen was said to have battered this poor woman to death.

'If he had, he would have been covered in blood from head to toe. The only blood he got on his clothes was from kneeling next to her when he found her. What's more, I know the ambulanceman who took Wendy to hospital that day. He carried her into the ambulance.

'He said *he* was covered in blood, as she was bleeding so much. He had to burn all his clothes afterwards, they were completely ruined. They were absolutely soaked in blood. You can talk to him. His name is Clyde Bateman. I used to work with him at Bakewell ambulance station. I was a senior ambulance driver and he was my boss.

'He was summoned to attend an appeal eight months after the trial but was never called as a witness. He wanted to talk about the bloodstaining. He's now retired, but every time I see him he maintains that Stephen didn't have enough bloodstaining on him to have committed the attack.'

Ray was still excited. He was sweating and slightly breathless. He eventually paused as I queried, 'How come you have Stephen's clothes?'

'They told me to take him down a change of clothes to the police station, and then they sent these off for testing. They gave us back the watch and the jewellery on the same night as the attack,' Ray said.

'The clothes came back later. It's obvious there's not enough blood on them, though.'

It was beginning to get dark and, as I had now spent several hours with the Downings, I decided to make a move, but Ray motioned me to sit back down. 'I've a lot more to show you. I've got more files and notes. You'll need to see them all,' he pleaded.

I had to take an urgent step back. It had been quite an afternoon. The Downing family had made this a personal crusade for the past 20-odd years, but I didn't want to be drawn in or build up their hopes before I got my bearings.

I politely declined Ray's offer. I told the pair I had to get back to work. I wanted to spend some time going through the files so that I could examine their claims in more detail. I decided I would make an early start the next day, and cancelled my weekend engagements.

For a split second I felt complete panic. Ray's papers were piled high next to my desk, and I wondered, *What if the cleaner has arrived early and dumped them, not realising their importance?*

When I returned to the office, the pile was thankfully still intact. I phoned Ray to arrange another meeting. He suggested I should go the day after next, as Stephen was due to ring from prison. He thought it would be good to speak to him directly.

By then everyone else had left the office. I had my coat on ready to follow them, my hand on the door handle to leave, when suddenly the phone rang. After such a busy day I was in two minds whether to answer it, but I reluctantly picked up in the end.

'Good evening, *Matlock Mercury*. Don Hale. Can I help you?'

There was complete silence.

I asked again, 'Hello, hello? *Matlock Mercury*.' Still silence, although I had the impression someone was listening at the other end. I thought I could hear someone breathing, and a slight background noise.

Then a mature man's husky voice shouted angrily, 'Keep your fucking nose out of the Downing case if you know what's good for you! Do you get my meaning?'

Before I had the chance to answer, he slammed down the phone.

CHAPTER 3

WHAT RAY SAW

I returned to the Downing household a day or two later. I decided not to mention my anonymous caller. I thought he was probably a local crank who had spotted me on the estate and just wanted to rattle my cage. Besides, there was a more important phone call at hand.

Nita put the kettle on and within a few minutes she had a piping-hot cup of tea ready. Stephen was going to phone from prison but would only have a few minutes to chat. The couple said all his calls were monitored and restricted to a few short minutes via a special phone card during breaks from work.

I knew very little about their son, other than what I had read in those dusty old cuttings and from listening to Ray and Nita's descriptions of him. I asked Nita, 'Had Stephen been working long as a gardener for the council?'

'No, no,' she replied with a knowing smile. 'He'd only been there for about seven weeks. He liked it, though. They'd shown him how to keep the hedges tidy, prune the trees, mow the lawns, keep the graves tidy, that kind of thing.

'Although he was left to his own devices, other workmen regularly visited him and Stephen would help them out. To be honest, though, he didn't seem able to stay in any kind of job for very long.'

As they spoke, I tried to imagine a young, immature Stephen Downing – a boy in many ways – convicted of brutally killing a married woman nearly twice his age at his place of work.

It seemed clear that he was not as bright as many other children of a similar age, and to me it seemed his struggle to cope with life continued into his teens and early working career.

Ray said Stephen loved model-making, needlework and cooking. Nita added that sometimes he would take over the kitchen to make everyone a meal, and he enjoyed baking. It appeared however, that Stephen had little in common with other teenage lads, and to many people he was considered odd and a loner.

As we chatted, I was startled out of my thoughts by the loud ringing of the telephone from the adjoining room. Nita rushed through and picked up the receiver, while Ray and I trailed after her.

She quickly passed the phone to Ray, who explained that I was there with them and wanted a quick chat. He then thrust the receiver into my chest.

Stephen sounded much younger on the phone than I had imagined. He was quite friendly but nervous, as he had never spoken with a journalist before. Initially he was slightly excitable, speaking at thirteen to the dozen, and it seemed he wanted to tell me his life story in one go, probably due to the limited time restrictions for a prison call. He seemed keen to accept my help and was almost emotional as he thanked me for my interest.

I told him I would appreciate as much help as possible from him and asked him to send me his personal account from the day of the attack. His parents seemed elated that after all those years someone had finally agreed to look into the case.

After the call, we sat back down in the kitchen, where Ray agreed to share his own recollections from the day of the attack. He grabbed another cup of tea and began.

'It was bitter cold that morning, that I do remember. I had woken early – about 5.30 a.m. I was a bus driver in those days for Hulleys of Baslow. I had the early morning route that day. I remember pulling back the curtains and being surprised to see a heavy frost.

'I had a wash and went down to the kitchen for some breakfast. Nita had come down by then.' He looked across to his wife for support. She must have heard the story many times before. 'You asked Stephen if he was going in to work, didn't you, Nita?' he said.

'Yes, there was a sleepy response, if I remember correctly,' Nita admitted. 'Stephen just couldn't get up in the morning. He had been off work on Monday and Tuesday with a heavy cold. I doubted whether he would make it to work that day.'

Ray continued, 'I knew Nita would wake him early enough, but she couldn't be behind him all the time. She also had to look after Christine. That day was important, because it was her first day back after the summer term. Christine wanted to be early, so Stephen had to fend for himself.

'He seemed okay the night before, and said he wanted to go back. I asked Nita before I left if she thought he'd be fit for work. She wasn't sure, but said she had his sandwiches ready if he decided to go in.'

'So, did Stephen get off to work on time?' I asked.

Nita was grinning, 'He was at the very last minute as usual. I called him at 7.20, and told him that Ray had been gone for ages and Christine was checking her school stuff. Even though we only lived a few minutes from his work, he was often still late.

'In fact, he was in such a rush that day that he put on the wrong boots. They were probably the first pair he could find in the half-light, but they were his best blue dress boots.

'He only realised this on his way in to work, and panicked, thinking his dad would shout at him. In any case, he changed them when he came home at lunchtime.'

'Anyway,' Ray coughed, resuming his story. 'By that time I reached the depot. I was pleased to see the coaches weren't frosted over.

'I was driving our old faithful bus Nell, which operated on the daily service round the local villages. I checked her over. She was always reliable, and I thought, *What a pity Stephen couldn't be more like her.*

'She started first time, and I drove out of the main yard but took it steady in case there was any ice about.

'As I approached Middleton-by-Youlgreave, I noticed some people huddled in a small group by the bus stop. One woman was stamping her feet to keep warm, and they were all wrapped against the bitter chill wind.

'"All aboard the skylark!" I shouted as the door swung open, and a cold breeze came in with the first passenger. I checked my change and adjusted the ticket machine ready for the next stop. The clock on the dashboard was visible to all, and the minute hand clicked to 8.05 a.m.

'I had arrived on time just before 8 a.m., but couldn't leave until the scheduled time of 8.10. I closed the door again, and while we waited I took a quick glance to admire the view.

'The engine shivered against the cold. The clock suddenly clicked, and it was 8.10 a.m. precisely.

'I asked if everyone was on – not really expecting a reply. I glanced in the rear-view mirror as I set off, and then suddenly this woman appeared directly in front of me. I had to stand back hard on the brakes, and the passengers were all tipped forward in their seats.

'I opened the door again and let on this young woman I recognised as Wendy Sewell. She had been totally oblivious to any danger and was fiddling for change inside her purse. She had actually brushed against the front radiator of the bus just as I was setting off. Still breathless with shock, I said to her, "You were lucky!"

'She replied, "Yes, I'd laddered my tights and had to look for another pair. I thought I'd miss the bus!"

'No, I don't mean that,' I said. 'I nearly knocked you over!' She seemed totally unconcerned, and then it dawned on me – she hadn't even realised her lucky escape.

'I then said, "You're not usually on this bus." And she replied, "No, but I've some business to attend to in Bakewell."

'Wendy sat on the front passenger seat by the door. She looked straight ahead and didn't acknowledge anyone. I glanced at her again as she sat down. She had long, dark-brown hair, which curled just above her shoulders. She was wearing a beige trouser suit with a black jumper.

'As she crossed her legs, her left trouser leg ran up slightly and I noticed that she was wearing tights underneath with small white ankle socks and rather dingy-looking white plimsolls.

'I thought she had probably put on the tights to guard against the cold. She carried a light-brown wicker-type shopping basket over one arm, and put her purse into a small handbag, which she placed under a cloth in her basket. I shook my head slightly and thought, *What a pity. A pretty young woman – shame about the shoes!*

I stopped Ray for a moment. 'You're sure about the purse, tights and basket?' I asked. I needed to be sure because I couldn't find any record of these items in the police scene-of-crime report. There was also no mention of any diary, which again was supposed to have been in her handbag – allegedly together with a black book.

It seemed rather odd that the victim was found without her handbag or any other important personal effects. I recalled that there was no mention either of finding her tights.

Ray thought for a moment and then said, 'Yes, I am absolutely certain. That very morning, she placed her purse into the basket and then covered it with a cloth.'

'So, what do you think happened to these things?' I asked him, adding, 'They were not found at her office, so are they still in Catcliff Wood?'

'Why not?' Ray replied. 'I don't think anyone bothered to look, despite it being right next to the cemetery. After they forced a confession out of Stephen the police made little effort to find anything, or to question anyone else.'

He was keen to continue with his story. 'I exchanged a few more pleasantries with Wendy but we were fast approaching Bakewell town centre. She was more intense as we came into Rutland Square. She seemed to have some things on her mind. As soon as we stopped, she was up and out in one, and ran down the street without saying a word. I shouted, "Cheerio!", half expecting her to wave back, but she didn't. I never saw her alive again.'

Ray wiped a tear from his eye – he was still emotional as he recalled these details – but soon regained his composure. He dipped his biscuit into his tea. 'I had a funny feeling it would be a memorable day. The strange thing is that I could have killed Wendy Sewell myself that morning, quite by accident, of course, and then we wouldn't have had 20-odd years of this bloody nonsense.'

Nita said she arrived home from work on the bus just after 1 p.m. She had only put the kettle on a few minutes before when she heard Stephen's key in the door. 'I shouted to him that it wasn't locked,' she said. 'Stephen said the shop had already closed for lunch, and he asked me if I could get him another bottle of pop and take it across to him later at the cemetery. He had an empty bottle with him to collect the refund, and he put it on the kitchen table with some money.

'I asked him if he was staying for a cuppa as I was making one for myself. He said no, as he had just come back to change his boots and feed the hedgehogs.

'I told him I had already fed them, and said I would get him another bottle of pop when the shop opened and take it down to him later. He stayed for maybe another minute or so, but said he had to get back to his work and would see me later – but he too never returned home.'

CHAPTER 4

THE CONFESSION

So far, I had only heard the Downing family's version of events, which, understandably, was all very cosy and supportive. I now had to examine the official papers to get some perspective on this. If Stephen really was innocent, I could only help if I thoroughly understood his best lines of defence.

Jackie had collated a massive bundle of paperwork from the courts and other key sources relating to the case. Among them was the Home Office summary, which included his original, alleged confession taken down by the police.

The police confession was stark and distasteful and gave Jackie second thoughts about becoming involved with the case. I told her to stick with it and wait until we received Stephen's documents with his version of events.

A copy of his confession was written down by officers on the night of the attack, dated 12 September 1973, and stated:

I don't know what made me do it. I saw this woman walking in the cemetery. I went into the chapel to get the pickaxe handle that I knew was there. I followed her, but I hadn't talked to her and she hadn't talked to me, but I think she knew I was there.

I came right up to her near enough. I hit her twice on the head, on the back of the neck. I just hit her to knock her out.

She fell to the ground and she was on her side, and then she was face down. I rolled her over and started to undress her. I pulled her bra off first. I had to pull her jumper up and I just got hold of it until it broke, and then I pulled her pants and her knickers off.

I started to play with her breasts and then her vagina. I put my middle finger up her vagina. I don't know why I hit her, but it might have been to do with what I have just told you. But I knew I had to knock her out first before I did anything to her.

It was only a couple of minutes. I was playing with her and there was just a bit of blood at the back of her neck. So, I left her, went back to the chapel, got my pop bottle and went to the shop, and then went home to see my mother and asked her to get a bottle of pop for me because the shop was closed. I suppose I did that so that no one would find out I'd hit the woman.

I went back to the cemetery about 15 minutes later and went back to see the woman. She was lying on the ground the same way as I'd left her, but she was covered in blood on her face and on her back. I bent down to see how she was, and she was semi-conscious, just. She put her hands up to her face and just kept wiping her face with her hand. She had been doing that when I first knocked her down.

I went to the telephone kiosk to ring for the police and ambulance so that they would think someone else had done it and I'd just found her. I hadn't any money, so I went to the Lodge and asked Wilf Walker if he was on the telephone, but he said he wasn't. So, I told him what I'd supposed to have found. He came to have a look and then he went to ask these other blokes in a white van outside the cemetery if they had seen her, but they said they hadn't, so one of them went to

*phone for the police. I just stayed because there was no place to
go.*

I noticed the immediate inconsistency with what Ray had told
me about Wendy Sewell having moved when Stephen returned
to the cemetery. There was no mention of this within his confession statement.

In stark contrast to his confession, I then received an interesting report from one of Stephen's prison officers. It had been sent
via a contact of mine at the Home Office. It related to a home
visit Stephen had made to Bakewell six months previously, in
March 1994 – the first time he had set foot back in the town
since his trial almost exactly 20 years before.

Downing had been accompanied by prison officer Clive
Tanner, who commented, 'He coped very well. There were a lot
of people there who knew him before and were coming up to
him and greeting him. It came across as very strange to me how
in a small community, where I assume a murder only takes place
possibly once every hundred years, when the offender returns he
is warmly welcomed by a great deal of the local people. Maybe
there is something in the point he is trying to make about not
being guilty.'

A copy of the trial judge's summary then arrived from Nottingham Crown Court. I had told Jackie to ask for a full transcript,
but was informed there wasn't one, which I found strange. A
check with the court clerk confirmed that no full record of the
trial existed. As a result, all I could do was work from the judge's
summing up.

The Honourable Mr Justice Nield began his summing up on
15 February 1974. He reminded the jury of their duty, pointing
out that Downing, who was soon to have his eighteenth birthday,
had a 'perfectly clean record'.

They were informed that manslaughter did not arise, because 'it is agreed that this unfortunate woman was murdered'. He explained, 'The issue is whether the Crown has proved it was this man who committed that murder.'

Turning to Stephen's confession he continued, 'One of the main planks of the prosecution case is the statement made by the accused and signed over and over again.'

He stressed that the prosecution had to establish that the statement had been 'voluntarily made' and 'accurately recorded', and went on to explain, 'If the jury thought there had been oppression, any improper conduct by the police to induce this young man to make a statement, or to threaten him if he did not that such and such things would happen, then the statement is valueless.'

While there was much to pore over in the judge's summing up, the most striking contradictions between Stephen's confession and the prosecution case were found in the medical and scientific evidence presented by the prosecution.

At 2.40 Mrs Sewell reached Chesterfield Royal Hospital. Mr Stillman, the surgeon, found multiple lacerations of the skull, and an X-ray confirmed there were fractures. Doctor Usher, the pathologist, performed a post-mortem examination on 15 September, the day after this woman died, and he found ten lacerations to the skull as if she had been violently assaulted by someone using the pickaxe handle. He took the view there must have been at least seven or eight or more violent blows and, whoever did it, would seem to have been in a frenzied state.

The judge pointed out that several witnesses had described Stephen Downing as 'calm and cool, certainly not frenzied' just moments after he was supposed to have carried out the attack. One witness, however, PC Ball, the first policeman to the scene, had not regarded him as cool. He had said, 'He was very excited. I told him to calm down.' This contradicted the evidence of other witnesses, who had seen nothing abnormal in Stephen's demeanour.

The judge turned to a report that the prosecution case relied upon heavily. It was written by Mr Norman Lee, a Home Office forensics expert. Mr Lee's evidence concerned the bloodstaining on Stephen's clothing and on the pickaxe handle, the murder weapon. He said:

> There were stains on his trousers on the knees where he might have kneeled, and on the front of the trousers mainly on the lower legs. There were also a large number of splashes and heavy smears.
>
> There was some blood on the right leg as high as the thighs. He said these stains would have been visible to the people in the cemetery. In addition, there were small spots of blood on his T-shirt and his gloves. An examination of Stephen's boots showed a lot of smears and small spots of blood, mainly at the front.

Stephen claimed at trial that, after finding Mrs Sewell, he knelt down and turned her over, whereupon she raised herself up and began to shake her head violently. That was the explanation, he said, for the blood on his clothes.

Mr Lee conceded that the blood on the boots 'might arise from somebody getting up from his knees and pressing on his toes on the ground'. He also went on to say that 'the blood-staining on the clothes, some of it, is consistent with someone turning over the body'.

However, the very small spots and splashes found on the clothes, boots and gloves were not consistent with turning someone over. And he did not accept Stephen's explanation that the small spots of blood flew on to his clothing from her head and long hair as she violently shook her head about.

He said, 'I cannot imagine how you could get splashings as small as those in the way Downing is suggesting,' and added, 'If she had flung herself about, then for such tiny spots a lot of energy must have been applied.' His preferred explanation was that the spots came from Mrs Sewell being beaten, 'and the harder you hit, the smaller the spot of blood'.

This was a complicated yet very vital point. I read and reread it to make sure I understood his argument. Norman Lee seemed to be saying that violent force produces a spray of blood, which would appear as tiny, almost microscopic spots, on any surface hit by this spray, such as clothing.

He did not believe Wendy Sewell could have shaken her head so violently as to produce these minute spots found on Stephen's clothing. He claimed they must have come from the blows of the pickaxe handle.

I could not see why Norman Lee was so sure. When cross-examined, he repeated that she could not have shaken her head so violently as to produce that result.

And yet it was not only Stephen who had described the victim thrashing around in an aggressive manner. The judge pointed out that the senior ambulanceman, Clyde Bateman, who arrived on the scene had also reported that, on the journey to the hospital, 'she became very restless, moving about a lot, throwing out her right arm all over the place, and his uniform was covered in blood but, according to that witness, she was not shaking her head'. And PC Ball told the court that 'she resisted violently with her arm'.

Although the ambulanceman had not noticed her moving her head, I believed this might have been due to her worsening condition. Stephen found her just after the attack, whereas she was in the ambulance almost an hour later. She soon fell into a coma due to her head injuries, from which she never recovered.

Norman Lee said of the murder weapon, 'The stains on the boots and lower legs of Downing's trousers were similar in size and proportion to the stains on the pickaxe handle.' He went on to conclude, 'There was very probably a close relationship between the handle and this man's trousers and boots, and I do not think this would come from offering succour. The boots and trousers were in close proximity when the deceased was battered.'

But doubt had been cast on Lee's conclusions even before the trial. I had been rummaging through Ray Downing's paperwork a few days previously and come across a forensic report written in January 1974. The contents were very dry and technical, and I had not realised its significance immediately. Now, as I retrieved it, there were things I urgently needed to check. The report, by Mr G.E. Moss of Commercial and Forensic Laboratories in Reading, had been written at the request of Stephen's defence team.

Mr Moss examined the murder weapon and various other exhibits in the presence of Norman Lee and police officers.

He found the pickaxe handle heavily bloodstained at the thick end, the end used to hit the victim, while the handle end was smeared with blood.

He agreed with the pathologist, Mr Usher, that at least seven or eight violent blows had been struck. He pointed out that, therefore, this was inconsistent with Stephen's confession.

I grabbed the Home Office summary of the case and turned again to the confession to double check. There it was in black and white: 'I hit her twice on the head, on the back of the neck. I just hit her at the back of the head to knock her out.' *Two blows!* The confession, relied on as the main plank of the prosecution case, contradicted the pathologist's evidence – also used by the prosecution – on this vital detail.

I turned to Moss's report again. The blood, he continued, 'on the back of the gloves could only be seen through a microscope and was not visible to the naked eye'. PC Ball and a council workman, Herbert Dawson, maintained Stephen said he was wearing gloves when he turned Wendy over.

Stephen was adamant he never said this, and claimed he told them his gloves remained in his back pocket all along. It was one of many apparent inconsistencies that might have made the jury doubt his account. It seemed to me that if he had been wearing his gloves, they would have been soaked in blood considering the extent of Wendy's injuries.

Mr Moss went on, 'The pattern of staining on the front legs of the jeans is consistent with kneeling in blood. This would be consistent with Downing kneeling beside the body some time after the attack.'

Mr Moss was also confirming that the blood was congealed and not fresh when it reached Downing's jeans. He went on, 'I assumed the linear markings on the inside right leg were probably caused by rubbing against a bloodied surface, possibly a boot while in the act of getting up from a kneeling position.

'The smears above knee level would also have been made by rubbing against a bloodied surface. Downing said he had turned the body over. If he did, the smearing might well have occurred at this time.'

Then I saw what I had really been looking for. It was in the matter of how the tiny spots and splashes of blood occurred that Mr Moss and Mr Lee differed most. Moss said, 'The blood splashing on the clothes could have resulted from head shaking, as Downing got up from a kneeling position.'

He concluded that the bloodstaining overall was consistent with Downing's version of events, including his assertion that there was a lot of blood about Wendy's face and on the path. Again, he insisted the forensic evidence was not consistent with the version of events in Downing's confession.

But there was no reference to Mr Moss's report or conclusions within the judge's summing up. I found it incredible that his evidence would not have been put before the jury.

Once again, I regretted the fact that a full trial transcript had not been located. It was so important to know whether Stephen's defence team used this vital forensic evidence. From the papers available to me it suggested they had not, but I couldn't be sure. And that was only one question among many that the judge's summing up would leave me to ponder.

CHAPTER 5

THE WITNESSES

The scientific evidence had certainly given me plenty to consider, and the witness statements, as presented in the judge's summing up, only posed more questions.

Mr Justice Nield described how several prosecution witnesses had claimed to have seen Wendy Sewell during the last walk of her life.

This grim story begins thus, does it not? Wendy Sewell, a young married woman, worked for the Forestry Commission at Bakewell. The Commission had an office in Catcliff House in Church Street, and the District Officer was Mr Osmaston.

At about 20 past noon Mr Osmaston was speaking on the telephone, and in came Mrs Sewell and handed him a note to say she was going out for a breath of fresh air.

Now that woman's movements are followed meticulously, until she reaches the cemetery – you may say, perhaps, it is a tribute to the thoroughness of the investigations.

We learn from Mr Read of the Department of Employment in the same building that he saw this woman leave at about 12.40. It is clear that she made her way along Butts Road. Two joiners, Mr Lomas and Mr Bradwell, who were working in that road and were having lunch at that time, saw her ...

three, four or five minutes after she left the building … and they exchanged greetings.

At about 12.45 Mrs Hill, in a Land Rover, came up to the cemetery gates where she always turned her vehicle, and saw Mrs Sewell walking into the cemetery, and there was no one else about. At about 12.50 Mr Orange saw Mrs Sewell walking on Butts Road towards the cemetery, and they exchanged greetings.

And about the same time Mr Carman, who was near the telephone kiosk just outside the cemetery gates, said he saw Mrs Sewell through the fence walking along the back path in the cemetery, the path along Burton Edge.

At this point the judge stressed that the timings given by witnesses had to be viewed as approximate. He then turned to the movements of Stephen Downing.

About 1.08 Mr Wilfred Walker, who was the cemetery attendant and lived in the lodge by the main gates, saw the accused who walked out of the main gates with a pop bottle under his arm. He appeared to be perfectly normal – this young man was not hurrying. Mr Walker did not notice anything about his clothing.

The judge pointed out that the jury had heard from Stephen Downing saying that he had greeted Mr Walker and his wife, who were at the door of the lodge. Mr Walker denied any such exchange had taken place. He continued:

At about 1.15 Mr Walker saw the accused again. This time he was coming back to the main gates and there was no pop bottle with him.

Just before that time Mr Fox and Mr Hawksworth,
workmen employed by the Urban District Council, had come
into the cemetery in order to go to the store.

At 1.20, or thereabouts, the accused came to Mr Walker's
lodge. He seemed very calm. Mr Walker said, 'He asked if I
was on the telephone. I said, "No, what is the matter?" He
said there was a woman who had been attacked in the
cemetery. I asked where she was. I went with him and he kept
pointing down there.'

At this point the judge drew the jury's attention to a further discrepancy in the accounts given by Wilf Walker and Stephen Downing. According to Mr Walker, as they approached the injured woman, Stephen told him, 'I don't want to lose my job. I like it.' When questioned, Stephen denied saying this.

The judge told the jury, 'Make up your minds, having seen Mr Walker, whether it is true.' He continued with his summary:

And so, these two reached the spot where this woman was
lying. Mr Walker said the accused told him, 'There was a pick
shaft handle covered with blood, and then I saw a van parked
by the store.' Mr Walker told you, 'I noticed this unfortunate
woman trying to get up. She fell back on the gravestone, and
never moved after that.'

Well, after some minutes Mr Walker and the defendant
called over the two workmen, Mr Fox and Mr Hawksworth,
to come and see what there was to be seen.

You were told by Mr Hawksworth, who arrived at the
scene, that they saw this body half-naked, naked up to the
thighs, and Mr Hawksworth went to telephone for the
police. Now at some time about this point two other people
arrived, also employed by the Urban District Council, Mr

Dawson and Mr Watts, and you have important evidence from them.

Mr Dawson told you, 'I went across and saw a person lying on the graves. The person was trying to wipe blood from the eyes with the back of his or her hand.'

Here the judge noted that Herbert Dawson had been unable to say if the victim was a man or a woman. He told how the witness had said he shouted for someone to fetch an ambulance, and that nothing struck him about Stephen's manner as he stood there with the rest of the group.

The judge then repeated the rest of Dawson's evidence, in which he had told the court:

'I [Dawson] said, "What the hell is going on?" I turned to the accused and I said, "Where are you working?" He said, "Just across here." I said, "Was it here this morning?" meaning the body, and he said, "No!" And then I saw that the woman moved again and was trying to stand up.'

The judge continued:

Mr Dawson went forward to try to save her from falling but was too late. Then the police arrived and the officer, Police Constable Ball, obviously rightly said to those assembled, 'Don't anybody touch anything,' and that the accused said, 'I did turn her over, but I had my gloves on.'

Mr Watts, one of the Urban District Council plumbers, told you he ran for the ambulance, having seen this body, and then 'I went back,' he said, and 'I saw the defendant.' He heard the defendant say to Mr Dawson that he touched the body, but he had his gloves on. 'Then I saw,' said Mr Watts,

'blood on the defendant's knees as if he had been kneeling
down, and I saw a pick handle on the path.' He said when he
first saw this woman there was blood on her face and body.

It was here that the judge highlighted a major difference between
the prosecution and defence accounts. Stephen Downing, he
said, had denied saying he made the remark about his gloves.
'Make up your minds about that,' instructed the judge, before
turning to the evidence of the next witness.

There came then Mr Fox, another of these workmen. He went
to the scene, and saw the body lying there partly clothed. The
accused told him he thought someone must have been in the
chapel and taken the pick shaft out. The accused added that
he had gone home at dinner time, and also that the woman
had moved. The accused then said, 'There looks like being an
identification parade.'

The judge pointed out a further 'sharp conflict' between the
Crown and defence cases. Stephen Downing denied making any
remark about an identity parade. He continued:

One turns to consider the weapon, the pick shaft handle.
*   Mr Hawksworth, the council workman who'd telephoned*
the police, told you about this. He said, 'I had been in the
cemetery about 11 o'clock that morning, and I saw the accused
coming away from the store with a pair of shears which he
would want for his work. I went into the store to check some
asbestos sheets and found something else we wanted, which
was a chimney cowl placed on top of the lectern. I noticed a
pick shaft nearby. I picked it up to have a look at it, then I
put it back.'

At this point the judge reminded the jury that Fred Hawksworth had identified the pickaxe handle he had seen in the chapel store as 'Exhibit 1', the handle shown to him in court, which the Crown claimed was the murder weapon. Hawksworth had agreed, 'This is it.' He had then gone on to say, 'Later on I saw the pick shaft on the pathway.'

After summarising the evidence given by the lodge keeper, the workmen and the ambulanceman, who were all present in the cemetery at some point, the judge told the jury, 'I think I am right in saying that, within the cemetery at the relevant time, no one else was seen,' although he reminded them, 'There are holes in the hedge, and another gate, where anybody could come in or out.'

He also drew their attention to the evidence given by two defence witnesses, both of whom had claimed to see 'a person, or two persons, coming away from the direction of the cemetery'.

However, the judge placed emphasis on only one of these witnesses, Mrs Louisa Hadfield, whose evidence, he said, 'was greatly relied on by the defence'. He reminded the jury:

> She told you she was walking in Upper Yeld Road with her dog at about 1.15 and saw a man running ever so fast towards her ... that means away from the direction in which the cemetery lay. She described his dress. She was very frightened. The dog snarled at him. She was so concerned that she had reported the matter to the police.

The judge then described the evidence of Mr Paling, which had been read out in court.

*Mr Paling, upon whom reliance is not so strongly placed, was
a long way down on the left of the plan. He was in Upper Yeld
Road and saw a chap coming up on the other side. He was
dressed respectably and was in a terrific hurry. This is all
about 350 yards off the plan. He was asked if he noticed any
blood on the man. He did not notice any. You may wonder if
that witness really helps you.*

He then spoke of the evidence given by Stephen's next-door
neighbour, Peter Moran.

*He saw Stephen coming from the direction of the cemetery
towards the shop at around 1.15. Mr Moran had left his
house and was on his way back to work in Bakewell at this
time. Stephen had told the court he saw Mr Moran outside
the cemetery gates.*

The judge then spoke about the police version of events, including Stephen's 'interrogation and confession', and the case
presented by the defence. I also wanted to examine the alleged
movements of key people in and around the cemetery that day,
and to check the timings given. Some of the accounts completely
contradicted each other.

Wendy Sewell's workplace was just a few minutes from the
entrance to Butts Road, which then became the public footpath
leading to the Butts. But where was Wendy between 12.20 p.m.
– the time she passed Mr Osmaston a note saying she was going
out – and 12.40 p.m., when she was actually seen leaving the
building?

And could Stephen really have only been away from the cemetery between 1.08 and 1.15 p.m., the times given for his depar-
ture and return by the gatekeeper? He seemed to have done a fair

amount in seven minutes – walked to the shop, then on to his house, where he stayed chatting to his mother for a brief time, and then back to the cemetery.

In addition to this, one of his neighbours, Peter Moran, claimed to have seen him at 1.15 p.m., walking towards the shop, the same time the gatekeeper said he saw him coming the other way, re-entering the cemetery.

There were many similar things that didn't make any sense and seemingly hadn't been challenged at trial by Stephen's defence. Why were only the police called in a first instance and then a second workman had to call an ambulance? It all sounded dubious. Many of the timings conflicted and were completely inaccurate.

I also noticed the fact that within this trial summary the judge also failed to mention a vitally important fact – that Wendy had moved from where she was first attacked, to another spot across some gravestones, where she was seen by the workmen. This fact was mentioned by Stephen Downing at trial. And it was also mentioned casually in at least one witness statement by a workman, but for some reason it was not challenged by the defence – even though it was part of Downing's revised statement made a few days after the 'confession'. I was determined to get to the bottom of all these inconsistencies.

Doing this with the assistance of Derbyshire police seemed unlikely, however, as around this time I received a reply from Derbyshire police HQ saying that all the paperwork and exhibits relating to the case had been burnt, lost or destroyed, including the murder weapon. I was furious. *How dare they destroy evidence before the man had served his time.*

CHAPTER 6

STEPHEN'S VERSION

I was about to visit a couple of potential witnesses when Stephen's personal account of events arrived. He also included a hand-drawn diagram of the cemetery layout, which roughly matched the one I'd made myself when I'd visited his parents. Stephen explained:

```
The cemetery always seemed empty even when there
were other people milling about - although I felt
particularly isolated when I was alone. The
creaking of the huge timbers in the roof structure
of the unconsecrated chapel gave the place an
eerie feeling, as if you were never quite alone.

    It was September and, while the day was warm
enough to work without a jacket, the chapel had a
chillness that cut to the bone. I wasted no time
in getting a fire going with the hope I could push
back the blanket of cold - at least enough to be
able to enjoy my break.

    I then collected the tools I needed. I don't
have any recollection of any unusual visitors to
the cemetery during the morning before my break,
although I do recall one lady who regularly walked
her dog in there. More often than not I would see
her in the afternoon, but on that day she came in
```

the morning. I never got to know her name but, as
was customary, she stopped by me and we chatted
briefly.

   She asked me where I had been for the past two
days, as she had not seen me, and I told her that
I'd been off with a cold. She told me to keep warm
and I informed her that I had a fire going in the
unconsecrated chapel.

   I remember the lady quite clearly, as it was the
first time I had seen her wearing a salmon-pink
wool topcoat. I think I may have commented on how
nice it looked and that it went well with her
blonde hair. I recall her saying it was a new one,
as she normally wore a beige coat. She went on her
way and I returned to work.

This particular section from Stephen struck a chord with me. His
very accurate recollection and description of a meeting with this
woman may indeed have been mentioned to his defence team –
although I could find no trace of it. The evidence from this
witness could have been used at trial to establish his state of mind
less than an hour before the frenzied attack on Wendy Sewell –
and at the very same location.

   It seems, however, that no effort was ever made to try to trace
her, or indeed that she was even considered for questioning. It
could be argued that she too was a similar vulnerable female, so
why didn't he attack her?

   Her knowledge that Stephen had been absent due to sickness
for the previous two days, and the fact the attack happened on
that Wednesday, his first day back at work, could again have
helped clarify and substantiate other additional claims from key
witnesses. Stephen's testimony continued:

I heard the clock strike noon and I stopped
clipping grass and took out the pocket watch I had
borrowed from my father.

I gathered my tools and returned to the
unconsecrated chapel where I had my lunch and a
cup of coffee. I followed this with a cigarette
and reluctantly pulled myself away from the fire's
inviting warmth to tinker with an old Allen mower.
I took out my father's pocket watch again and saw
that it was about 12.55 p.m.

I then lit another cigarette and went to smoke
it standing by the steps to the right of the
unconsecrated chapel. I noticed a woman walking up
the path towards the junior school. I had never
seen her before, so I continued to watch her until
she went behind the hedge surrounding the Garden
of Remembrance.

There had been some damage caused to some of the
graves, nothing too serious, just childish
vandalism, so I was asked to look out for any such
behaviour. By the time she passed behind the hedge
I had finished my cigarette and, realising she would
not be the kind of person to do any damage, I went
back inside the chapel where I stoked up the fire.

I then put on my jacket and picked up my
lemonade bottle with the hope of getting to the
shops before they closed for lunch.

By the time I left the unconsecrated chapel it
would be about 1.05. The shop I was heading for
normally closed at 1 p.m., but had on occasions
been known to stay open for a few minutes longer
if they had customers in already being served.

As I walked along the main drive I soon noticed that the woman, who I later learnt was Wendy Sewell, was walking along the bottom footpath that runs alongside Catcliff Wood. She was a little way ahead of me and seemed to be in no rush.

She appeared to be looking from side to side at the inscriptions on the headstones. I estimate that it would have taken around two to three minutes to cover the length of the path, with the woman disappearing behind the consecrated chapel moments before I drew level with the building. As I went past she did not continue on her journey and I naturally assumed that she had turned around to retrace her steps. I didn't turn around to look.

When I came level with the lodge I saw Wilf Walker and his wife at the door. I don't think his wife acknowledged me, but Wilf and I nodded to each other. I turned left outside the gates and passed Peter Moran crossing the road on his way back to work.

We both said hello to each other without stopping. As I got nearer to the shop I passed Charlie Carman, also on his way back to work. We both greeted each other and again neither of us stopped. Moments later, I realised the shop had already closed so I went home.

I would later come to learn that Stephen had received a good education in prison and took several exams to improve his English and writing skills, so he was a far cry from the boy with a reading age of 11 when he first went to prison. As I studied his personal account, something struck me as very odd. I thought

Charlie Carman, a trial witness, could perhaps have helped Stephen establish his alibi, yet he was only called as a prosecution witness due to his sighting of Wendy Sewell. And he only gave written evidence for the prosecution. It was only ever said in court that Stephen saw Moran, not Carman. I found it strange that Carman had not been called or even cross-examined by Stephen's defence team.

I continued reading.

Upon arrival I went to unlock the door and my mother called to me to say the door wasn't locked. I went in via the back door where my mother greeted me. She was in the process of making herself a cup of coffee and explained that she had not long arrived home.

I asked if she would buy me a bottle of lemonade when the shop reopened. My mother said she would. I then counted out the money – minus the allowance on the returned bottle. She asked if I would like the bottle of lemonade bringing down to the churchyard and I said something along the lines that it would be all right either way, as I could always take it with me the next day. I then asked her if she had fed my baby hedgehogs, as that was one of the main reasons I had gone back home. She said she had.

A couple more minutes passed and then I said I had better be getting back. My mother offered to make a cup of coffee, but I refused. I never liked to be away for too long in case anyone checked up on me and I had to explain the reason for my absence, as I had perhaps spent about five minutes or so with my mother before leaving and making my way back to the cemetery by the same route.

As I entered the main gates of the cemetery, I noticed that Wilf and his wife had gone into the lodge and closed the door. After going a little further, I took my jacket off and carried it over my shoulder. It wasn't until I was passing some of the first graves that something caught my eye, so I looked to my left. It took a few seconds to realise that it was someone lying on the bottom path, so I walked over. It was impossible to see the blood from the main drive or any of the external signs of injury.

I threw my jacket down at the victim's feet and then I knelt at her side. It was not possible to check for any signs of life while she was lying on her front, so I rolled her over towards me. There was quite a lot of blood on the path and her hair was heavily soaked in it. I don't recall seeing any facial injuries.

I felt for a pulse at the neck but found none. It came as a shock when she raised herself up, and I too reacted by getting to my feet.

It was at this point that I had something sharp pressed into the small of my back and I began to turn to try to see who was behind me.

I was ordered not to turn around and was told if I was to say anything my sister would get the same. The man said something along the lines of 'have you found it?', as if to address another person. No reply came and then the next thing I knew was that the person had left me, and I turned

at the sound of rustling foliage as they made
their escape down into the woodland area.

I gave him and his companion no more attention
but picked up my jacket and ran over to the lodge,
whereupon I asked Wilf Walker if he was on the
phone.

He said he wasn't and asked me why I should
enquire. I informed him that a woman had been
attacked. He asked me to show him where and he
followed me to the corner of the lodge. I pointed
in the direction of where she lay. He said some of
my work colleagues had come into the cemetery and
we should check first to see if they had already
called the emergency services.

As we got to within a few yards of the chapel we
were met by other workers carrying out sheets of
asbestos and leaning them against the outside of
the building ready for loading on to a Land Rover.
They had arrived in Watts's white van.

Wilf asked them if they had seen anything or
called the police or an ambulance. They said they
hadn't and one of them went off to make the call.
Shortly afterwards Dawson arrived in the Land
Rover. As I recall, Dawson made to go over to
where she was, and at the same time shouted she
was getting up.

I had my back to her and turned to look. She
was already on her feet and managed to take a
few steps, perhaps two or three, before losing
her balance and falling forwards, banging the
left side of her forehead on the corner of a
headstone.

Dawson was slow to react and had taken only a couple of steps by the time she was falling over. Watts shouted to Dawson he should just leave her alone and not touch anything.

We then stood outside the unconsecrated chapel near to the steps leading to the bottom footpath. It must have been about 10 to 15 minutes before a police officer, PC Ball, arrived on the scene and came over to where we were standing. He asked a few questions as to who had found her, what we were doing there, then asked where she was. We indicated, and he went over to her and had a look and then walked part of the way back before calling me over to where he waited. He asked if I had been the one who found her, and I said I was. He then went on to ask me to say where, and I told him, and even pointed out the place from where we stood.

Finally, he asked if I had touched anything. I said I hadn't except for turning her over, and I showed him my bloodstained hands. I asked if I could wash the blood off my hands, but he said no, it would be needed for forensics. We then went over to where the rest of the group stood. I seem to recall him asking a couple of questions – if any of them had seen or touched anything. They all answered no.

I think it was Dawson who asked if it was all right for me to help them load the Land Rover and the policeman said it was. The policeman then went back and placed his tunic over the body before going to his car and making a call on the radio.

It would be a good 15 to 20 minutes, at a guess, before anyone else arrived and maybe as much as another 5 to 10 minutes before a Detective Inspector Younger came to ask me the same questions that PC Ball had just asked. I gave him the same answers.

He went back to the others for a brief moment and then came back with someone else in a suit. I was asked if I would be willing to go with them to the station for further questioning, which I agreed to do. I was led over to a blue and white police car where I sat in the back with one of the policemen, while the other got in the front with the driver. As we were about to go through the cemetery gates the ambulance arrived.

I already had many queries and misgivings about the case. This latest account from Stephen threw me into even greater turmoil.

The thing that immediately stood out was his description of someone assaulting him and threatening his sister, as he knelt by the injured woman. If this were true, and this unidentified person had a companion as suggested, then who were these people? And why was no mention of them made at the trial? Could one of them be the man who trial witnesses Louisa Hadfield and George Paling saw running away from the direction of the cemetery? I also wondered why so little effort was made on the part of the police to establish who this running man was.

Of course, this latest account was at serious odds with Stephen's original confession, which he had retracted after 13 days. However, apart from the omission of someone in the cemetery threatening him, it was same story he had told the police during the first nine hours in the police station, and in subsequent years in prison. I needed to know why Stephen had briefly deviated from this version and admitted in his confession to attacking and sexually assaulting Wendy Sewell.

When I re-read Stephen's alleged confession statement, there were various bits and pieces that simply did not and could not match the facts. Stephen said he hit Wendy twice on the back of the head to knock her out. The Home Office's own summary confirmed that Wendy had been hit 'seven or eight times' with repeated, savage blows to the head.

I also questioned how, after such an attack, any jury could have imagined Stephen Downing walking out of the cemetery appearing 'calm' and 'perfectly normal', with no apparent blood-staining after such a frenzied attack. There was also no mention in his 'confession' of Wendy having moved from the path to the graves. In fact, he said, 'She was lying on the ground the same way I had left her.'

One of the workmen, Hawksworth, said he had picked up the murder weapon earlier in the day. In which case his fingerprints would have been on it as well as those of the murderer. Were any fingerprints or blood samples taken from the murder weapon? Or from the workmen, who were also allowed to carry on working in and around the chapel even though the supposed murderer had gone back there after committing such a violent attack? If the pickaxe handle had come from the council store, any of the workmen's fingerprints could have appeared on it quite innocently, even Stephen's.

Another important factor taken from Stephen's account of the day was that, on his way home from the cemetery at 1.08 pm, he spoke words of greeting to one of the prosecution witnesses, Charlie Carman. He said he saw him between the shop and the cemetery, walking in the direction of town on his way to work.

Unfortunately, Carman was now dead, but I found out that at the time he had been employed, like Stephen, as a gardener with the council.

That day, Carman was working in Bath Gardens in the town centre. I checked his evidence. It confirmed he was heading back into town that lunchtime, but made no mention of seeing Stephen Downing.

Carman said he looked over the hedge of the cemetery somewhere near the phone box and saw Wendy walking along a path. At this point on his route he would have already passed Stephen, who was heading to the shop. So, Wendy must have been uninjured after Stephen had left the cemetery. Why then had Carman not been quizzed over this anomaly? Had Stephen ever queried this with the police or his defence team?

I also noticed a major time discrepancy. Carman said he had spotted Wendy at 12.50, but everyone agreed that Stephen did not leave the cemetery until around 1.08. If Stephen saw Carman, and vice versa, then Charlie's timing was well out.

There were many parts of this puzzle that didn't make sense. But I also needed some more answers from Stephen. Why did he change his story at the police station? Why admit attacking and, moreover, sexually assaulting Wendy? Why did he wait 13 days before retracting his confession?

I was also interested in knowing more about Nita's assertion that he changed his boots when he came home at lunchtime.

She claimed it was because he had put on the wrong boots in the morning. And I also needed to clear up the allegation concerning this mystery man in the cemetery who had poked Stephen in the back and threatened him. Why on earth had that allegation not formed part of his defence? I knew I would still need to ask some difficult questions, which many people, the Downings included, might not like.

I wrote to Stephen again and asked him if he could answer some additional queries. In particular, I wanted to hear his version of the interrogation at the police station. Ray told me the confession was forced out of him, but I needed to hear it all directly from Stephen.

CHAPTER 7

BELIEVING THE BEEBES

I realised my presence and my nosey-parker attitude was making an impact around Bakewell. Perhaps I was beginning to upset some locals who thought their secrets had been buried with Wendy Sewell.

I noticed it far more on the council estate near the Downings' home, where quite often people would stop and point at me as I drove past, no doubt muttering something about me under their breath.

I was apprehensive about becoming involved in such a delicate and controversial case. I knew my involvement was likely to make enemies in this small rural community, and was bound to reawaken many thoughts and emotions that had been suppressed for decades.

One morning as I breezed into work, Elsie, the receptionist, who was on the telephone, began frantically beckoning to me with her free arm. I was about to ask her what the matter was when she put a finger to her lips.

I hurried through the door and round the back of the counter to where she was sitting.

'Really, young man,' she was saying in her best telephone manner, 'now do go away and stop being so silly!' With that she slammed the receiver down.

'Who was it?' I asked.

'I don't know, Don. But he said he wanted to kick your head in,' she replied, raising her eyebrows. Elsie had been with the *Mercury* for donkey's years and was used to dealing with irate callers. She was not easily fazed.

'Did he say why?'

'He just said you would know why.'

'Well, I might.'

She peered at me over her glasses. She was a tall, thin woman with a quick temper who was in her late forties and was always impeccably dressed. She didn't suffer fools gladly and had a real bee in her bonnet about 'time wasters' interrupting her regimented routine.

Elsie then added casually, 'To be quite honest, it's the second time he's rung.'

'When was the last?' I enquired.

'A couple of days ago. I wasn't going to mention it. He was more abusive the first time, rather than threatening. But if he's starting to talk about beating you up, well, you should know. It was definitely the same chap. He didn't sound particularly old.' She paused, obviously waiting for me to explain.

'I'm sorry, Elsie. If you get any more, don't talk to him. Just put him straight through to me. Or if I'm out, hang up.'

I walked through to my office, leaving Elsie burning with curiosity. I was angry that someone was upsetting my staff, but if they thought they could put me off that easily, they had another thing coming.

Even at that early stage, I had a gut feeling about the case. Lots of people kept singing the same tune – Downing was serving time for someone else. I had an overwhelming desire to seek out the truth once and for all. If Stephen Downing was guilty and I could prove it, then it would at least end the mystery.

But what if he was innocent?

Certain prominent local characters and traders began to show a peculiar interest in my preliminary enquiries, displaying a curious nervousness about the victim's past. Calls came in to me from a publican and several shop owners in Bakewell, asking me why I was suddenly 'digging up dirt' about this old case.

Feedback about my investigation also came from my advertising reps. They felt that pressure was mounting for me to drop the case. Advertisers were becoming nervous that it could have an adverse effect both on advertising revenues and the tourism trade, as Bakewell was not that sort of town.

More interesting to me, however, was the reps also confirming that the town was buzzing with gossip about the victim's love life. It was being said that she had had several boyfriends, echoing what Ray and Sam Fay, my deputy editor, had told me the first time the Downings came to my office, and there was even mention of a love child, despite it being said at the trial and in the Home Office report that the Sewells had no children. I would have to look more closely at the life and times of Mrs Wendy Sewell.

My reporters also added that the local 'plods and pips' weren't happy about me kicking up dust over an old case like this, which was already long gone and forgotten.

Reputations were on the line. I asked Jackie to make an approach to the duty inspector, but he seemed to be advising us to leave well alone. I asked her if he gave a precise reason. She shook her head and replied, 'All he said was that Downing was guilty. A right little pervert.' This claim was something I would come to hear a few times – but why?

'It's strange,' I said. 'But that's what some other contacts have said. All very interesting, but I can't find anything to substantiate their claims.'

All this was happening despite the fact that I had not yet published one word in the *Mercury* about the case. I did, however, start to gain a lot of support from many people who were starting to express their doubts and opinions about the case. The residents of some houses that overlooked the cemetery had lived there for years and confirmed that no routine house-to-house enquiries were carried out at the time.

Marie Bright, an elderly lady, asked to see me urgently. When I visited her home, she told me she was still worried – even now – about possible repercussions. She explained she'd seen a 'pasty-faced' man with a bright orange T-shirt hanging around the main entrance gates about an hour before the attack.

She claimed the man got off the bus from Bakewell at about noon. Mrs Bright said, 'This man was aged about 40 to 45 and was acting rather queer. I hadn't seen him around before and I think he was a stranger because he kept looking around, and at his watch. He looked suspicious, as though he was waiting for someone. I saw this man coming over the top of the wall, out of the cemetery, about an hour later.'

She said she had also seen another man parked up in a dark-coloured van near the phone box by the cemetery gates some time that lunchtime. She described him as a fat, bulky figure.

Margaret Richards, another elderly woman who lived close by, told me she too had seen a man standing close to the beech hedge by the cemetery gates. Her description of him was almost identical to that given by Marie Bright of the man in the orange T-shirt. She claimed he appeared to be acting suspiciously, looking at his watch, and was very nervous.

Both Bright and Richards said they had been to Bakewell police station to report their sightings. They had seen PC Ernie Charlesworth, who hadn't seemed interested and told them they already had someone in custody charged with the murder. I knew Charlesworth and believed him to be an arrogant and lazy beat bobby. He was considered something of a bully by junior colleagues.

I wondered why he had not referred these witnesses to a more senior investigating officer. What I wasn't aware of at that time was the fact that he had been the one who got the confession out of Downing, which he had boasted about for years.

I wondered, too, whether the noon bus driver had been questioned, or whether he had seen any suspicious characters running around. In those days everyone knew everyone, and a stranger would be noticed.

I was then contacted by another witness, a Mrs Gibson from a neighbouring road, who said the police did call at her home on the Saturday night after the attack and actually took a statement. She claimed she was told not to tell anyone or say anything to anyone else. But she too confirmed the police didn't make general house-to-house calls.

This was agreed by housewife Pat Shimwell, who explained she had been chatting with a friend at the door of her house on Burton Edge, overlooking the cemetery, and noticed Stephen Downing leaving by the main gate at about 1.10 p.m. with his pop bottle.

She was standing at her garden gate with her arms folded as we spoke, relating her story in a matter-of-fact manner. Like many of the women who were eager to talk to me, Pat Shimwell was in her mid-fifties and had been at her home near the cemetery all day on 12 September.

I believed the police would have had a ready-made set of witnesses with any one of these plain-speaking women who apparently noticed everything – if only they had bothered to talk to them. Pat Shimwell later told me that she was in her bedroom tidying up when she heard a 'commotion in the cemetery', with several workmen yelling at each other.

She remembered someone shouting out something like 'leave her!' At about 1.30 she saw the policeman in the cemetery. She told me that a bobby asked if she had seen anything. And then claimed that she was quite remarkably told, 'If anyone asks, I haven't been here.'

I asked her if she could be sure that Stephen had left the cemetery at around 1.10 p.m. She said she could because she had seen the bus at its scheduled stop at the same time. Once again, I had reason to thank Hulleys buses for helping to plot the course of the day's events.

Pat Shimwell asked if I'd spoken to any of the youngsters who were playing around the area that lunchtime. I recalled Ray saying something about children when we walked around the cemetery.

She suggested I should track down Ian and Lucy Beebe. The story was that something 'horrible' had frightened them in the cemetery that day. Shimwell admitted that they were very young at the time, and told me they used to live along Burton Edge but had since moved away.

I soon discovered that the Beebe family played a crucial but often maligned role in this murder inquiry. The eldest daughter was Jayne Atkins, a fifteen-year-old at the time, who was a half-sister to little Ian and Lucy, then aged four and seven. Jayne appeared as a major new witness at the Court of Appeal in October 1974 to give evidence in support of Stephen Downing.

Jayne told three appeal court judges she had seen 'a man and a woman with their arms round each other' in the cemetery on the day Wendy Sewell was attacked. She confirmed the man was not Stephen Downing.

She explained that only a few minutes before she saw the couple embrace, she had seen Stephen leaving the cemetery. She said the couple were standing on the lower path, behind one of the chapels, and not far from the very spot where Wendy was later found bleeding to death.

Jayne told the court she had been afraid at first to tell the police about what she had seen, for fear the man had recognised her – and that she might become a victim as well.

At a pre-trial hearing, the three law lords decided she could not be believed. They maintained that, had she been a credible witness, she would have come forward much earlier with such vital information. They decided her evidence was therefore 'not credible' and rejected it, and Stephen's appeal against his conviction was hastily dismissed.

I wanted to meet Jayne Atkins, and to see if her story had changed over the years. I was also keen to track down and interview the younger children and find out what had frightened them.

This proved no easy feat. Former neighbours told me the Beebes had moved to a new house because they had been so terrified of reprisals after Jayne had given her evidence to the Court of Appeal. They said the family had received several anonymous threats.

Back at my office, after spending much of the morning on the estate, I received a telephone call on my direct line. 'Been snooping around again, then?' a man's voice sneered.

'Who is this?' I asked. It was not the same voice as before. This man sounded much older.

'Never you mind. That little sod got what he deserved. If I see your car on that estate again, you're dead,' he claimed, before slamming down the phone.

My heart was pounding, and my thoughts turned to Kath and my two boys. What if this person knew where I lived? Not for the first time, I wondered just what I was getting myself into.

*   *   *

Later that week, I finally tracked down the Beebes. They were living on the outskirts of Chesterfield, in a council house in Renishaw, on the road out towards Sheffield. Margaret Beebe opened the door. She was a very pleasant lady in her fifties with a strong local accent.

She greeted me with a friendly smile. When I told her the purpose of my visit she appeared enthusiastic and ushered me inside. She told me that the children, by now in their twenties and thirties, had all left home. She and her husband Ken lived on their own.

Once she started talking about past events, her mood changed. She told me that she and her family left Bakewell in 1977, moving first to Lichfield in Staffordshire before ending up here in Renishaw, about 15 miles from Bakewell. She confirmed what I had already been told – that they were forced to move because they believed their lives were in danger after Jayne gave evidence at the Court of Appeal.

They had received anonymous threats for more than two years, and could take it no more.

'The worst thing was,' she said, 'no one believed us. No one took us seriously, except for our immediate neighbours. We were just left to get on with it and deal with all this bother on our own. It was very upsetting. And it was terrible for the little ones.'

'So, tell me what happened that day, Margaret,' I said.

'The children, that's my Ian and Lucy, and their little friend Pam Sheldon, were all out playing on waste ground, then in the cemetery, when something frightened them. I think they told me at the time that somebody with blood on them jumped over the wall out of the cemetery and frightened the life out of them. They wouldn't go into the cemetery for a long while after that.'

'What time of day was this?'

'Ian and Lucy had come home at lunchtime from infant school and were out playing on their bikes,' she said. 'Then Ian came in as white as a sheet. He'd left his bike somewhere. He couldn't say anything at first. I sat him down on the couch. He was very scared and talked about a man with blood on him.

'He had nightmares for a long time afterwards. He couldn't go back to school and had to stay at home.'

Margaret Beebe was sitting on the sofa next to me but was talking thirteen to the dozen, and flailing her arms around like a windmill, as she became more and more engrossed in her story.

I had to duck several times.

'I put my little one, Adrian, in the buggy,' she continued, 'and took Lucy back to school. As I passed the cemetery there were police there, and an ambulance. I remember seeing them putting a body into the ambulance.

'When I went back home, Ian had messed himself with fright. I thought I'd fetch a doctor, then he calmed down a bit and said, "Mummy, that man got blood all over him!"'

'Were the police told about all this?' I asked.

'They came around on the Friday night, two days after the attack, but didn't take any statements. Ian was in bed asleep, so they said they'd come back to talk to him. They never did, though.'

'And this was the first time the police came to your house? They didn't come on the day itself?'

'No, the Friday was the first time. They didn't go to any of the houses on Burton Edge on the day it happened.' Margaret added that some time after 1.10 on the day of the attack she popped her head round the perimeter hedge of the cemetery to look for the family's pet dog.

Her daughter Jayne had already gone out to look for it. Margaret said, 'I didn't see anyone.' A few minutes later, though, she recalled hearing a shout, something like 'Hey!' or 'Help!'

'It must have been a shocking experience for your family,' I said.

'Well, later that day, when I went to work at Cintride at six o'clock, I heard all about this woman who had been battered in the cemetery. I kept Ian off school till the following Monday, but he continued to suffer with his nerves until 1977. It was four years of misery until we moved to Lichfield.

'I had a breakdown after all this. Our family was called a pack of liars by the police. We only said what we saw. I used to work at Cintride on the 6 till 10 p.m. shift. One night, when I was walking there on my own up Bagshaw Hill, a car came alongside me and slowed down.

'There were people in the front and back, and someone wound down the window and shouted, "You had better keep your mouth shut or else things will happen to you and your girl!" I think this was after the trial but before the appeal. When Jayne gave her evidence, the judges basically called her a liar.'

Margaret Beebe added one other interesting fact to my ever-increasing portfolio of information. Her husband Ken, a quarry worker, had been approached by a workmate during one of his breaks, some two or three years after the murder, who told him, 'It's a shame Stephen Downing is doing time for someone else. I know who did it.'

This gem of information was typical of many statements I was to encounter over the next few years. If it was all true, then the identity of the murderer of Wendy Sewell had been one of the worst-kept secrets in the Peak District.

The more I talked to people, the more it appeared that half the population of the town and its surrounding villages knew what had 'really happened', and were 'certain' who the murderer was. About half-a-dozen names regularly cropped up.

I quickly came to realise that in a small community during that period, gossip and rumour spread like wildfire. Yet if you attempted to trace it back to its source, a wall of silence would suddenly descend, the more usual response being, 'I don't want to get involved.'

Amazingly, I was to encounter tales of drunken boasting in the town's numerous pubs of many men claiming to have been 'involved' with Wendy and/or her killing. Many of the claims were contradictory, yet one remark was uttered consistently: 'Stephen Downing didn't do it.'

I thanked Margaret Beebe for her help and asked if she could put me in touch with her children, Ian, Lucy and Jayne.

Ian and Lucy were a possibility, she said, although how accurate their memories would be after 21 years was debatable, considering their tender ages at the time.

She wrote down my number and said she would pass it on to them. She added that they both lived nearby. Jayne, however, was another matter. Mrs Beebe confirmed that Jayne was now in her late thirties, but had lived in fear of her life ever since she was a teenager.

Despite the passage of time, Jayne remained convinced that the person responsible for Wendy Sewell's death still meant to harm her after she had dared to speak out at the appeal. Mrs Beebe said she had promised her daughter that she would not reveal Jayne's whereabouts.

*   *   *

Lucy Beebe, or Lucy Wood, to use her married name, telephoned me a few days later at the *Mercury* office. She was very helpful and described the events quite clearly, saying, 'I went into the cemetery looking for my brother Ian and my friend Pamela at lunchtime on the day of the murder. We used to play there all the time. We were little devils. We used to play with the flowers on the graves. Ian and I were playing hide-and-seek that day.'

'So, did you see anything unusual on that particular day?'

'I saw Ian. He was pale and shocked, and I helped him back home. He didn't or couldn't say anything. I remember that it took him a while to recover. He even left his bike in the road. He'd obviously seen something that really frightened him.'

'Did he say what had scared him so much?'

'He spoke later of a bloodstained man on the graves.'

I didn't press Lucy any further, or ask her any leading questions, as I wanted her memories to be untainted by suggestion as far as possible.

So many rumours had flown around Bakewell for the past 20 years or more, and I was acutely aware that someone who had been a child at the time may have been influenced by half-overheard adult gossip or repeated theories.

I asked Lucy to get in touch with me if she remembered anything else, and I remained determined to speak to her half-sister Jayne Atkins. I had been making strenuous efforts to discover her whereabouts, pressing the family to let me know where she was. I was still convinced Jayne could be a vital witness, as she had recalled seeing Wendy embracing a man after Stephen had left the cemetery.

Jackie, who had been eavesdropping on my call, obviously felt as I did. Once I had put down the receiver, she said, 'Don, we really must talk about Jayne Atkins.'

For the past week or so, Jackie had immersed herself in the details of the failed 1974 appeal. Margaret Beebe had agreed to talk to her on the telephone, and Jackie had spent hours questioning her about Jayne and talking to the Downings about the case that had been prepared for the Court of Appeal.

She had studied the newspaper reports and court papers from the time, as well as old police notes provided by my friendly informants in the force. They all confirmed that Jayne's evidence was rejected mainly on the grounds that too much time had passed before she came forward. I was desperate to chat with Jayne to find the reasons why.

I was delighted by Jackie's enthusiasm. 'We'll arrange a proper meeting, Jackie,' I replied. 'We need to go through everything with the team.'

* * *

A few days later I met up with Allan Taylor, a presenter on Central Television, in a pub far away from the madding crowds of Bakewell. Allan was tall and wiry, and spoke in a deep, slow Scottish drawl. I had known him for many years, and during my time at the *Mercury* we had co-operated on many stories.

I outlined the case and my findings to date. Allan was particularly concerned about Stephen Downing's original statement and the amount of time he was detained without support. Over the next few days he began making some enquiries of his own and even went to see the Downings.

On his way back to Nottingham one day, he called in at the *Mercury* offices. Jackie got her chance to tell us about her research on Jayne Atkins. She filled in Allan with the background, explaining how Jayne was a 15-year-old girl at the time, living in a house on Burton Edge, along the topside of the cemetery.

Jackie explained, 'She had come home during her school lunch break from Lady Manners and was looking for her pet dog. She remembered she had left the house after listening to the one o'clock news headline on the radio. She had turned right along the path by the top of the cemetery towards the junior school.

Halfway from her home to the end of the cemetery there's a bit where the hedge stops, and then there's a wall.

'Just then, she looked into the graveyard and saw a woman near the Garden of Remembrance. In her statement she told police the woman was young and slim with dark hair and wearing a beige-coloured trouser suit with dark brown matching jumper. She didn't know her.'

She continued, 'Jayne continued walking along the path by the cemetery. By the beech hedge at the far end, she looked into the open fields beyond. There was still no sign of her pet dog. The dog often went into the cemetery, so she decided to have a look in there. As she walked along to the side gate at the junior school end, she remembers seeing a dark-coloured van – she thought it was brown – parked on waste ground close to the school.

There was a man sitting inside, a biggish bloke. Then she went into the cemetery and walked along the top path towards the workmen's store at the unconsecrated chapel.

'When she reached the main drive, she saw Stephen Downing walking out, a good way in front of her towards the main gate. She knew Stephen by sight, as he lived on the same estate. He didn't see her.

'She passed the unconsecrated chapel and, as she got about level with the little grass island near it, some movement caught her attention. She glanced across and noticed the woman she had seen a few minutes earlier standing behind the consecrated chapel on the bottom path with her arms round a man.

'Later, when she saw newspaper photographs, she was able to identify this woman as Wendy Sewell. She told police she didn't know the man, but said he had sandy-coloured shoulder-length hair, was about five feet eight inches tall and was wearing denim jeans and a jacket.

'She couldn't see her dog, so she turned around and retraced her steps along the middle path. She then spotted the dog at the end of the cemetery near the far wall, which bounded the fields, and, after a few minutes, she said she managed to catch him near the bottom gate.

'While putting on his lead she heard the sound of a motor vehicle and, on looking round, saw that a white van had come into the cemetery. She left by the side gate near the school and turned right towards her home. As she walked along the path she heard a shout. She couldn't see who it was because the boundary hedge at this point was about six feet high. She didn't think much of it.

'As she continued back to her house on Burton Edge, she saw Stephen again, this time walking back across the road and heading towards the main cemetery gates. She thought it must have been about 1.25 p.m. when she got home. She went back to school and was late.'

Allan was fascinated by this witness. He had been scribbling down notes the whole time Jackie had been talking. 'She confirms Downing's timings too!' Allan said. 'Her account of seeing this woman in the Garden of Remembrance coincides exactly with what Stephen wrote to you, Don – and the time he left the cemetery and Stephen returning. It all fits! And the description of Wendy Sewell's clothing was accurate, although she could have got that from newspaper reports, I suppose. But why didn't she say all this at first?'

Jackie held the Jayne Atkins file aloft. 'Plenty of reasons,' she said. 'In the Court of Apeal, Lord Justice Orr made the point that she didn't come forward with her story for many months after the murder, even though the police visited her house and asked if anyone had seen anything.'

Jackie paused and studied the paperwork more closely, searching for Jayne's exact words. She said, '"I was afraid the man in the cemetery might have recognised me, and I might be the next one!"

'Now, we know the judges didn't accept this as a good enough reason for her keeping quiet for several months,' Jackie continued. 'But there were things that were never said about Jayne Atkins.

'For a start, she was only 15 when all this happened, and a very vulnerable 15 at that. I don't know the exact details, but she had quite a troubled home life. Soon after the murder, in early November, Jayne ran away from home.

'She was eventually placed with foster parents in Buxton. I know it's only ten miles away, but it would be like another world, away from the estate and all the neighbours gossiping about the murder and Stephen Downing. She simply lost touch with developments on the Wendy Sewell murder case.

'That is, until she saw an article in the newspaper. She had a Saturday job at the Barbecue Cafe in Buxton, and this article had been left lying open on a table by a customer.'

With a flourish, Jackie produced a copy of the *Derbyshire Times* from 23 February 1974. She turned to page six.

YOUTH ON MURDER CHARGE FOUND GUILTY

Stephen Downing, aged 17, was found guilty of murdering 32-year-old typist Mrs Wendy Sewell in a cemetery at Bakewell, Derbyshire, by a unanimous verdict at Nottingham Crown Court last Friday.

'Look at the last paragraph!' Jackie insisted.

He had told the jury that he found the victim lying semi-conscious in the graveyard after going home during his lunch hour, but the prosecution said his lunchtime walk was only an alibi after he had carried out the attack. Downing pleaded not guilty to the murder.

'When Jayne read it,' continued Jackie, 'she knew Downing had told the truth at his trial. That phrase – "The prosecution said his lunchtime walk was only an alibi after he had carried out the attack" – she knew it wasn't like that.

'She had seen Stephen leaving the cemetery on his lunchtime walk. Wendy Sewell had been very much alive at that point – she had been in the arms of another man.

'It dawned on Jayne that there were probably only four people who knew that Stephen had told the truth – herself, Stephen, the victim, who was now dead, and the man Wendy had been embracing before she was attacked. The mysterious sandy-haired man had not come forward, for whatever reason.'

'So, is that when she went to the police?' asked Allan.

'No, not straight away. It was in March. It kept playing on her mind, though. You see she'd always assumed that Stephen must have attacked Wendy later that afternoon, after she saw him going back to the cemetery. I mean, the police were so confident they'd got the right man, that's what they kept telling everyone on the estate – "he's confessed, he did it" – so why should Jayne query it?

'She only heard about the attack when she got back from school later that afternoon, and no one had told her the exact time it was meant to have happened. And, of course, she was terrified. This mystery man was out there somewhere. But who could she tell? Remember, she was only 15, cut off from her family, and maybe knew she wouldn't be believed.

'Eventually she told her foster parents what she knew. Ironically, her foster-father was a Buxton policeman. He told her she should go home and tell her family, and the Bakewell police, everything she had told him. So that's what she did. She then visited the regional HQ at Buxton and spoke with CID officers there.'

'And did they believe her?' Allan asked.

'Well, partially,' said Jackie. 'Talking to her family, it seems the police basically believed her story about seeing Wendy with this other man, but they told her she must have got the wrong day.'

'Even if they thought she'd got the days mixed up, they should still have tried to track him down. If Wendy Sewell had been meeting someone in the cemetery and knew him well enough to be putting her arms round him ... well, surely the police should have found out who he was,' Allan pointed out.

'Yes, but she hadn't got the wrong day,' Jackie said, desperate to make her point. 'It was her first day back of the new school term. Jayne was actually wearing her school uniform and had gone looking for the dog in her school lunch break. It couldn't have been an earlier day, because that would have been in the school holidays.

'And in any case, Stephen had been off with a cold for the previous two days. And it couldn't have been later, because Wendy was in hospital and then died. All they'd needed to estab-lish was that Jayne was in her uniform and had been at school.'

I also realised that confirmation of that fact that Jayne was perfectly correct about the day in question could also have been verified by Stephen's own work records. This was a Wednesday lunchtime, and he had been off sick for a couple of days before, so this was first day back at work. It could not have been any other day.

Additional verification of this fact could also have been obtained from the blonde-haired woman with a dog who met and chatted with Stephen in the cemetery less than an hour before the attack on Wendy Sewell.

Stephen said she was wearing a distinct salmon-pink wool topcoat, and the lady asked him where he had been for the past two days. She could also have accounted for his state of mind immediately before an alleged frenzied attack on another female visitor.

* * *

It took me several more visits to Margaret Beebe's home and some additional telephone calls to Lucy, during which I stressed that Jayne's testimony might be vital in getting Stephen out of jail if only I could convince the authorities to allow another appeal, before I persuaded them to tell me where she was staying.

Shortly after the 1974 appeal failed, she had fled the country in fear for her life. By early 1995 she was living and working in a small hotel on a Greek island. I now had her telephone number.

A few days later, I called the hotel bar in Greece where Jayne worked. I spoke with an English woman who was having a drink. I explained that I was calling from the UK and needed to speak to Jayne.

She knew her and said she would try to find her. I fully expected her to come back with a negative response, but, after waiting a good five minutes, I was taken aback when Jayne answered.

Her first reaction was one of shock that I had managed to trace her. This quickly gave way to fear – if I could find her then so could anyone else. I reassured her that her family had been concerned for her safety and wanted to protect her. I told her not to worry as they were certainly not giving out her number at random. Lucy had been in touch with her so she at least knew something about my investigation.

Jayne then repeated the story she had told the Court of Appeal 21 years earlier, standing by it in every detail. She said she didn't know the man Wendy had embraced, but she had clearly seen him.

She said she was still fearful because he knew who she was, stating, 'Not only did I see him, but he saw me.' Jayne knew he must have read everything in the papers about her giving evidence to the Court of Appeal at the time, and confirmed there had been nasty, anonymous threats made to her family.

'I was told to keep my mouth shut, or I'd end up like Wendy,' she recalled, with her voice now trembling. 'And after the appeal I was warned that there was a contract out on me if I opened my mouth again – I was told that I would be shot!'

It really shocked me to realise that this 37-year-old woman was still living in fear for her life as a result of a murder that had taken place more than two decades previously.

*   *   *

I was awoken by the local police in the early hours of the morning to tell me that a large skip full of rubbish, just outside the *Mercury* offices, had been firebombed and set ablaze.

Pulling on my clothes, I immediately rushed down to the office. It was a few minutes after 3 a.m. I was just in time to see a fire crew hosing down the skip. Luckily the flames had fallen just short of the building, and there was little or no wind.

I returned home and, after a few hours of tossing and turning, I finally struggled back to the office. This was Tuesday, the busiest day of the week, as the paper was going to press.

I was shocked to see that a front window had been smashed.

Arrangements were made to have the window boarded up and we waited for the police to arrive again. The floor was strewn with broken glass, and a large house brick lay in the middle of a desk belonging to the advertising manager. It must have been hurled though the window shortly after we had all left once the fire in the skip had been put out.

I wondered if the culprit had been watching us and waiting, and I presumed it must have been the same person who started the fire outside. I was grateful the brick had landed in the early hours of the morning rather than in the middle of the day.

In the afternoon the telephone rang in my office, straight through on my direct line. I recognised the voice from the last time. 'There'll be more to come if you don't drop this Downing case,' the man threatened.

'So you know about the skip and the brick?'

'You'll get more than a brick next time! And mark my words, there will be a next time if you don't stop. You might get blown away.' Down went the receiver again.

I admit, I was getting scared. Not only was the *Matlock Mercury* building a target for attack, but now I was, too.

CHAPTER 8

THE RUNNING MAN

The identity of at least one person placed near the scene of the crime was proving elusive. Two defence witnesses at trial had described someone running 'ever so fast' and 'in a terrific hurry' away from the direction of the cemetery. Who was this running man?

The testimony of one of these witnesses in particular, Louisa Hadfield, had been highlighted by the judge as indicating 'someone else might have been responsible'. It seemed this line of enquiry had never been properly investigated.

I called on Louisa Hadfield, a wiry yet lively old lady. She was a widow in her late seventies, and she had called the office after seeing my car on the estate and hearing about updates in the local post office.

She was quite a fiery character who didn't suffer fools gladly, and spoke of a distrust of the local police. She walked with a stick, and at first glance appeared physically frail, but her eyes still sparkled and she had a real passion for justice. She asked me to sit down in the living room of her house on Yeld Road, and began to recall the events of that day.

The bizarre happenings still remained fixed in her memory, as they did with so many other people. 'I saw everything!' she said indignantly. 'I can remember it all as clearly as if it were yesterday.'

'Tell me about this running man, for a start,' I said.

'Well, I was out walking on Upper Yeld Road with my dog Polly, when this big healthy-looking young man came running at me like a bat out of hell. I was frightened because he was running so very fast, scared-like, and the dog didn't like him one bit. She went for him, and he went up on to the grass verge and looked right into my face.'

She put her hand to her face, with her palm a few inches from her nose, and stared back into it, as if to demonstrate just how close the man had been to her.

'Can you describe exactly what he looked like?'

'Yes, he was over six feet tall, fair hair and youngish. His hair was long in the modern style of that day, and he was a well-built lad with denim jeans and a denim jacket.'

'Did you notice what colour T-shirt he was wearing?' I asked, mindful of the reference to a bright-orange T-shirt in Marie Bright's description of the man hanging around the cemetery.

'I didn't notice a T-shirt. But something I did notice, he had blood on him. On the left side, underneath his kneecap, and some other scratchy marks on that side too. I remember blood in the shape of a horseshoe on his jeans. I could draw you a picture. As I said, it's as clear to me as if it were yesterday. I was very frightened. He scared the living daylights out of me. I thought he was going to hit me.'

This was all fascinating stuff. The judge's summing-up had not mentioned anything about a running man having blood on him. Yet it practically tallied with what the Beebe children told their mother.

'So which way did he go?' I asked.

'He carried on running at top speed up the road, towards Lady Manners School.'

'Did you tell anyone?'

'I told my husband about it. He said not to get involved. But it worried me. I couldn't sleep after I heard about the murder. Eventually he said, "Right, get your coat," and we went to the police station.'

'So what happened there?'

'They didn't seem too bothered. They said they'd already got someone. They told me he'd already admitted it. They took my statement and it appears others had also seen this running man. Mr Paling saw him too as he was about to cross the road with his grandchild, and I think he gave a statement. But he didn't want to get involved.'

'Do you remember what time it was?'

'The 1.20 Hulleys bus had just pulled up at the stop.'

'Was anyone else about?'

'Well, just before I saw this man running, I saw Mr Orange.'

She gave me his real name, but here we'll call him Mr Orange. I remembered that Mr Orange was one of the witnesses who had given brief written evidence at the trial, to the effect that Wendy had passed him near the Kissing Gate on the Butts on the way to the cemetery some time before one o'clock.

Mrs Hadfield continued, 'Mr Orange was heading down towards the cemetery, maybe five minutes or so before I saw the running man. I gather he saw the running man too. He must have done.'

This was interesting. At trial, Mr Orange didn't mention seeing a man running away – but I wondered if he had ever been asked. I made a note to speak to him. 'So, at what point did you think this might have had something to do with the murder?'

'My neighbours, Mrs Wilson and Mrs Corbridge, told me about the attack on the woman in the graveyard at about 3.30 the same day. I didn't connect this man with it at the time.'

'So, when did it dawn on you that it might be relevant?'

'It must have been a day or two after the event,' she said. 'I was sitting here like I'm sitting here today.' She paused and stared ahead, as if looking back into the past. 'As I've said before, I was so upset and bothered that my husband said, "Well, that's it, lass. Get your coat and we'll go down." And that's what we did. We went to the police, but they said someone had admitted it.'

Mrs Hadfield shrugged her shoulders with a sigh of resignation. It was a story she must have retold to people many times. 'So that was the end of it, then, as far as the police were concerned?' I asked.

She gave a wry laugh and stood up. She shuffled across to her sideboard and started to rummage through a top drawer.

'What are you looking for?' I asked.

'You'll see. Wait a minute – I have a photo of this running man,' she replied. I was astonished.

'Here it is,' she said with glee as she pulled out an old newspaper cutting and offered it to me. 'This is him. This is the man I saw running away that day.'

The cutting included a faded photograph and a report from the *Derbyshire Times*, dated some 20 years previously. I turned to Mrs Hadfield with a quizzical look.

'I was looking through this paper one day when I suddenly saw this picture,' she said. 'My heart missed a beat. Here was the bloodstained running man!'

She leaned over and jabbed her finger at the centre of a group of people, at a smiling youth with blond hair. The caption underneath didn't include his name.

'This is the man I saw running away,' she repeated, rather angrily, and sat back in her favourite chair. This drama obviously brought back some mixed emotions for her, and reminded her of her late husband.

I didn't want to exhaust Mrs Hadfield, but I needed to clarify some other points before letting her rest. I asked her, 'Did you find the cutting after the trial, and did you tell the police again?'

She took a deep breath. 'Well, I was down visiting at a block of flats in the town when I bumped into Ethel Wright, who was a cleaner at the police station.

'She was at the flats visiting her brother-in-law. Anyway, I told her all this, and she went and told them at the police station. The police phoned me up that night and asked me to take the picture in to them the next day.'

'So, did you?'

'Yes. I knew I'd seen him, and I knew it was him. I went to the police station and had to go upstairs. Ernie Charlesworth, our local bobby, was just sitting there speaking casually on the telephone.

'He saw me and just seemed to ignore me, and carried on talking to some mate of his. I was kept waiting a long time, and I wondered if he remembered me from my previous visit at the time of the murder.

'He didn't seem very interested. He just took the photograph from me, had a quick glance, and then just shoved it in a filing cabinet. He hardly asked me anything. He didn't take down my statement or ask me any questions.'

'And did the police follow it up?'

'No. I never heard from them again. Even at the time of the murder, the police never came around. That's what I could never get over. It just looked as though you were making it up or telling lies. I hadn't told a lie. It was the truth! That's why I went out and bought another paper, so I could keep a copy. It's been in that drawer ever since.'

I later managed to obtain a copy from the archives and sent it to Stephen in prison to see if he recognised the man. I then asked

Mrs Hadfield if she had seen this running man again on the estate, or anywhere else around town since.

Quite surprisingly, she responded, 'Yes, I saw him up here just a few weeks after the murder, and before all this business in the paper. He was walking on the other side of the road, and I opened a window to let him know I'd seen him. And when he walked on further, I dashed downstairs and went to the front door to watch him.'

'Do you know his name?'

'I didn't at the time, and when I found out it meant nothing to me. It was just that face I remembered. And I'll remember it to my dying day.'

'So, what is his name?' I asked.

She looked me intently in the eye and gave me the running man's real name. For now, I will just call him Mr Blue.

*   *   *

Following my conversation with Louisa Hadfield, I attempted to talk to the other trial witness, George Paling, who also claimed to have seen a man rushing up Yeld Road in the direction of Lady Manners School at around the same time.

Paling was reluctant to speak to me. Now in his late seventies, he said he had already given a statement to the police and said his evidence had been read out at the trial. He seemed frightened, and he told me he did not want to get involved.

Fortunately, in the bundle of paperwork the Downings had left with me I found a copy of the actual statement he had given to the police at 11.50 p.m. on the night of the attack, when they visited his home.

He said that at around 1.10 p.m. on the day in question he saw: 'A man hurrying along the road from the direction of the cemetery towards Lady Manners School. I looked at him because he seemed harassed. He was walking as fast as he could without running, his arms were swinging and his mouth hanging open. He was sweating, and he looked queer – so much so that I nudged my wife to look at him. He then went out of sight along the road.'

Paling claimed he saw this man again some five or ten minutes later as he took his granddaughter for a walk in her pushchair along by Lady Manners School. His statement confirmed: 'As I approached the main entrance to the school I saw the same man standing in the entrance, looking towards the school, and he had his hand on the wall. He gave me a glare, and, because of his whole attitude, I gave him a wide berth, although he didn't speak. I carried on walking about three or four hundred yards and then turned round. On my return he had disappeared completely.'

In his description of the man Paling said he was 'about 28 to 35 years old, about 5 foot 8 to 5 foot 9' but on the stout side, with dark hair, clean-shaven, flushed complexion, no hat and clean-looking.

'He was wearing a navy-blue sports shirt and trousers, no jacket. I couldn't say what colour trousers, greyish if anything. He had a good head of hair, but not long. Thinking about it, I can't think where he went unless it was into the school grounds.'

I was interested but slightly confused by the description Paling had given. A stout, dark-haired, smartly dressed man in his late twenties to mid-thirties and of medium height was nothing like the tall, fair, denim-clad youth of Louisa Hadfield's memory.

In Paling's statement there was no mention of any bloodstaining. His description also failed to match the man Marie Bright and Margaret Richards saw hanging around the cemetery; they saw a man wearing an orange T-shirt, while Paling's wore a navy-blue sports shirt.

So why would two different men be running or hurrying up the road in a state of agitation at around the same time of day? An obvious theory is that one was chasing the other, or they were both somehow involved in the attack.

I wondered if Paling had deliberately failed to give a true description because he either knew who this running man was, or that he had been frightened, or even warned off by him, and as he was with a young child he didn't want any repercussions.

I later revisited Louisa Hadfield and told her Paling had refused to speak with me, and that his original description differed greatly from her own. She was very critical of him and reaffirmed that this running man character had definitely scared her. She agreed that he may have been concerned that the man perhaps knew him.

The tale of this running man became something of a folk tale on the estate. What was known, however, was the name of this person, and that he had moved out of the area not long after the murder. I thought it might be worth trying to locate him for a chat.

*   *   *

I discovered that Mr Blue lived down south and had a very good job. He wasn't too hard to locate, and when I called he answered the telephone and gave his name. I told him who I was, and explained that I was investigating the murder of Wendy Sewell and Stephen Downing's claims of innocence.

Suddenly there was absolute silence. You could have heard a pin drop. I knew he was still on the line as I could hear him breathing. When he eventually spoke, he replied angrily, 'How the hell did you manage to trace me?'

I thought it was a very odd reaction. I told him it had only taken me a couple of days to track him down, but privately I wondered why he appeared to be so anxious. I wondered if he had been in hiding, or if the running man was still on the run.

I tried to engage him in conversation, but I could feel the tension and some shakiness in his voice. I said several witnesses claimed to have seen a running man on the day of the attack in 1973, and mentioned that one witness in particular said she had recognised his face from an old newspaper article.

He was stuttering and stumbling for answers. I asked if he had been near the scene of the crime in Bakewell cemetery on that day, and as a real long shot I asked him if he knew Wendy Sewell.

Mr Blue denied knowing her and denied being anywhere near the cemetery, and said he couldn't remember where he was on that day. He also claimed he didn't know anything about the murder and had never heard of Stephen Downing.

It all sounded a bit far-fetched to me. Nearly everyone else I'd spoken to said they could practically recall every detail of that dreadful day in September 1973. He admitted he'd probably left the area shortly after that date, but insisted it was not due to anything sinister.

He said the key witness must have been mistaken, and denied being the running man. He surprisingly added, 'If the police thought I had anything to do with the murder, surely they would have questioned me at the time?'

It was a valid point, but, unknown to me at that time, one possible reason for this alleged oversight by the police lay buried within confidential Home Office files for decades and even now I believe that allegedly the most plausible explanation still remains protected by severe restrictions.

I wondered if this was the same reason the police didn't interview Mr Blue at a later date, after Mrs Hadfield had shown PC

Charlesworth the newspaper cutting. The constant and worrying links back to Charlesworth, and his reluctance to accept any fresh information or evidence, suggested another probable and more logical explanation.

*   *   *

Some months later, I obtained Louisa Hadfield's original police statement, and a note claiming to have positively identified Mr Blue as the running man. Also recorded was the fact Paling's statement had been taken down by Detective Constable Bagshawe at 11.50 p.m. on the day of the attack. By then, Downing had already been detained at Bakewell police station for over nine hours.

On examining the police paperwork it seemed a strange anomaly that detectives were clearly alerted to at least one young, harassed and sweaty man in a 'hell of a hurry' dashing away from the direction of the scene of crime, at about the exact time of the attack, and yet reports suggested no attempts were ever made to verify his identity or to question his actions. It implied that all police enquiries were terminated once Downing had been forced in to signing their 'confession'.

CHAPTER 9

PERSONS OF INTEREST: MR ORANGE, MR OULSNAM AND MR RED

During a conference with my team at the *Mercury*, we ran through a list of potential witnesses – rather than suspects – who might have seen Stephen Downing leaving or returning to the cemetery.

One of the many names who cropped up regularly was Mr Orange. Within official trial reports he was the witness who claimed to have said 'hello' to Wendy at 12.50 p.m. near the top of the Butts, about 200 yards down from the cemetery gates.

Ray Downing had been urging me to read copies of numerous police statements from the early eighties relating to Mr Orange in his bundle of paperwork.

At that time there had been a short-lived flurry of activity surrounding the case in preparation for the second appeal. I had not had time to study all the statements in detail, but at a glance several seemed to be from bar staff at the Castle Hotel in Bakewell. Now Louisa Hadfield's latest statement to me raised some additional queries about Mr Orange.

He was interviewed by police shortly after the attack because allegedly several people had mentioned seeing him around the area. He told them he was on his way home and had not seen Wendy again after greeting her near the top of the Butts.

In 1973 Mr Orange was, by his own admission, a petty crook in his early thirties who had served a spell in prison, and had a reputation for drinking and womanising. He was said by some women of his age group to have had 'film-star good looks' at the time.

By the early nineties he was still living on the estate, had married and separated from his wife, and was now living with a girlfriend – we'll call her Ms Yellow. I was told he still enjoyed a drink or three. He apparently scraped a living doing building jobs, gardening or painting and decorating.

It was time to pay him a visit. During the last few months of 1994 I called several times at his Bakewell home, but he evaded all my attempts to see him.

My trips to the estate were never wasted, though. People were often waiting for me to appear, so they could come forward to offer information. Some of Mr Orange's neighbours, observing my visits and no doubt putting two and two together, told me they believed Mr Orange had once had a brief fling with Wendy. They said Mr Orange's mother told them. And I was told by another witness that they had seen a man making a phone call at around 2 p.m. on the day of the attack from the phone box outside the cemetery gates. They thought this was odd, as he was wearing gloves.

I still found it incredible that, after all these years, people could remember such details and were still eager to pass them on. Many residents were now singing from the same hymn book, claiming they had provided information directly to the police – and especially to PC Charlesworth – only to be rebuffed and told, 'We've already got him,' or, 'He's admitted it.' I was given the impression that some officers had tried to rubbish Downing's reputation at the outset by describing him as a 'weirdo', 'pervert' or 'peeping Tom'.

*   *   *

An elderly lady approached me one day and thrust an old bit of card from a torn cigarette packet into my hand. She said, 'Here, I've kept this for 20 years. You may as well have it.' Descriptions of vehicles and even some registration numbers were scribbled on it.

She said she wrote down all the various makes and colours of cars or vans that she had seen in the road the morning or lunch-time of the day of the murder.

'I was trying to find a policeman to give it to. I expected them to come round all the houses, but they didn't. Eventually I offered it to a policeman near the scene, but he didn't want it either. So see if you can do anything with it,' she said, before shuffling off.

Another woman told me she had seen a large fat man sitting in a brown van near the phone box. This rang a bell, as I remembered Marie Bright a couple of weeks before telling me about a similar sighting. I then double-checked the old lady's cigarette packet, and sure enough she too had made mention of a 'Brown van, Austin make'.

Jayne Atkins had also mentioned a brown van parked close to the cemetery on waste ground along Burton Edge, near the junior school end. She also reported seeing a large man sitting in it. She said this was about 1.05 p.m. Again, I pondered why the police had not traced this man. In a small town like Bakewell it is difficult to remain anonymous.

When I mentioned the brown van and the fat man to others on the estate, I was told almost unanimously, 'Oh, that'll have been Syd Oulsnam.' I thought it strange his name didn't appear within any trial notes, though the name seemed very familiar to me.

Oulsnam was certainly a familiar figure on the estate at the time of the murder. He had a reputation for being lazy and always eating. He was often described as a rather odd odd-job man, preferring to watch others do the work while he just sat in his van with his elbow leaning out of the window.

He lived in an isolated house on the outskirts of Ashford-in-the-Water with his sister and brother-in-law. I was given directions and drove up there one day after visiting Ray. It was an old whitewashed cottage that had obviously seen better days.

Next to it was an outbuilding, which was being used as a garage. An elderly lady opened the door. She had a rather surly, unfriendly expression. She seemed protective of something and didn't open the door very wide. Instinctively, I looked over her left shoulder, and I could see movement in the background and then a fattish man scampering about.

'Hello, I'm from the *Matlock Mercury*. Is Syd Oulsnam at home?'

She looked surprised and rather nervous, as if she was not quite sure what to say. 'Syd?' she queried. 'No, he's not home.'

I looked behind her again and saw the man grabbing his jacket. He looked to be making an exit to the rear. 'So, when will he be back?' I asked.

She turned slightly, trying to look behind her as if for some reassurance. 'Syd?' she repeated. 'I've no idea. He's … No idea, he has been out all day.'

I felt slightly embarrassed for her. Although I had never met Syd, the description seemed to fit the man hiding in the hallway. I handed her my business card and then noticed a van suddenly speed out from the garage yard and drive off in the direction of Ashford.

'Was that Syd?' I asked, waving my hand at the driver as he roared past. I was convinced it was him.

'No, he'll be home later,' she said, sounding rather dismissive.

'Well, that looked like him to me, Mrs …' But she didn't want to give her name or any details.

'Ask him to call me, please? You have my card and numbers. Thank you.'

She closed the door, and I went back to my car grinning.

If Syd didn't want to talk with me at this stage I could wait. I made a note to visit him again.

I made a few more attempts to visit Oulsnam without success. If he didn't want to talk, there was little else I could do.

*   *   *

A week or so later, much to my surprise, Syd Oulsnam phoned the *Mercury* office and asked for me. He sounded nervous and was a little breathless. He asked me why I wanted to see him and innocently enquired, 'I gather you've been round to my house?'

I asked him about the day of the attack on Wendy. He said he couldn't remember much about it as it was so long ago. He was determined to distance himself from the area and said he was away that day. I thought it odd. If he couldn't remember then how did he know he was away?

I told Oulsnam that his name had been mentioned, together with a description of him in his van parked near the back of the cemetery.

'No, no, not me,' he insisted. 'I wasn't anywhere near Bakewell that day.' He then queried what day it was again, which was strange after just giving me a categorical assurance that he wasn't there.

'Wednesday, 12 September 1973.' I said. 'Wendy was attacked at lunchtime. Does that help your memory?'

'No. I was *miles* away from town that day,' he replied.

'So, Syd, how do you explain the fact that your van was seen there?'

He sounded very nervous again. 'No, not me. You must be mistaken.'

I asked him if he had been questioned over the murder. He remained vague and then agreed he had given a statement, adding, 'So had everyone else.'

'And what did you tell the police, Syd? Did you say you were miles away?'

'Yes, I think so,' he spluttered. 'I went there of my own free will.'

'Are you sure, Syd? Your own free will, you say? And not because people had reported seeing you and the van?' I paused for a reply. None came.

'Syd, I want you to put the record straight. People keep saying these things. Did someone suggest you were up there that day? And you do admit you were questioned by the police?'

'I went of my own free will,' he reiterated. 'They said it was nowt to worry about. They already had the lad that did it, Stephen Downing. A right little pervert. He killed her!'

Syd sounded more defiant now. And here again were the same false police claims about Downing. I paused for a moment, just to keep him in suspense, before saying, 'So, Syd, just to confirm. You were not parked anywhere near the cemetery that day? You were not in fact parked on waste ground at the back of the cemetery? You were not in Bakewell that day?'

He was very hesitant to reply. 'Not me. No,' he said with an air of finality. My call had shaken him, but I was on a fishing exercise at this stage. 'So that's it, is it?' he asked. 'I've got to get on.'

'Okay, Syd. No problem. Thanks for the call. Perhaps we will talk again? Shall I come round when you've a bit more time?'

'Yeah, maybe,' he said, squirming. 'I must go now.' He put down the receiver.

*   *   *

When I mentioned my chat with Oulsnam to Ray Downing, he too said he had seen him driving down Yeld Road, away from the cemetery and heading off back towards town at about lunchtime on the fateful day.

Ray said that after taking a coachload of pensioners to Chatsworth House, he headed home for some lunch. There was a scheduled Hulleys bus coming down the hill, which reached the same junction and was turning right.

He explained that bus drivers are notorious clock-watchers, as their job demands, and he instinctively glanced at his watch to check whether the other bus was on time. Ray thought Nita would have just been dropped off further up the road after doing some shopping. The two drivers greeted each other with a wave and a smile.

Ray said, 'At that split second I noticed a man in a brownish-coloured van at the junction just in front of the other bus. He too raised his hand up to me. He mistakenly thought I was waving to him. As I peered at the driver, I recognised it was Syd Oulsnam. I thought no more of it, and reached home about 1.25. Nita said I'd just missed Stephen. I was disappointed because I wanted to show Stephen my new coach.'

Unaware of what was happening in the cemetery, Ray returned back to work that afternoon.

Ray asked me if I had found the chance to go through all the paperwork he had left at the office. I told him I had not read all of it. He pulled a face in frustration and asked, 'Have you come across anything in there about Syd Oulsnam?'

I had to admit that I had not seen any reference to the man so far.

Ray then went on to give me some further, fascinating information. He explained that on 19 October 1973, some five weeks after the murder, he had received a phone call from a young man who said he had been at the same school as Stephen, and claimed to have some important information about a local landowner and farmer – someone we'll refer to as Mr Red in this story.

The man on the line was reluctant to give his name, but Ray was sure he knew who he was. He explained that he had been speaking to a small boy who often hung around Mr Red's farm and enjoyed helping out with the animals.

He said the boy had told him Mr Red had had a 'terrific row' with Wendy on the night before the attack and had arranged to go to Bakewell the next day to 'try to put things right with her'.

Ray said another man, Syd Oulsnam, was going to drive him there. The boy claimed Mr Red told him all this, and instructed, 'If anyone asks where I was that day, just say I was anywhere else but Bakewell.'

Some alarm bells started to ring. Was it just another rumour, Chinese whispers, or malicious gossip? Wendy definitely told Ray she had some business to attend to in Bakewell that day.

Ray continued his story. He said he went to the police and relayed the phone call to DC Oakes that very day, 19 October. 'I managed to persuade my informant to tell me the name and whereabouts of the child who made these allegations,' Ray explained. 'He was the son of an acquaintance of Mr Red, who also lived in the area.' I will just refer to him as a 'businessman' in this story.

*   *   *

Working late again at the *Mercury* office, I rummaged through a mountain of cardboard files, scraps of paper and some original paperwork left by Ray, and others collated by my own people.

I opened a thin file labelled 'Ervin'. This was a unique collection of work undertaken by private investigator Robert Ervin, whom the Downings had employed for some ten years after the case.

Ray told me there was a lot more of Ervin's work somewhere, but said he had lost track of him following his retirement. Ervin was now dead. He had passed away at least ten years before. The file contained a few copies of statements and scribbled remarks, but still no mention of Syd Oulsnam.

However, I noticed a file with the title Police Documents. Inside was another batch of official papers, including a pile of police statements from some bar staff at a Bakewell pub, apparently all taken in the early eighties. They mentioned Mr Orange but, again, I couldn't see any mention of Oulsnam.

I continued thumbing through the papers and was thinking of picking up the phone and asking Ray what he was on about, when two names emphasised in capital letters finally jumped out at me: OULSNAM and MR RED.

It was a copy of a police memo dated 19 October 1973, in which Detective Constable Oakes of Bakewell police reported back on Ray's new information, and offered some insight into the day of the murder.

> *Sgt Hodgson and myself interviewed MR RED during the evening of the murder, who told us that he had been to a sheep sale all day at Craven Arms, Shropshire, having left early in the morning and returned home during the early evening. This was checked out by interviewing other people who had travelled with him to the sale.*

The memo ended with a reminder to check on:

(a) The businessman
(b) Mr Red
(c) Syd Oulsnam of Ashford

in order to 'see what they have to say about this new story'.

I wanted to get this straight in my head. On 19 October, Ray had been given a tip-off about Mr Red's movements on the day of the attack. Yet the police had already questioned Mr Red more than a month before, just a few hours after the attack.

I had only recently been informed that Wendy had an affair with Mr Red shortly before she was killed. Was Ray's contact implying the 'terrific row' the night before her death was a lovers' tiff?

I had heard stories from Ray and also from Sam Fay, my deputy editor, and more recently from my advertising reps that the gossip about town was all about Wendy and her alleged 'reputation'.

She was considered promiscuous by many people. If this memo was genuine, it was proof that at least one of Wendy's alleged former boyfriends was interviewed on the night of the attack.

I wondered what prompted the police to pick him up. In a small town like Bakewell it was probable the police already knew about this alleged relationship, and they might have wanted to eliminate any lovers as suspects. It seemed Mr Red had an alibi for the day in question. I wondered if any other men she knew had been questioned.

I looked for further information in the file, and soon found another memo from DC Oakes. It appeared that the day after speaking with Ray, he went to a number of addresses in villages around Bakewell where three men on the list – the businessman, Mr Red and Oulsnam – lived.

He had made the following report of his visits:

*At 2.15 p.m. on Saturday, 20 October 1973, I saw the
businessman, and there outlined the nature of the enquiries.
The businessman denied having discussed this matter with
anyone, or of having any knowledge of the alleged agreement
as per telephone message. The businessman stated that Mr Red
had been at the Craven Arms, Shropshire, sheep sale on the
day of the murder ... and this has been confirmed previously.*

*At 2.30 p.m., on Saturday, 20 October 1973, I saw Syd
Oulsnam, Ashford-in-the-Water, and outlined the nature of
the anonymous telephone call. He informed me that on the
day prior to the murder, he had been muck carting for Mr
Red, and knew he was going to the sheep sale the following
day.*

*On completing the work for the day, Mr Red told Oulsnam
not to bother going the following day, as he would be in
Shropshire. However, for whatever reason, Oulsnam went up
past Mr Red's house the next day, on the off-chance Mr Red
would be there, only to find he had gone. Mr Oulsnam denied
having seen Mr Red at all on the day of the murder, or of
taking him down to Bakewell.*

*So far as related to Mr Red, he still maintains he did go to
Shropshire to the sheep sale and his statement, corroborated by
others, includes such details.*

There was something very peculiar about the police memos and
the timings. I wondered how an officer could possibly conduct
two different interviews within 15 minutes when they were about
10 miles apart.

I also queried why they had all been typed out on lined paper
that bore no official police heading.

I saw Ray the next day and asked him how he had come across them. He said Ervin traced the official statements years ago, but had never been able to disprove Mr Red's alibi.

Ray confirmed that Stephen had copied them all out himself as a record. He kept a note in prison of everything Ervin, or anyone else, had discovered.

'Unfortunately,' said Ray, 'Ervin kept all the original copies.'

I realised that an alleged police memo copied out by a convicted murderer was unlikely to prove credible at an appeal. Ray pulled another long face and looked disappointed again. Another dead end.

*   *   *

The following week, in the middle of the night, the *Mercury* office came under attack again. A lighted roll of paper was pushed through the letterbox, setting fire to some leaflets and the carpet. We also suffered a couple of minor break-ins, yet on each occasion nothing obvious was taken.

Clearly my investigations were ruffling feathers. The warnings prompted me to move my portfolio to a safer place.

And then I received another threat, a late-night call – this time in my own home. A man jeered, 'We know where you live. You and your family had better watch your back!'

The message was clear: stop digging dirt.

The situation was clearly getting more serious, and I was unwittingly becoming part of the ongoing story. I was shocked that someone had found my personal telephone number and decided to threaten me at home. I suddenly began to question whether any of this was worth the risk to my wife and family. The attacks on the office and threatening calls to staff also continued, but for some bizarre reason it only strengthened my resolve to carry on and to see who was really behind all this. Why was someone trying very hard to stop me investigating Stephen Downing's claims of innocence?

I was frustrated that the police were not interested in any of my claims, and, after discussion with my wife, she insisted that I should continue if I believed what I was doing was right and proper. She told me I was good at my job and would sort things out, eventually. And her support was vital to me.

All I could do was continue my investigation, and to do so I needed to find out more about Mr Red.

I understood that in the early seventies he had several irons in the fire locally and employed half a dozen or so men on a casual basis. I also learnt that Syd Oulsnam was one of the men he regularly hired.

Mr Red had married in the late sixties. His wife ran her own business from the farm. The couple had no children by the time they separated. And at about the time of the murder Mr Red was said to be around 30 years old and living on his own. He was fit, with youthful looks for his age, and had remarried in the mid-seventies.

I had already been given the official line that no relevant paperwork existed about this case. I still thought it was worth making unofficial enquiries, so I asked one of my police contacts if he could do some digging about the Mr Red connection. I wasn't very confident about tracing any documentation, until my informant came back to me, saying excitedly, 'I've got them, Don. Where do you want to meet?'

I had three very good contacts within the local force at both Matlock and Bakewell. None of them knew that the others were also supplying information and paperwork to me, and they each worked independently.

I was a keen runner and often ran round the district to keep fit. I was also a football fan – as were many of my police contacts – so we arranged to have a number of unique drop boxes available behind stone walls, or behind a gate in the woods, coupled with the names of football teams, such as Chelsea, Spurs, Port Vale, to reflect their particular favourites. This worked well, as when each informant would contact me they would give their code name so that I knew certain key information would be left at one of the drop sites. They would place copy statements or police documents in a plastic folder so that I could pick them up on my runs, or via my car, to avoid the possibility of them being seen with me.

Thanks to my informer Port Vale, I now had firm evidence on official Derbyshire police headed notepaper from 1973 that an alleged ex-boyfriend of Wendy Sewell's was questioned on the night of the attack.

This official police memo also provided a statement from one of the men who stated Mr Red had attended a sheep sale in Shropshire. It claimed he was a farmer from near Buxton. The statement was taken on 27 October 1973 by DC Oakes, a week after Ray's new evidence was disregarded.

I have known Mr Red for over ten years, and he has done a bit of building for me on the farm. On Wednesday, 12 September 1973, Mr Red called for me at about 8.45 a.m., at the farm. He was driving his uncle's car and, together with his two uncles, we all drove to Craven Arms, Shropshire, where we attended a sheep sale. I didn't buy any sheep but both Mr Red's uncles bought about 70 sheep between them. I don't know if Mr Red bought any himself, but he made payment with one of their cheques for the sheep his uncles had bought.

> *We had our dinner at a public house at the sheep sale and left, arriving back here at home at about 4.45 p.m. the same day. Mr Red was with me and his uncles all day. He didn't leave the sheep sale at all. We didn't stop off anywhere on the journey there or back, other than when we filled up with petrol.*

This broadly corroborated what Mr Red, the businessman and Syd Oulsnam had all said; however, I spotted at least one potential discrepancy. The farmer said Mr Red had been driving his uncle's car. Oulsnam said Mr Red's own car was missing from outside his home that day. So where was Mr Red's vehicle that day? Did he leave it somewhere or did they go in separate cars?

I didn't find any other statements from anyone involved with the sheep sale, nor did I locate Mr Red's original police statement made 'during the evening of the murder'. However, I noted a reference that one of the key witnesses, who provided Mr Red's alibi, had died in 1975.

DC Oakes's memo made it clear that both Mr Red and his alibi had been checked, and that he was interviewed some weeks before Ray contacted the police on 19 October. For years, until the appearance of this memo, Ray had been under the impression that Mr Red's name only entered the frame on information he had given to the police.

Ray remained critical of DC Oakes, and after I told him about my latest findings, he explained, 'I'm not surprised the businessman denied any knowledge of Mr Red and Wendy having a "terrific row". It was not the businessman who was supposed to have heard the argument, but his son. Oakes interviewed the wrong man.'

CHAPTER 10

WHO WAS WENDY SEWELL?

Someone else had been held in the cells for several hours on the night of the attack on Wendy – and at the same time that Stephen was being interrogated. The victim's husband, David Sewell.

I had a great deal of sympathy for him, and hoped he would work with me and give me his version of events. He was obviously very reluctant to talk to me, though, given that I was seemingly trying to defend and even free his wife's convicted killer.

At first he was quite hostile and refused to see me at his house, but he agreed to a brief telephone interview. I told him what I was doing and why, and asked him if he knew anything about some fresh evidence that hadn't been put before the jury.

He replied, 'No, I have not heard about any new evidence. Nothing at all. I wasn't aware there was the slightest doubt from the start. A lot of do-gooders are trying to make criminals look good. I was left in no doubt and the police were left in no doubt. How you hope to prove something 20-plus years later is beyond me.'

I said this new information might shed more light on the murder.

He disagreed. 'The police went at length through the evidence at the time. They were left in no doubt.'

I asked if he knew who Wendy was meeting that day. I suggested that he must have been aware of the rumours concerning his wife's alleged promiscuity, and the possibility of meeting someone in the graveyard.

'No one. It was a very simple and straightforward situation. Her father had died a few years earlier. They never got around to putting up a headstone for him and she simply went up there one lunchtime to have a look at the gravestones. That's all there was to it,' he insisted.

I wondered if he knew why Wendy caught the early bus that morning. He said he couldn't remember but admitted, 'She was certainly here when I went to work in Derby. I don't know why she went at that time. In any case the police were well up on this fellow and the type of offences he'd already committed. There were no end of them.'

I asked him what he meant. He told me he had spoken to PC Ernie Charlesworth who gave him an assurance they had the right man.

He said, 'I'll quote from the police. They told me, "We knew what he was and were waiting for him to do something to convict him." That was said to me at the time.'

I reminded him, 'If we're quoting facts, at trial it was stated that Downing had "a perfectly clean record and was of good character". There was no evidence to the contrary.'

These innuendos and claims that Stephen was a 'little pervert' or such like kept cropping up, usually from people who didn't really know the lad. I wanted to get to the root of it all.

Had the police told others the same false story that David Sewell had just repeated? The prime source of most of these false smears on Stephen's character came from PC Ernie Charlesworth. The estate was his patch, and I got the impression he liked to throw his weight around – a police bully playing the big fish in a small pond.

I had heard that three years before the murder, when Stephen was just 14, he was one of several children grilled by Charlesworth over obscene phone calls and an alleged assault on a woman.

Stephen, however, was exonerated on both counts. He had a good alibi – he was at a school presentation at the same time as the assault – and the real culprit, who had dropped his Air Training Corps cap badge near the scene, eventually admitted the offence.

This particular individual only received a mild rebuke from Charlesworth and was let off, but the officer still held Downing responsible, and for years afterwards he kept repeating this false claim, telling people he was questioned over the assault. Yes, that was true, but he forgot to mention that about a dozen or so other boys were also questioned until the cap badge proved someone else was responsible.

As time went by, David Sewell eventually spoke with one of my reporters and at least two journalists from the nationals. He told my reporter, 'I remember the day the assault happened. As usual we had breakfast together in the kitchen here. I kissed her and said goodbye.'

The next he heard about his wife was when the police phoned him at his office in Derby. He said he dashed home to Bakewell and, despite the fact that he had a good alibi, he still found himself in a cell next to Stephen Downing – and being grilled as a potential suspect.

'I wasn't free to go,' said Sewell. 'I was helping with enquiries. I felt my treatment was inappropriate. I only had a cup of tea and a biscuit before I was allowed to leave early the following morning.'

He still seemed to be in denial regarding rumours about his wife's alleged love life and extramarital affairs – despite numerous court papers confirming matters to the contrary.

He said, 'People will say, no doubt, that there is no smoke without fire, but it's just not true. I was with her at the time, and

I'm sure I would have known if she had been having all these affairs that are being suggested. She was no more than a normal woman of her time.'

He seemed to contradict himself, however, when he said, 'Some of the people she was associating with, I didn't feel were good for her. She was troubled and unsettled. There was quite a social life going on in Bakewell, and she was mixing with people of her own age who weren't a good influence on her.

'I told her quite forcefully that I wasn't happy with the situation. I felt her behaviour was not appropriate for a married woman. Whether she was pregnant or not before she left home, I can't be certain. I knew very little about the child but I knew who the father was. He was a businessman in the town from an influential family.

'He was single, and she could have gone to live with him, but whether she got short shrift from him I'll never know.

'Then she contacted me and said she wanted to come back. We were apart for about a year, and in the meantime she had had this baby.

'It was of no interest to me. She said that she would have liked me to adopt her child. I could not do that. I said if she wanted to keep the baby she wasn't coming back to me, and if she wanted to come back she would have to make other arrangements for the child. I didn't want anything to do with the baby.'

Wendy was forced into making the heart-wrenching decision to give up her child, Thomas, for adoption, and return to her husband.

He confirmed, 'It was entirely her decision. The situation wasn't easy for either of us. She had given up her only child and it seemed she wouldn't have any more. Wendy wasn't happy in herself. I think she was unfulfilled.'

He then explained how they bought an old farmhouse cottage

after they got back together again to provide her with a renovation project.

And it was from this same property in September 1973 that Wendy left home for the very last time, catching a local early bus driven by Ray Downing. She travelled to work in Bakewell, and never returned.

* * *

Working so hard to help Stephen's efforts to clear his name could have made it easy to forget that there was another victim in this story, one who had no possibility of a second chance. I kept wondering why Wendy Sewell was so horrifically murdered. Who was she, and who else was involved in a relationship with her? Did she have any enemies? Did she have any problems at home or at work? Who was the person who visited her office just before she left for the cemetery?

Wendy was, to a certain extent, a forgotten piece of an enormous jigsaw puzzle. It was important to continually tell myself that, while Stephen appeared to be the victim of a terrible miscarriage of justice, Wendy was also the victim of a brutal, life-ending attack.

The dramatic police photographs of her frail, lifeless body covered in cuts and bruises brought home the grim reality of her ordeal. She had suffered a savage beating and was unrecognisable from the attractive young woman I'd seen in photographs. I was not surprised that one witness had been unable to state whether the victim was a man or woman, it was that bad.

When I was first shown the mortuary photographs of Wendy's body I was almost physically sick. But it brought home to me the importance of my investigations. The images reflected the sheer brutality of this horrific attack on a young, innocent and defenceless woman in the middle of the day. I couldn't recognise her at first, and wondered if there had been a mistake. She looked so thin and lifeless. I wondered what had triggered such a vicious assault. I couldn't believe Stephen Downing at the tender age of 17 would be capable of such violence. I needed to get some fresh air to clear my head and carry on with my work.

I believed her injuries were not only inflicted by the pickaxe handle. Some of the bruising to her body was more reminiscent of a severe kicking, and the images displayed extensive bruising to her neck and shoulders.

The injuries did not match Downing's forced confession, but they fully illustrated the ferocity of this frenzied attack, and a deliberate intention to kill this defenceless woman.

It must have seemed quite evident that it was certainly not the actions of a simple-minded youth during his lunch break. I believe the police simply based their initial theories around what they thought had happened and gave Downing a script to sign.

Reports of the trial from old newspaper cuttings portrayed the victim as a young, married typist whose lifestyle was nothing out of the ordinary. And yet the official Home Office files on the case made for far more interesting reading:

The victim, Mrs Wendy Sewell, was married to David Sewell in March 1964. The marriage was not a success, however, and in September 1967 she left her husband and moved into lodgings.

Subsequently, she formed associations with other men and, although she and her husband were reconciled in July 1971, and from then on lived together reasonably well until the time of her death, Mrs Sewell continued to associate with other men.

The gossip about Wendy started almost as soon as I began my own investigations. Bakewell in 1973 was just a small rural market town, and everyone knew everyone else's business. Nothing much seemed to have changed. After several months of enquiries, I had been provided with an extensive list of supposed boyfriends. Gossip was rife, but I soon learnt to take a lot of this rumour-mongering with a pinch of salt.

David Sewell met Wendy Crawshaw, as she was then known, in Sheffield, where he was living with his family shortly after graduating from Imperial College London. She was an only child living at home with her parents and was three years his junior. They became engaged and were married in 1964. They moved to a bungalow in Bakewell.

David's job meant he was away from home all day, leaving his young wife to find her own amusement in a new town. It was claimed that she left one job as a secretary to the magistrates' court in Bakewell due to a scandal involving an alleged affair with a co-worker.

It was just one of many similar claims from the rumour mill. It was also alleged that she had relationships with some other important local men, including a senior police officer and a solicitor, among her new circle of friends.

The name of Mr Red came to light several times, and a former close friend of hers believed she enjoyed the thrill of sex in open places. She claimed Wendy knew of, and was even amused by, her nickname 'the Martini Girl'. Anytime, Anyplace, Anywhere!

Another insisted Wendy kept a secret 'black book' in which she recorded the names and even rated the performance of her lovers. Some suggested this was a possible motive for her murder. I found much of this gossip rather distasteful, however, as Wendy was unable to defend herself.

What was known in local circles, but not necessarily evident to the jury at Downing's trial, was that her marriage collapsed in 1967, and she moved into rented lodgings in Bakewell, before telling friends she was pregnant.

Details of the separation from her husband and her associations with other men were also kept secret, and it was even stated in court that the Sewells had no children. So, was it deliberate and calculating not to inform the court of the true facts, that she did have a child out of wedlock?

At that time in a town like Bakewell her behaviour would have been considered fairly scandalous, and may even have swayed the jury to consider other motives, other potential suspects and other key factors. I believe many important details regarding her life and her movements were deliberately overlooked or suppressed at trial.

Judging by the report Ray Downing gave me about the day of the attack, Wendy was definitely in a hurry. She caught the early bus into town and had also confirmed to Ray that she had 'some business to attend to'.

Was this business the reason for her murder? There was no mention again in court as to why she caught this early bus, or any other hint as to why she had an early appointment or some task to attend to.

Ray later told me another bus driver had mentioned seeing Wendy Sewell shortly after she had exited his bus, claiming 'Wendy was heading back towards the Square from the Buxton Road end of town' before walking a few hundred yards back to her job with the Forestry Commission in King Street, just off the Square but in a completely different direction.

This early arrival implies she had some sort of agenda, and had every intention of making this detour or liaison before work, and yet no enquiries were ever made to ascertain where she went, who she met or what business she had to attend to.

A friendly copper I called Chelsea promised he would try to locate any relevant statements given to the police in 1973 relating to her movements that day. His success in doing so proved once again that the police were wrong when they said all the paperwork and exhibits had been lost, burnt or destroyed.

One of the first he came up with was that of John Osmaston, her boss at the Forestry Commission office in Bakewell, who had been called by the Crown as a trial witness.

Osmaston's statement contained much more detail than the one sentence highlighted in the trial summary, where it was merely mentioned that Mrs Sewell had handed him a note at 12.20 saying she was going out 'for a breath of air'.

The biggest revelation was his telling the police that Wendy had a male visitor just before she hastily left the office at lunchtime. Osmaston's statement read:

> *I heard someone in the other office speaking to Mrs Sewell. I only heard two or three words.*
>
> *Trying to recall, it seemed slightly abrupt. It was not a voice that I recognised at all. I cannot say whether this person left the office, but a few moments later Mrs Sewell came into my office, while I was still on the telephone, and gave me a small piece of paper on which she had scribbled, 'I'm going out for a breath of air.'*
>
> *I nodded my head and she went out, presumably out of her office too? She had gone from her office a couple of minutes later when I finished the phone call.*

This was vital evidence. Why was this mysterious male visitor never traced? The man was 'abrupt'. Mr Osmaston later said he was 'speaking in a raised voice'.

Osmaston continued:

I crumpled up the piece of paper on which the note was written when I finished the call and I threw it into the waste-paper bin. I can say without doubt, the writing on the paper was Mrs Sewell's.

As soon as I finished the phone conversation I went out for lunch. The town was busy. I returned to the office about 1.15. I was surprised Mrs Sewell had not returned by then.

I remained in the office and carried on with my work, and between 2 and 3 p.m. telephoned the home of Mrs Sewell to see if she was there. All I could think of was that she had gone to her mother, who had been ill and may have got worse.

I remained in the office until 3.15, when the police told me something serious had happened to Mrs Sewell. I retrieved the piece of paper on which she had written the message, and later handed it to the police officer who called on me.

Mrs Sewell had not had a holiday away from home with her husband this year. All her leave had been taken in odd days and I notice, while I was on holiday, her leave card shows two hours per day off between 10 and 25 July between noon and 2 p.m. I have an idea Mrs Sewell had an interest in a wool shop on Buxton Road at Bakewell, although I am not aware of her exact connection with it.

The reference to Wendy's holiday arrangements in relation to her husband struck me as curious. I wondered why David Sewell was not asked about this matter, and I also wondered why Osmaston chose to mention it.

Was he implying that a happily married woman would have taken more orthodox holiday leave than the odd day here and there, or a couple of hours at lunchtime? The hours 'between noon and 2 p.m.' jumped out at me. Wendy had met her killer between these times. I realised my thought processes were wandering into the realms of pure speculation.

Osmaston's mention of a wool shop on Buxton Road also reminded me that Wendy had been spotted that very morning walking back towards the centre of Bakewell from the 'Buxton Road end' of town by one of Ray's fellow bus drivers, after getting off the bus in the town centre.

Osmaston then surprisingly mentioned another important point:

> *I also received a recorded mail delivery for Mrs Sewell after returning from lunch. The mail was handed to me by the postman who said he had been unable to deliver it to Mrs Sewell at home.*

In a tight community like Bakewell, especially around that period, the postman would have known everybody and probably every aspect of their lives, yet it still seemed odd that he would deliver a package to Wendy's workplace – some two or three miles from her home. Did anyone check what was in the delivery? Was it a parcel or a letter? Again, I could find no mention of it.

Osmaston's statement generated more questions than answers, and I considered whether any of Wendy's friends or work colleagues would be able throw any light on these anomalies after all these years.

*   *   *

The situation with the threats, phone calls and attacks on the office reached a climax just before Christmas. I had been out jogging on a cold, dark night, along the A6 through Darley Dale on the road towards Bakewell, on one of my regular routes.

I noticed a sports car parked in a lay-by close to the Red House Stables and St Elphin's School. A few seconds later, as I crossed the main road heading home, the car suddenly accelerated out of the lay-by and, still without lights, skidded towards me.

Instinctively, I jumped onto the pavement and watched it speed past. I stopped for a moment to gain my breath, but it was some time later before I realised what had happened – I'd almost been killed.

At first, I put it down to my own negligence, but deep down I had a nagging doubt. I told Kath and my colleagues at work what had happened. I think I wanted confirmation of what I already feared. They all said I should report this near miss to the police.

I telephoned CID and was promised a visit the same morning. Shortly afterwards, I received a call to say that the detective asked to call had lost his car keys, so he wouldn't be able to make it. I felt like asking if he'd also lost the use of his legs too, as our offices were only just around the corner from the police station.

Just before Christmas, I received this letter from Stephen Downing:

```
                    HM Prison, 7 North Square,
                         Dorchester, Dorset.


Dear Don,
I would like to say thank you to you and your
staff for taking an interest in my case, but above
all for believing in my innocence. I appreciate
that it is quite an undertaking for a small paper
to take on, also in view of its limited number of
readers. I hope that I am able to help you with
the investigation as much as I possibly can. I
trust that what I have sent will be enough to get
you started. Please feel free to ask more of me. I
```

don't see why I should sit back and let you do all
the work.
   Stephen Downing

I found it almost impossible to fully imagine what it must have been like for Stephen to be given an indefinite life sentence for a murder he did not commit. A child put in a man's prison, who eventually became lost in the system due to his constant denial.

I wondered what his feelings were when the former army investigator Robert Ervin stopped work on his case, or the time he lost his appeal. It must have been heart-breaking for him to wonder if he would ever be free.

I worried about giving Stephen and his family false hopes. I could guarantee very little, apart from doing my very best to investigate his claims of innocence, but as this was all a new, exhausting and at times frightening experience for me, I kept wondering if I was doing the right thing, and often wondered if I would I ever find sufficient fresh evidence for another appeal.

At Christmas I decided I would present a new portfolio of evidence to the Chief Constable, John Newing, and to the authorities. If nothing else, I was determined to make people aware of all the inconsistencies and anomalies, and also make the public aware of the facts.

During the festive break we received numerous calls offering further information about the Downing case. I found that I couldn't switch off. I was phoning back and forth from home and chasing new leads, until Kath suddenly shouted, 'That's it! It's four o'clock in the morning. Leave it till the New Year.'

We knew it was only a brief respite, but neither of us could have imagined then just how this case would come to totally dominate our lives.

CHAPTER 11

ANATOMY OF A FALSE CONFESSION

Stephen sent me his personal recollections of his interrogation by Bakewell police in 1973. I had been eager to see this, ever since reading his alleged confession statement. I wanted to try to understand what had been going through the mind of this naïve teenager.

He said he had been questioned for over nine hours without being allowed a parent or solicitor present. I was wondering just what had finally made him change his story and confess to this most brutal attack on a young woman.

Stephen explained:

A few minutes after arriving in the police station I was escorted upstairs and shown into a room on the left of the upstairs landing. It was quite a large room and one wall was dominated by two large sash windows. The sparse furnishings consisted of two desks, four or five chairs which looked like dining-room chairs and a couple of filing cabinets.

I was told to sit on one of the chairs that had been left in the centre of the room. The uniformed police then left the room and Detective Inspector Younger and another detective whose name was

Johnson came in. They immediately began to ask me questions. One sat in front of me at the desk while the other sat behind my right shoulder.

They took it in turns to ask questions. This went on for between 10 and 15 minutes before they got up and walked from the room saying, 'We'll be back.' As soon as they left the room a couple of uniformed police would come in.

On other occasions PC Ernie Charlesworth would come in alone. He would position himself just in front of me and would speak as if he was my father giving me advice. He told me that if I co-operated he would do what he could to make the penalty less severe.

As I was being questioned I looked out the window and saw a workman up a ladder wiring something up. When I asked what he was doing, I was told the phone people were installing extra telephone lines as a result of the case – and he seemed to suggest this disruption was all my fault, as if I had caused the whole town and its inhabitants to change their well-ordered and disciplined routine.

I asked on at least two occasions to see a solicitor, and I also asked to see my family. I was told that I didn't need a solicitor as I was only being questioned, and I wasn't going to be allowed to see my family, although they did inform me that they would be told where I was. That was about 10 p.m., or perhaps even a little later.

It struck me that Stephen had been detained at the police station for so many hours at that point, and been made to sit on a very hard chair in a bare room while Johnson, Younger and Charlesworth took it in turns to question him.

I also noted the unusual reference to PC Charlesworth, who seemed to be playing the 'good cop', a friendly father-figure type, deliberately left alone with Stephen, trying to appear all chummy and conspiratorial, dangling the bait of a less severe punishment. But why was Charlesworth talking of punishment? Why was he even talking to Stephen at all? Who the hell was this Charlesworth? It was also evident Stephen hadn't been cautioned or even informed he was a potential suspect.

He continued:

> I was told I didn't need a solicitor as I was only being questioned. I have a feeling that even then they only contacted my family because they wanted me to change my clothes so that what I had on could be sent off for forensic testing.
>
> I believe it would be about 11 p.m. when my father arrived with a change of clothing, but he was kept waiting. I knew nothing about the call to my family or of his arrival. At the time I was alone with Ernie Charlesworth. I was cold, tired and hungry and in constant pain from my back. I had got to the end of my endurance and I finally gave up. I told him I would make a statement.
>
> As soon as I said that, Charlesworth left the room and within seconds came back with the other detectives. Then they began to question me further. Moments later my father was shown into

the room. I was asked to change into the clothes that had been brought for me.

Charlesworth remained by the door watching every move and I could see he was hanging on to every word that passed between me and my dad.

I vividly recall my father asking me if I had done it – and I said that I had. He told me that he was proud of me for having the guts to admit it, though not for what I had done. It was all so confusing.

One moment he was proud and the next he wasn't. I don't think we were allowed more than about ten minutes together before he was asked to leave. He said he would be back soon and would get a solicitor.

Younger and one of the other uniformed police officers came in and I was asked to make my statement. I was asked if I would like to write it or have someone write it for me. I was deeply embarrassed at my poor spelling so I asked them to write it for me. I only learned later that this was another foolish error on my part.

I took the view that the woman would be able to tell them who it was that had attacked her or at least give some kind of description, so there would be no harm in fabricating parts of the jigsaw.

I stopped reading and scored a very thick red line under the last sentence. It was so important to remember that, at this point, Stephen had not confessed to murder, potentially just a serious assault, and Wendy Sewell was still alive.

For a frightened teenager who was 'cold, tired, hungry and in constant pain' there was logic in his thought process. He fully believed the victim would tell the police that it wasn't him who attacked her. He was so desperate to sleep and rest his injured back, and didn't want to be questioned throughout the night.

Stephen continued:

Younger began by asking me to tell him what happened while the uniformed guy wrote it down. During the course of the statement being taken I was stopped, and Younger made a few suggestions and led me on several occasions, saying that it would mean the same but it would read better.

It may seem unlikely that I could allow myself to be so foolish or naive, but I only had a limited reading ability. It's only now when I look back at some of the letters I wrote to my solicitor, or the forms I was required to fill in, that I realise just how backward I really was.

I guess it would be well after midnight by the time I dictated my statement and they persuaded me to believe that what they had suggested would be the best wording - if only to suit them. I was so tired in the later stages of my questioning that Younger put his hand on my shoulder twice to wake me up, or just to shake me.

A uniformed officer wrote it down in pencil and read it back to me. Afterwards I was given a ballpoint pen and asked to sign it. At the time I didn't realise the full implications of what I was signing. If I had actually carried out the attack, I wouldn't have lied about the number of blows.

```
     A number of witnesses saw me leave the cemetery
with my pop bottle in my hand and without a single
bloodstain on my clothes. The police seemed to
think I was capable of committing such an act and
walking away calmly.
```

I had consistently pointed out these absurdities and anomalies within my analysis of Stephen's confession statement. He said he had hit her twice, but the prosecution's own experts agreed she had been struck seven or eight times. And after that 'frenzied' attack, where was all the blood on Stephen's clothes?

Stephen continued:

```
When I read the statement later I knew there were
things in it that I should change, but my reading
was poor and I was very embarrassed. I had been
told I would be questioned all night if necessary,
and I just wanted it all to be over so I could get
some sleep. I know it sounds silly now, but I knew
I hadn't done it and that I wouldn't be kept in
for long. I was very naive.
```

On reading Stephen's varied responses to my questions, I was thankful he had put some of his prison time to good use by educating himself with correspondence courses and the like, as this proved invaluable in understanding his predicament and reactions from years before. It also helped him to obtain work in a trusted position as a librarian and later as a Samaritan listener.

I studied the trial notes again, to compare the police version with that given by Stephen. The police evidence began in the cemetery with the arrival of PC Ball, who tried to give Wendy first aid. This was around 1.42 p.m. He described Stephen as being 'very excited' and added, 'I told him to calm down.' This contradicted all other descriptions of Stephen's demeanour in the cemetery by his fellow workmates and the gatekeeper.

PC Ball said he noticed three small spots of blood on the inside of his left forearm, about which Stephen remarked, 'These came when I turned her over.' Detective Inspector Robin Younger admitted at trial that it was around 9.30 p.m., when he again questioned Stephen, that he pointed out bloodstaining on his clothes and boots.

Why, I wondered, had it taken Detective Younger so long to notice this? I didn't really need to ask myself that question, though. The answer was quite obvious: there was hardly any blood on him to notice.

I had seen the clothes, and I'd only noticed the tiny splash marks because they were highlighted by a bright yellow forensic marker.

So all the senior detectives, and even the infamous PC Charlesworth, had had a main suspect sitting in front of them for more than seven hours, after he'd supposedly carried out a frenzied attack on Wendy Sewell, and yet they didn't notice any bloodstaining to his clothing? It all seemed preposterous.

I was astounded by what I had read from Stephen, and compared it with the police interrogation and subsequent confession. The confession seemed to consist of mainly one-word answers, and even a shake of his head was considered by officers to mean 'yes'.

*   *   *

My research revealed two compelling and supportive psychiatric reports on Stephen Downing – both prepared before his trial in February 1974. They seemed to confirm the same conclusions I had come to.

On 29 November 1973, Dr A.R. Jones, a consultant psychiatrist at Scarsdale Hospital, Chesterfield, stated:

He was probably of low intelligence. I could find no evidence of mental illness.

His deputy headmaster described Downing as a 'lazy child with a low IQ, always late for school and a loner'. He was not a bully and he did not bully others. He did not exhibit behaviour that suggested there was a violent side to his nature.

I asked him why he had made a statement to the police admitting this offence. He told me the policemen had informed him that he would be charged with attempted murder and he did not think there was anything else he could do.

One can imagine the possibility of a tired, frightened youth making a false confession under pressure. He said he had not been frightened or pressured except on the one occasion when the policeman shook him briefly by the shoulder of his jacket.

No one is entirely satisfied with any definition of psychopathy. If in fact Downing committed this offence, I would place him in this category and consider him to be suffering from a mental disorder as defined in the Mental Health Act. I have some slight misgivings on this score, however, in that I think it would be unusual for the psychopath to commit a major offence without previously having given some indication of antisocial tendencies of violence.

Stephen Downing was again examined on 1 February 1974, this time by Dr J.C.M. Wilkinson, who was a consultant psychiatrist at the Pastures Hospital in Derby.

His report was perhaps more specific and stated:

It is not surprising from my point of view that after being arrested and questioned for many hours, probably feeling cold and hungry and having difficulty in expressing himself, he should ultimately confess in order to escape from the worst experience of harassment he had in his life.

Having confessed, he was immensely influenced by the fact that his father, far from rejecting him, stood by him and told him how proud he was that he had, at least, owned up under very difficult circumstances.

When the victim died, and Stephen realised he could not be exonerated by her naming the attacker, from what he says he seems to have resigned himself to be a victim himself, until his father made it clear to Stephen he did not believe him to be guilty. Stephen Downing at this point cried and stated thereafter he had not committed the crime.

Stephen Downing does not suffer from any psychiatric disorder. There is no evidence whatsoever in his past to suggest that he suffers from a personality disorder, nor that he has any abnormal sexual or aggressive urges.

On the contrary, his life history would seem to indicate that it is highly unlikely that someone with his passive personality would impulsively attack a female and then proceed to sexually assault her.

These reports could and should have greatly added to claims of oppression during the initial police interviews, mentioning, as they did, his 'low intelligence, a passive personality and the worst experience of harassment he had in his life'. But the contents of these reports weren't fully revealed to the jury until after they had reached their verdict.

I was interested to read Dr Wilkinson's assessment of why Stephen took 13 days to retract his confession. How he was immensely influenced by his father, who had said he was proud of him for admitting to it – Stephen said he had found this 'so confusing' – and how he had resigned himself to be a victim himself until Ray made it clear that he believed him to be innocent.

I asked Ray about the conversation when Stephen had first told him he hadn't done it. 'In my heart, I knew Stephen hadn't killed this woman,' he said. 'Initially, I said I was proud of him for admitting to it, but as things progressed I became convinced he was innocent. One day during my visit to Risley prison, I said to him, "Stephen, why do you keep saying you've done it?" At this he broke down and told us the truth.'

I told Ray that Stephen had sent me a detailed account of his interrogation at Bakewell police station, which I hoped to use as grounds for an appeal.

Ray saw the document and agreed with it. He confirmed that he and Nita had visited the police station several times during the late afternoon and early evening while Stephen was being held, and were repeatedly prohibited from seeing him.

He said, 'They kept saying he was just helping with enquiries. They assured us he would be home soon and there was nothing to worry about. We kept going back and forth but still they wouldn't let us near him. There was nothing else we could do.

'Eventually, we were asked to bring a change of clothing. The police wanted to do some forensic tests. We could hardly say no. It was only after he had made this so-called confession that we were finally allowed to see him.'

I believed there was much more Stephen could tell me about the day in question, especially those hours spent in the police sttion, if only I could meet him face to face. The next day I applied for a visiting order to Dorchester prison.

*   *   *

I became sick and tired of hearing various witnesses going on about PC Ernest Charlesworth. Most people trotted out the same script: Ernie always said Downing was 'a right little pervert' and that he had been watching him for such a long time and was just waiting for him to do something.

This same rubbish had been told to the victim's husband, David Sewell. Even worse, Charlesworth allegedly dismissed a considerable amount of potentially fresh evidence presented to him in the early days, including that of Louisa Hadfield about the 'running man', plus similar evidence from Mr Paling and at least two other neighbours.

I decided to confront him. I'd heard that he was now retired and working as a part-time court bailiff. I smiled at this, as it finally dawned on me what Ray and Nita had been referring to when they mentioned a bailiff they didn't care much for who lived in the area on my very first visit to their home.

I went round to his home in Bakewell and knocked on the door. As he opened it he could see it was me and tried to shut it again quickly. 'No, you don't,' I shouted. 'I want a word with you.'

'No comment, I can't say anything,' he squealed like a frightened mouse.

I stuck my foot in the door so he couldn't quite close it. *So this is the infamous police bully who is too afraid to face me.* I tried to talk to him but he was terrified of being exposed for what he was – a liar and a cheat, who I believed should have faced justice himself. He became very agitated and refused to answer any questions.

I tried again on another occasion. He claimed he had been told not to talk to me. He seemed nervous and was deliberately evasive. A bully often backs down when confronted, and I was determined to fire difficult questions at him, but I received no coherent answers.

A few days later, some of the beat bobbies in Matlock were having a pop at me about Charlesworth, saying he'd sent me away with a flea in my ear. That seemed to be the tale he'd told his police mates. When I heard this again from one of my friendly coppers, I thought I'd try to confront the old sod again.

He was involved with a darts contest for Bakewell Carnival. I'd heard that the committee were meeting in a particular pub one night, so I decided to go along to see if I could have a word with him again after their meeting.

I went into Bakewell quite late and found Charlesworth propping up the bar, surrounded by some very big lads. I was fairly angry after hearing about this 'flea in my ear' rubbish and beckoned him to come over. I told him I needed a word. He sauntered across, looking smug and over-confident. But when I told him he was a liar he turned almost purple with rage.

There was a sudden buzz around the bar and some nasty looks were exchanged. 'Sent me away with a flea in my ear, Ernie – is that right? At least that's what you told your police mates,' I said.

'I gather you didn't tell them you were too scared to talk to me and explain yourself? You had to hide behind your front door and refused to speak. I just want to know the truth, Ernie – you can tell me in front of your pals. What did you used to say about Downing and why?'

He gave me daggers, as did the rest of his group. They were muttering to each other. Someone mentioned sorting me out, and I suddenly realised they were all coppers.

I was already public enemy number one in the Bakewell cop shop, but I felt that I had to confront Charlesworth, even it meant embarrassing him. I was anxious to destroy his hard-man image once and for all. 'Come on, Ernie. Surely you can tell me the truth now?'

He swore under his breath and mumbled something about still not being able to talk about the case. Official secrets. 'It'll all come out later. Downing's guilty. He admitted it to me,' he said.

'Did you caution him and read him his rights, then? I hope it does all come out eventually, and you will be standing in the dock in place of Downing.'

He turned away.

'Okay, Ernie, I get the message. I've not changed my opinion of you one bit. You've a lot to answer for. One day I hope to put you on the stand for perverting the course of justice. Until then, I hope you can live with yourself.' With that I turned and left. My heart was thumping and I was sweating, and as I made my way back to my car I half-expected someone to attack me from behind.

CHAPTER 12

ON THE TRAIL OF MR ORANGE

After all my efforts to investigate the case so far, I decided that it was finally time to go public and see if I could encourage any other potential witnesses to come forward with information. As I was preparing to write my first article for the *Mercury*, I received a very interesting telephone call.

A woman asked if we could meet to talk about Mr Orange. She said she was one of his former lovers. I will call her Rita, although it is not her real name, as she is still terrified after having spoken to me.

I arranged to meet her at her home. She gave me directions but told me to park on the next road, as she didn't want anyone to know I had called. She stood by her window throughout our meeting, shielding herself behind the thick curtains and nervously peering out to see if anyone was watching the house.

'Why are you so scared, Rita?' I asked.

'I'm scared that Mr Orange will find out you're here,' she replied.

'What do you want to tell me?'

'Mr Orange told the police a pack of lies about what he saw that day,' she said. 'At 12.50 he was nowhere near the cemetery gates when he saw Wendy. He was much further down the hill, by the Kissing Gate with Ms Yellow. Wendy passed them on her way up the Butts and he said hello. Mr Orange knew Wendy very well. She was well known to a lot of men.'

'Who's Ms Yellow?'

Rita explained that she was another girlfriend of his. He had arranged to meet her at the Kissing Gate, a rusty old wrought-iron contraption which marked entry from the Butts path into the secluded Catcliff Wood. It was also known as a popular lovers' meeting point, about halfway up the pathway between the town and the cemetery.

I interrupted her to ask, 'How far is this from the cemetery gates?'

'It's a five-minute walk, but it depends on whether you are going up or down. It's probably longer on the way up.'

'How do you know this?'

'Mr Orange told me all about it years afterwards. He knew what time it was when they saw Wendy because he remembered Ms Yellow saying, "It's 12.50, I'd better be getting back." Rita explained how Ms Yellow went off towards town, while Mr Orange carried on up the hill behind Wendy.'

One thing I knew for certain was that if Wendy had been at the Kissing Gate at 12.50, it must then have been around 12.55 at least before she reached the cemetery. This information alone could possibly have destroyed the prosecution case, which assumed that Stephen attacked Wendy between the time she was seen entering the cemetery at around 12.50 and the time Stephen was seen leaving the cemetery at around 1.08, some 18 minutes in total.

It was claimed his trip home via the shop was just to establish an alibi, so that he could return to the cemetery later and pretend he'd found Wendy lying battered and dying. The limited timeline for this attack now seemed to have been reduced from 18 to just 13 minutes.

I was enthused by Rita's claim but wanted to check other factors before getting too excited. 'When did he see Wendy go into the cemetery?' I asked.

She didn't know, and couldn't remember now, but added, 'He told me he met Charlie Carman up there.' Rita was unable to tell me exactly when or where Mr Orange and Carman met.

She seemed to think that, contrary to the evidence read out at trial, Mr Orange did not go straight home. 'I think he hung around,' she claimed.

Carman's whereabouts and his part in this drama were becoming crucial to my unravelling of this crime. His written evidence to the court said he was near the cemetery gates by the phone box at 12.50, and he saw Wendy, who was already in the cemetery. But Stephen claimed to have seen Carman some 20 minutes after that, walking towards the cemetery on his way back to town.

Now Mr Orange was also said to have seen Carman. If Rita was telling the truth, neither Wendy nor Mr Orange could have arrived at the cemetery gates at the top of the Butts before at least 12.55.

If he had, in fact, 'hung around' for whatever reason, there was no telling what time Mr Orange saw Carman. If it was some time just after 1 p.m. then it would lend more weight to Stephen's story about seeing Carman. How could Charlie Carman have got his times so badly mixed up? It was a shame he was no longer here to ask.

'If Mr Orange didn't go straight home, where did he go?' I asked Rita.

'I don't know. I think he hung around the estate. He went along Yeld Road and, after heading back towards the cemetery, he said he saw a man running away.'

'What?'

'He saw a man running away from the cemetery. I'm sure he told me that.' She threw another quick glance towards the window.

'Have you ever told anyone else about this before?'

She wrung her hands, looked at me and shook her head. She was visibly upset, choking back the tears. I reached into my pocket, pulled out a clean handkerchief and handed it to her.

'Did he know this running man?' I asked after a few seconds.

'He never said.'

'Did Mr Orange see Stephen Downing at any point?'

'I'm sure he said something about seeing Stephen going into the cemetery after Wendy had been found by someone else.'

I was astounded by Rita's claims. 'Try to remember exactly what he said,' I insisted.

'I can't. It's so long ago,' she replied wearily. 'But I know that pretty soon afterwards he went down to the Castle Hotel in Bakewell and told people Wendy had been attacked. He said she had head injuries.'

'How on earth did he know?'

'I can't quite remember. I think he said he had seen someone and they'd told him – one of the workmen in the cemetery, I think? But I remember him saying it wasn't Stephen.'

It was said in evidence that the only time any workman had left the cemetery was to phone for the emergency services. I had some considerable doubt about this claim, and have always wondered why only the police were called and not an ambulance, which I would have deemed essential.

My mind was racing again. I wanted to ask her a dozen more questions but she was becoming rather vague, confused and visibly worried about any repercussions. I thought it quite possible that a workman or even the gatekeeper could have mentioned something to Mr Orange, but why didn't he clarify this – and particularly in relation to the running man and Stephen Downing?

Rita added, 'He told Charlie Carman and another worker too.'

I was puzzled and asked her, 'So where was Charlie Carman?'

'He was back at work in Bath Gardens. I think the gardener's afternoon shift started at one o'clock.'

'Rita, I'm going to have to see Mr Orange. Is there anything else you remember him saying?'

'No, only that Stephen didn't do it. He's often said that. Please don't tell Mr Orange I've said anything – or Ms Yellow.'

'Ms Yellow?'

'Yes, I told you, she's the one he was meeting that day Wendy was attacked. He lives with her now.'

If Rita was correct then I believed Mr Orange's evidence could prove vital in this confusing saga. Why did he not speak out at the time? And who was this running man?

I recalled Louisa Hadfield insisting that Mr Orange must have seen a blond-haired youth running up Yeld Road. She saw this running man at about 1.20, and said she saw Mr Orange about five minutes before on Yeld Road heading in the direction of the cemetery. That would also add further substance to the theory that Mr Orange was not at his mother's house at 1.10.

The report of Mr Orange allegedly seeing Stephen going into the cemetery after Wendy's body had been discovered could have proved decisive – again, if true. It would also have placed Mr Orange closer to the cemetery some time between Stephen leaving at 1.08 and returning between 1.15 and 1.20, the period when I believed the attack actually took place.

I wondered which workman told Mr Orange it was Wendy who had been attacked – and perhaps mentioned head injuries. I was also trying to work out the time he visited the Castle Hotel and was allegedly telling bar staff all about it. The timings raised some serious questions.

CHAPTER 13

WALKING WITH WITNESSES

A few days later, I asked Ray Downing to meet me at the Kissing Gate. Rita claimed Wendy passed Mr Orange and Ms Yellow at this very spot at 12.50 p.m. I had a stopwatch with me to investigate the timings of that day.

Ray and I began to walk up the hill. It was a steep climb and I had to hold back for Ray, who decided this was the time to tell me about his angina and diabetes.

We tried to envisage the pace a healthy 32-year-old woman might have managed, and even I became slightly breathless on the incline.

Ray by now was panting for breath, and we had to stop for a moment, so I pressed hold on the stopwatch. He made his efforts worse by constantly talking as we climbed. As we reached the cemetery gates I looked at my stopwatch: 5 minutes and 20 seconds.

If Rita was right, Wendy would have arrived at the cemetery at more like 12.55 p.m., and perhaps not 12.50 p.m., given a few minutes here and there, which could have made a huge difference to Stephen's claims of innocence. The gatekeeper, Wilf Walker, and other witnesses had been in no doubt whatsoever that they had seen Stephen walk past those very same cemetery gates on his way to the shop and then home at 1.08 p.m., leaving at most only 13 minutes between Wendy entering the cemetery and the time Stephen left.

I reset my stopwatch. I wanted to check 13 minutes against the account given by Stephen in his so-called confession. According to the prosecution, Stephen had noticed Wendy in the cemetery, followed her around, gone to his store for a weapon, carried out the attack, undressed and sexually assaulted her, then returned to the chapel to collect his pop bottle, put on his jacket and leave the cemetery, witnessed by several people who all agreed he was calm and his normal self.

I went to the unconsecrated chapel first, which was about 250 yards from the main cemetery gates in a straight line. I started my watch. I allowed Wendy a couple of minutes to have been walking about the cemetery before Stephen saw her.

The prosecution version said he spotted her on the lower path walking towards the main gates. At some point she must have retraced her steps.

Stephen's latest detailed recollections claimed he first saw her walking towards the Garden of Remembrance at the far end, about 400 yards or so from the gates, after which he went into the unconsecrated chapel store to stoke up the fire and collect his bottle of pop.

Jayne Atkins also spotted Wendy in the Garden of Remembrance when she was close to the far end of the cemetery looking for her dog. When Stephen went outside again, he said Wendy was walking along the lower path in the direction of the consecrated chapel and the gates.

This walk to the Garden of Remembrance and back would have taken Wendy much longer than two minutes, more like eight, as she was wandering along looking at headstones, according to Stephen. But at this point I decided to stick to the prosecution's version, which made no mention of such a walk.

In his confession Stephen said he 'watched Wendy'. I added on another minute for him to have observed her on the lower path and then make the decision to attack her. I could not recreate his next action, however, as the unconsecrated chapel store was now locked, but I allowed another 50 seconds for Stephen to have entered, selected and then picked up the murder weapon – the pickaxe handle.

So far my total was 3 minutes and 50 seconds, from Wendy having entered the cemetery to her would-be attacker standing ready with the weapon in his hands.

I then followed the most direct route from the unconsecrated chapel to a spot on the lower path near the consecrated chapel where Wendy was attacked. I walked along the middle path, and then crossed diagonally over rough terrain, through the gravestones, to reach the lower path. I didn't rush, as Stephen was alleged to have attacked Wendy from behind and would have had to creep up on her so as not to attract her attention.

It took me 2 minutes and 30 seconds. So far a total of 5 minutes and 20 seconds.

The violent attack on Wendy, with seven or eight blows being struck, plus the subsequent sexual assault after undressing her must have taken at least five minutes.

One of the old newspaper cuttings also alleged that Wendy once had a black belt in judo, so I believed that unless she had been struck hard from behind by surprise, she would have put up a struggle – which we later found that she did.

I had not met Stephen by this time, but from photographs I had seen of him and from chats with his parents I knew he was only just over five feet tall. I also remembered that he complained of having a bad back, which had plagued him during the hours of police interrogations. By now I already had an accumulated total of 9 minutes and 20 seconds.

I then retraced Stephen's route back to the unconsecrated chapel, where he went to collect his pop bottle – another minute and 30 seconds. I deduced he would have probably run a little quicker on the way back if he had just violently assaulted a woman, so a running total of 12 minutes and 20 seconds so far.

A further minute perhaps to compose himself, then the long walk from there to the main gates, which took me 2 minutes and 30 seconds. Ray then advised that, if I were to time Stephen's walk properly, I would need to reduce my pace, as his son had a slow and ambling gait.

I remembered the trial witnesses saying he left the cemetery looking the same as usual, perfectly normal and not agitated, and certainly not running as one might have expected. So I added a further 20 seconds. That gave me a final time of 15 minutes and 10 seconds for Stephen to have done all the things he was meant to have done.

The initial few minutes from Wendy entering the cemetery and Stephen deciding to attack her would most likely have taken longer than the two minutes I had estimated, especially if the sightings in the Garden of Remembrance were correct. My timings now confirmed that Stephen couldn't possibly have carried out the attack within this time frame.

I was still concerned as to why some other witnesses, apart from Mr Orange, had given different times for seeing Wendy in or around the cemetery. At the trial a Mrs Hill said she saw Wendy enter the cemetery gates at 12.45. Yet a Mr Read said he saw her leave her office in King Street at 12.40. Even Usain Bolt couldn't have tackled that steep hill in five minutes.

Moreover, two joiners, Lomas and Bradwell, roughly confirmed the time at which she left the town centre. They saw her, having entered Butts Road, at 12.45 p.m.

So now it seemed she had only entered the cemetery at about 12.55. I believed Charlie Carman's statement was inaccurate, as he claimed to have seen Wendy in the cemetery at 12.50, but from what Stephen and Rita had told me, Carman probably passed the cemetery much later than this, possibly well after one o'clock.

If Stephen was correct, I believe Carman must have been heading back at about 1.10 p.m. Moreover, if Mr Orange was a few minutes behind Wendy climbing the hill and had then 'hung around' the area, it would have placed Carman at the scene much later, especially if he saw him too.

Then it struck me. Rita said the gardeners' shifts started at one o'clock sharp. I wondered if Carman deliberately mistook the time in his police statement because he was late back for work.

There were some major discrepancies within a handful of key witness statements. And I recalled that in the trial summary the judge made it clear that all timings given by witnesses should only be taken as 'approximate'.

I was slightly annoyed by this, as in my opinion the timings were absolutely crucial to proving Stephen's alibi. To me there seemed considerable doubt about the time Stephen spent away from the cemetery.

It was agreed by all parties that he had left by around 1.08 and returned between 1.15 and 1.20, when he was spotted by Wilf Walker re-entering the gates. A few minutes later he dashed back to Mr Walker, claiming he had found an injured woman.

This would only have allowed between 7 and 12 minutes to walk from the cemetery gates to the shop, then onto his house, chat to his mother, change his boots and return to the cemetery.

I estimated that he would have been away from the cemetery for at least 12 minutes to have done all that. As the time of 1.08 now appears undisputed, I believed it would have been at least 1.20 when he returned.

I remembered a pile of police statements still unread in my office relating to Mr Orange, taken from bar staff at a Bakewell pub. Could they be crucial to my enquiries? Maybe they held the clue to the time Mr Orange was really back in town talking about the attack.

I also noted from the original trial notes that it took 12 minutes before a policeman arrived. Many of the workmen also claimed that when PC Ball drove into the cemetery he started asking questions before checking on the victim. Perhaps he assumed she was already dead.

It was said that it was only after Wendy Sewell started to move and began groaning that the officer finally called for an ambulance. It was 1.55 p.m. before the ambulance arrived – nearly an hour after Wendy had been brutally attacked.

I could hardly believe all these claims, and even today I still wonder why it took so long to ask for medical support. Why was an ambulance not sent for immediately, before calling the police?

It is still my belief that Wendy might still be alive today if urgent medical aid had reached her much sooner. Unfortunately, many witnesses are no longer alive, including some of the workmen, plus Wilf Walker and his wife, and Charlie Carman.

In the trial notes there were several serious discrepancies between their different accounts and what Stephen was alleged to have said or not. This included Stephen speaking to Wilf and his wife, and whether he said he was wearing gloves and was worried about losing his job, and about him saying there looked like being an identity parade, and whether he spoke to Carman as he walked to the shop. It all remained most frustrating.

I wanted to find out what Mr Orange had been saying about the attack on the afternoon it happened. I wondered how and precisely when he found out the information. From further copies of police statements provided by informants, I read that Charlie Carman said he first heard of the attack from Mr Orange at about 3.30 p.m., while he was working in Bath Gardens.

According to Ray, about six months after the murder two women who worked in town at the Castle Hotel, Cynthia Smithurst and Yvonne Spencer, told him they too had first heard of the attack on Wendy from Mr Orange on the day it happened. They alleged that Mr Orange had been in the bar that lunchtime. They said they finished work at 2 p.m., so believed he must have mentioned it to them before then.

In the early eighties there was a resurgence of interest in the case, largely due to Ray's persistence in trying to unearth new information. Robert Ervin was also collecting new evidence in preparation for a second appeal. It appeared that Cynthia and Yvonne were interviewed by the police. Some police statements were also taken from the hotel's proprietors, Arthur and Muriel Duplock, along with their son, Robert.

These statements were part of the huge pile of documents Ray had collated over the years. But when I went through them with one of my police informants, Port Vale, I found some of the contents rather strange. I was astonished when I discovered the truth about them. The statements were actually written up in the eighties, when the police had allegedly panicked about a possible appeal, but based on notes taken in 1973. The dates now appeared to be a complete fabrication.

Yvonne Spencer's statement, which included her hours of duty as being 8.30 a.m. to 2 p.m., read:

> *It was during the lunch hour that my friend Cynthia Smithurst told me that someone had been battered in the cemetery. I was working in the kitchen at the time. I remember saying, 'How do you know?' and she said, 'Mr Orange's been in and told me.'*

Cynthia Smithurst's statement, which included her hours of work as noon till 2 p.m. and a comment about Mr Orange – 'I am certain he was in the bar' – read:

> *I finished cleaning the bedrooms about 1.45 p.m. and went into the bar. I remember seeing Yvonne in or around the bar, and also Arthur, Muriel and Robert Duplock.*
>
> *As far as I can remember, given that it was about eight years ago, someone in the bar said, 'There's been a murder in the churchyard,' or words to that effect. I cannot remember who said this.*

The two statements were similar to what Ray Downing claimed to have been told by these two women in 1974. However, the statement of the proprietors' son, Robert Duplock, contradicts their version of events.

He recalled:

> *As far as I can remember, the first I heard of the murder was towards the end of the lunchtime closing on the 12th. Lunchtime permitted hours were from 10.30 a.m. to 3 p.m., and, as far as I can recall, it was towards 3 p.m., perhaps 2.45 p.m., that someone came into the pub and said something like 'there's been a murder in the churchyard'.*
>
> *I cannot for the life of me think who came in and said this, nor of any other persons who were in the hotel at the time. Thinking back, I seem to remember that all the women who worked at the hotel had left at around 2 p.m. I remember thinking when the murder was mentioned that it was a pity they weren't there because they would have liked to hear such gossip.*

*I feel sure that if the girls had heard of such a murder
earlier than myself then they would have told me about it.
They didn't. By the evening, reporters had booked in at the
hotel and gossip surrounding the murder was rife.*

Robert's parents, Cynthia and Arthur Duplock, confirmed they
were many hundreds of miles away at the time, visiting Mrs
Duplock's parents in Brighton. Arthur Duplock stated:

*I positively recall that this was the day that Wendy Sewell was
murdered as, on our return to the Castle Hotel at
approximately one o'clock the following morning, I saw that
the pub was still lit up and press reporters were in the bar of
the hotel. This was the first that I had heard of the attack on
Wendy Sewell.*

The attack on Wendy was constantly referred to as a 'murder'
even though Wendy had not then died. And I couldn't help
thinking it was odd that the press had arrived so quickly and
booked into the hotel. It didn't make sense. At this stage it was
still only an assault. National newspapers wouldn't send reporters
all that way just to investigate an assault on a young girl in a
country graveyard, let alone pay for them to stay in a posh hotel
overnight.

Documents now confirmed that the police spoke with both
barmaids to confirm their recollection of events and to check
their timings. From my own estimation of their accounts, and
bearing in mind this eight-year gap with their interviews, I felt
they might have been persuaded to amend their statements
slightly, for whatever reason.

On reflection, Cynthia stated, 'It may be that on the day that
Wendy Sewell was murdered Mr and Mrs Duplock had the day

off and left Robert in charge. If this was the case, I would most likely have stayed behind to help, and it could be any time up to 3 p.m. that someone mentioned the murder.'

Yvonne Spencer stood by her story, and even admitted she was being influenced by police officers who had told her she might have got her times mixed up. In her second, later statement, she said, 'It could have been just after 2 p.m., and more like 3 p.m., which is closing time. On occasions I worked later, particularly if the Duplocks had the day off.'

Both women were neighbours of the Downing family, and the police implied that this might have tainted their evidence. The officer who interviewed them even mentioned this in his report, saying, 'With the best will in the world, they told Ray Downing what he wanted to hear.'

My own enquiries – and from evidence presented by my police informant Port Vale – later indicated something quite extraordinary. When I spoke with one of the barmaids, she confirmed that neither of them had ever made or signed a formal police statement. And when I checked the final 'revised' versions, I noticed all references to Mr Orange had been removed. I also wondered why they had all been re-typed up from original notes – eight years later.

*　　*　　*

Official papers confirmed the police re-interviewed Mr Orange in 1981. He repeated his earlier account, saying he first heard about the attack between 4 and 5 p.m., in Bakewell Square from Charlie Carman.

There was no mention, however, of any essential cross-check to Charlie Carman's own contradictory statement, which alleged it was Mr Orange who told him about the attack at about

3.30 p.m., in Bath Gardens, with no reference to acknowledging Stephen Downing, and nothing further about anyone else coming in or out of the cemetery.

Mr Orange's statement claimed:

> It is possible I went into the Castle before it closed at 3 p.m. on the day of the attack, but I couldn't have spoken to anyone about it because I didn't know it had happened at that time.
>
> I didn't see any activity at the cemetery during the afternoon to make me think anything had happened there and, although I did go back into town from my mother's house, it is quite likely that I walked down Moorhall, Yeld Road and South Church Street, which is in the opposite direction to the cemetery.

He also told police that he had never been out with Wendy Sewell, nor had she ever been to his home.

*   *   *

When Ray called in early 1995 to tell me that Mr Orange wanted to set up a meeting with me, I was quite shocked. Mr Orange obviously knew I had been on the estate many times asking questions and interviewing previous eye witnesses, and must have known that his name had continually cropped up. I suppose he must have thought it was his way of clearing the air; I thought it could be a breakthrough at last and might help to resolve a few anomalies about this complex case.

I had been given mixed descriptions about him, including his stature, his drinking habits, his work and his record, and in some ways I was looking forward to the meeting. But I was also wary, and wondered if it could be a trap.

It was a wild, drizzly day as I drove along the A6 to meet Mr Orange at his home. My wife and colleagues were certainly a little apprehensive about me going to interview him, and I was somewhat relieved when I realised he would be there with his girlfriend, Ms Yellow. She was the very same woman he had been with near the Butts in 1973 when Wendy passed them on her way to the cemetery.

Mr Orange met me at the door. He was a rather scruffy-looking and stocky individual in his mid-fifties. I remembered someone saying he was once believed to be a ladies' man with 'film-star looks' when he was much younger. I found it hard to imagine, as he now struggled with a large beer belly and thinning hair.

He showed me into a rather sparse living room and introduced me to Ms Yellow. She sat on a sofa, smoking a cigarette and continually coughing.

Ms Yellow seemed nervous and fidgety. She sat hunched and awkward and continually chain-smoked. She told me she was at the Kissing Gate about half-way down the Butts with Mr Orange on the day in question, saying, 'Wendy passed us, and then I said, oh, look – it's 12.50 p.m., I'd better be getting back down to Bakewell.'

Mr Orange nodded in agreement, but seemed surprised and perhaps a little agitated by my interest in the case some 21 years after Wendy Sewell's murder.

He emphasised the long passage of time and queried the purpose of my visit. He said: 'I mean, nobody comes and asks you anything for years, and now this, so what can anyone remember now?'

He confirmed, however, seeing Wendy with Ms Yellow by the Kissing Gate and admitted that after leaving his girlfriend he then walked back up the Butts, just a couple of minutes or so behind Wendy, following her exact route towards the cemetery gates, but claimed she soon disappeared out of sight. He could not have reached these gates before at least 12.55–12.58 p.m., as it was a hard five-minutes-plus climb.

When I asked him if he'd seen anyone else about that day, he quickly replied, 'I saw no one, apart from Wendy.' He then suddenly paused for a moment, and added, 'The only other person I saw on the Butts either coming up or down was Mr Carman on his way back to town.'

Mr Orange said that despite my challenge of an alleged sighting of him by at least one other key witness about ten minutes later, and at another location nearby, he insisted he went straight to his mother's house and didn't hang around.

I then carefully explained that it was in fact a neighbour, Mrs Hadfield, who had recently told me – and said this same information would have been included within her original police statement – of her seeing a bloodstained young man running away very fast from the direction of the cemetery some time after 1.10 p.m. I explained Mrs Hadfield said she also saw him at about the same time as this running man, and fully believed he too must have seen both her and this other person.

Mr Orange pulled a face at my query, and vehemently denied ever seeing Mrs Hadfield, or any running man, stating: 'No, I didn't see anybody running at all – I saw nobody! I told the police exactly what I saw. I told Ray Downing that if I knew anything else I would have told them.'

There was now some slight anger and frustration in his voice, and I felt my question may have touched a nerve, and that he may have had to deny this claim many times before. It was a relatively small estate and similar gossip had been rife for decades.

From what Stephen's father Ray had told me, Mr Orange always claimed that Stephen 'didn't do it', so I wanted to know his reasons for saying this.

He repeated his belief that he thought Stephen was innocent, but couldn't really offer any explanation, apart from claiming he was 'not the type'. He then confirmed that although he knew Stephen Downing, he said he hadn't see him at all that day.

Mr Orange explained, 'He was a quiet lad, and a bit of a loner. He must have had a hell of a time in prison. I know, I've been there,' and added: 'You just couldn't imagine Stephen doing anything like that. I mean, when you know somebody that you see quite regularly walking about – he was a lot younger than me, and he was only a kid – you can't imagine that he could have done something like that.'

He obviously knew it was Stephen who had first found Wendy lying badly injured in the cemetery, and said he wasn't aware of anyone else being around at the time she was found, but then I felt slightly puzzled, and wondered how he could know that for sure, if he wasn't there? I let that go unchallenged.

'I have a report that you went into the Castle Hotel in Bakewell later that same lunchtime, and told bar staff that Wendy had been attacked, and that she had suffered head injuries,' I then told him.

Mr Orange was quite taken aback. He ran his hand over his face and looked to Ms Yellow for support before he flatly denied the allegation, and argued that in fact it was Charlie Carman who had told him about the incident later that afternoon – and insisted it was Carman who said he thought it was Wendy!

He explained: 'I did used to go into the Castle. I was friendly with the landlord and landlady there. But no, I didn't know it was Wendy. The first time I heard about Wendy – and he didn't say it was, but he thought it was her – was from Mr Carman, who I saw when he was working in Bath Gardens. This was much later on, in the afternoon. He said to me, "Did you see that girl today on the Butts?" And I asked, "Do you mean Wendy?", and he said yes, then he told me they think it's her that's been attacked in the cemetery. That was all I knew about it.'

His claim was in stark contrast to Carman's original police statement, in which he said Mr Orange told him about the attack – and thought it was Wendy – about 3.30 p.m., in Bath Gardens, where Carman was working.

And Mr Orange's allegation also contradicted at least two other original 1973 police statements from bar staff at the Castle Hotel, who also believed that he had first mentioned the cemetery attack in the pub before 2 p.m., saying he thought it was Wendy.

Mr Orange had an answer for everything, or insisted he couldn't remember certain points after all this time, but denied all the allegations from his ex-lover Rita, and some unfounded allegations allegedly made about him and contained within some anonymous letters sent to the *Matlock Mercury*.

He did, though, admit to knowing both Mr Red and Syd Oulsnam, and claimed Mr Red had been a former lover of Wendy Sewell, and said that coincidentally he had also been at school with Mr Red.

When I asked Mr Orange if Wendy had once been his girl-friend too, he flatly denied it, although he confirmed he knew her well, and said he was always friendly to her whenever they met in town. At that remark, I noticed Ms Yellow quickly look up and glare at him. She started spluttering again. I wondered if this had perhaps triggered something she too had once wondered about from his past associations. I then regretted not interviewing them both separately.

I later pressed him again to see if had remembered anything else from that day. We had been chatting for quite a while, so I wanted to know if anything unusual had suddenly sprung to mind. Or had he noticed any suspicious characters hanging about?

He pondered for a moment, looked hard again at Ms Yellow, and in a surprise update to what he had previously said, he muttered: 'I did have a fuzzy recollection of seeing someone who said they saw a man leave the cemetery to phone for help. I think they said Wendy had been attacked.' Mr Orange added that he didn't know who this person was now, and couldn't remember much else.

I considered whether this remarkable throw-away comment may have unwittingly provided a potentially plausible explanation about what really happened at the Castle Hotel in September 1973, and at his later meeting with Carman. I thought that perhaps on hearing these words near the scene of crime, plus perhaps with the boost of a few pints in the Castle, he had suddenly become more informative, vocal and yet forgetful.

Mr Orange, however, stuck to his previous comments of not knowing anything else for sure, and insisted he didn't tell anyone else about the incident in the pub, or in Bath Gardens, repeating his claim that it was Carman who told him about the attack and Wendy.

*   *   *

My extensive interview with Mr Orange seemed to raise more questions than answers, and I was left with a raft of inconsistencies and anomalies to consider.

I read statements from all the workmen in the cemetery who had been with Downing when they came across the injured victim. The one who phoned the police from the phone box claimed he hadn't seen or spoken to anyone as he left the scene to dash for help, but unfortunately most of the workmen – and even Charlie Carman – had since died, so it was impossible to verify the true facts. And I still wondered why they didn't call for an ambulance rather than the police.

I had also seen Charlie Carman's original police statement and knew he claimed Mr Orange had told him. His statement was vitally important, as he also said he looked over the cemetery hedge on his way back to work and saw Wendy alive and well. He made no apparent mention, though, of seeing Downing.

Stephen, however, claimed he saw Carman and Peter Moran on his exit from the cemetery at 1.08 p.m., a time verified by the gatekeeper, Wilf Walker. I considered whether Carman was ever asked about this brief encounter, as it could have supported Downing's alibi, and confirmed the victim was still mobile and uninjured.

With thoughts of a potential conspiracy theory, as I believe Downing had been forced into signing a false confession, I also wondered whether details of this short meeting had been conveniently omitted, as this later timing could have discredited the 'confession'.

It seemed yet another strange anomaly had been totally ignored by Downing's defence team and, in addition, there was no apparent inquiry or comparison of evidence to examine the dispute about who really told who about the attack and the fact it was Wendy with head injuries. It was obvious that both witnesses couldn't be right.

I then realised that perhaps the most important query of all relating to Carman's statement had escaped scrutiny. I knew Mr Orange had mentioned passing Carman, which I previously suggested might have been closer to 1 p.m., as Carman headed back down to town. Carman said he saw Wendy alive, yet Mr Orange said he didn't see her again, so I wondered: why?

Then I studied both accounts again, and I believe that if Downing saw and perhaps spoke briefly with Carman at 1.08 p.m., then Carman must have retraced his steps, and possibly returned home for something he had forgotten.

He perhaps saw Wendy after passing Stephen. I felt Carman must therefore have been late back for work that afternoon, and perhaps didn't want to admit this in his statement. And I wondered again why this additional anomaly had not been fully examined.

The conflicting statements between Mr Orange, Carman and Downing provide a fascinating conundrum within this murder mystery. My theory is that if Mr Orange did in fact see Carman before 1 p.m., and Downing saw him later at 1.08 p.m., then he must have doubled back for whatever reason. But, if Mr Orange saw Carman some time after 1.08 p.m., then Mr Orange must have been mistaken with his recollections, and perhaps his own whereabouts at that slightly later time, which might also explain why Mrs Hadfield was certain she spotted him some time after 1.10 p.m.

I felt that clarification of all the witness timings identified around the scene of crime was vital to establish a precise timeline, and to determine exactly when Wendy Sewell was attacked. The analysis of Mr Orange and Carman's statements and timings adds further credibility to my belief that the victim was really attacked between 1.10 and 1.18 p.m., when Downing was at home, and that it could NOT have been before 1.08 as the police have always believed.

Within a couple of weeks of conducting this interview, and following a similar blitz on the estate to talk with many other 'persons of interest', I then started to receive a series of nasty, threatening phone calls, and received some extreme intimidation from people trying to warn me off investigating the case.

I then faced the most frightening experience of my life, when after being enticed out onto a bleak moorland road in my car at night by a hoax call, I was chased and continually bumped from behind by a huge great quarry lorry for mile after mile on a deserted, narrow roller-coaster road, only to escape with both my wing mirror, and my life, left hanging by a narrow thread.

*   *   *

The strange thing about my investigations around Bakewell at that time was that it remained a very close-knit community where everyone knew everyone else as neighbours, friends, relatives or workmates. People naturally had differing opinions of this crime, and bizarrely for Ray Downing, as a local taxi driver he was still in demand to transport former suspects, witnesses or other persons of interest around the area, without any threat of animosity. I felt like I was an intruder in some sort of public soap opera.

For Ray and Nita Downing it had been mission impossible to find anyone willing to help with their quest to free their son. They had a distrust of the police, the press, politicians and even Stephen's original solicitors. Perhaps this was why they later hired the services of amateur sleuth Robert Ervin, a former army investigator. Although they initially did much of the leg-work and enquiries themselves, it was difficult to remain impartial when quizzing neighbours or following up on any relevant gossip.

The police believed they were their own worst enemies, and claimed they may have tainted the evidence of key witnesses by interference. This was considered a probable issue during the lead-up to an appeal in October 1974, when Jayne Atkins presented her evidence.

In an effort to discredit her, the prosecution implied the Downings had encouraged Jayne to come forward. They also said they were friendly with the Beebe family, and said that Nita had actually accompanied Jayne and her mother Margaret to Bakewell police station in March 1974.

Lucy Beebe contacted me again to add further information. She was able to relate how she and Pam Sheldon had been in the cemetery playing with Ian at around 1.10 p.m., and left via the hedge. Lucy's brother Ian remained on his own. On a further occasion she explained that both she and Pam saw a bloodstained person jump over the cemetery wall and run off. She gave me a telephone number for Ian and said she had persuaded him to talk to me.

I interviewed Ian Beebe in January 1995. He was then in his mid-twenties. Although his recollections from September 1973 were blurred and slightly uncertain due to his young age at the time, he remained adamant he saw something 'horrific' and said it would stay with him all his life.

He explained, 'I was only about four at the time. I went out of the house on my pushbike and was going into the cemetery by the main gates. Pam and I were playing a game of hide-and-seek. I was pedalling up and down the paths when I saw this lady slumped on a gravestone. She was covered in blood and groaning. It really gave me quite a start and frightened the life out of me.'

I challenged him, 'Are you sure it was a woman, Ian? At the time, your sister said you told her it was a man.'

'I panicked. I must have been in shock. This person came over the gravestone. It was definitely a woman covered in blood. I might have said a man at the time, I can't remember. I think it was because everyone had long hair in those days. I couldn't speak!'

I recalled that workman Herbert Dawson had also displayed some confusion as to whether it was a man or a woman seen staggering about the gravestones, so I wasn't too surprised that a four-year-old child would also struggle to see the difference too.

'Did you see a man with a woman?' I asked.

'Pam said there was a bloke with blood on him.' He paused for a moment. 'It was lunchtime and my mother let me stay off school for a long time afterwards – but I had nightmares. It took me a long time to get over it, and I couldn't go back into that cemetery again.'

The complicated puzzle of what children and adults actually saw that day in the cemetery was finally beginning to fit together.

*   *   *

My television-presenter friend Allan Taylor had begun to take a real interest in the Downing case, and when I told him I had spoken to Jayne Atkins a couple of weeks ago he asked if I could give him the details of her whereabouts so that he could speak directly with her.

At first I was reluctant, but I eventually agreed to contact her to see how she felt about doing a television interview. To my great surprise she agreed, on condition that her exact location was not revealed.

Allan called her the following day, and she permitted him to do a taped interview over the telephone. That same evening it was broadcast on Central Television's regional news programme, together with an old photograph of Jayne. She added little or nothing to my own interview with her, but reiterated her claims in support of Stephen Downing, while a voiceover updated viewers on other developments in the case.

To my horror, Jayne telephoned me a few days later in blind panic. Despite my assurances that her whereabouts would not be disclosed, she informed me that her interview had been broadcast on Greek TV and her cover was blown. She would now be forced to move on again.

I didn't understand. Despite repeated requests by the police for me to provide the details of all my informants, I had constantly refused.

Allan Taylor assured me that he had told no one else from Central TV of Jayne's whereabouts, although he agreed that anyone in authority could have traced his call. He confirmed that Central didn't sell on the story, and he believed the broadcast in Greece was intercepted by someone keen to keep tabs on this particular witness.

I made my own enquiries, and a reliable Home Office source told me the taped interview had been pirated.

When I caught up with Allan again, I asked him what he had made of Jayne. He said, 'I spoke to her at length, and can't totally dismiss her claims. She's not the sort of person to embellish or distort. There's no doubt she was a crucial witness. Okay, it took her a long time, but even so, her troubled childhood should not be forgotten. It can't have been easy for her to come forward.'

I agreed. It took a great deal of courage for a teenage girl from a troubled home and a rural background to make her first ever trip to London and appear in such intimidating surroundings. She knew the risks involved, and to her credit she did what many other people could and should have done.

CHAPTER 14

THE BOMBSHELL

I had to wait a long time for permission to visit Stephen Downing in prison. The authorities were reluctant to allow a journalist to talk with him directly. On 22 January, however, a letter finally arrived from him, replying to my latest questions about his recollections at the scene of crime.

He wrote back, using my questions as headings:

WHAT CAN YOU TELL ME ABOUT THE MAN WHO THREATENED YOU?

I only saw the man who threatened me from the back as he ran off into the woods. He was wearing denim trousers and jacket, and I could see he had on a lemon-coloured T-shirt.

From the back view I calculated he would have been around five feet ten to six feet four, heavily built though not overweight, and agile for his size. I didn't see his face, but I feel it must have been someone who knew me because he knew I had a sister.

I would say he had a local accent. That is to say, I didn't notice anything to indicate he was an outsider. His voice was fairly deep in tone, though this could have been distorted as

he spoke through clenched teeth in a vicious
manner.

As for the sharp instrument I felt in the small
of my back, I had the impression that it could
have been a knife. However, a knife was not used
in the attack on Wendy Sewell.

The police found two splinters of wood from the
pickaxe shaft, each said to be around six inches
in length. He could have pushed one of them into
my back.

WHY DID YOU TELL NO ONE ABOUT HIM AT THE TIME?
I didn't tell the police or my solicitors because
I thought I would eventually be released, and I
was frightened because the man had threatened
the same would happen to my sister if I told
anybody.

WHEN DID YOU FIRST TELL SOMEONE ABOUT HIM?
The first person I told was my father in February
1974 after I had been convicted. I think he told
my solicitors.

**WHY DID YOU WAIT 13 DAYS TO RETRACT YOUR
CONFESSION, AND WHAT PROMPTED YOU TO DO IT AT THAT
POINT?**
I strongly believed that I would not be kept in
Risley for very long before being released. I know
this seems rather silly, but I was that naive as
to believe it. It was several days before I
realised that I was not going to be let out. And
with Wendy Sewell dying, it had reduced my chances

of the police finding out who was really responsible, as she was not able to tell them.

This was quite devastating for me. It was like not being able to swim and getting thrown in the deep end. You believe someone will come along and save you, but when they don't you realise it is up to you to do something.

I had been terrified of saying anything about the man who threatened me in case the same happened to my sister. A few days after my arrest I had asked my parents to get police protection for Christine on her way to and from school and so on. But the police had refused.

When I realised I was going to be held in prison and couldn't do anything to protect her, I had to change my plea so I would be released and could watch over Christine. That's when I changed my plea … I broke down and cried and told my father I hadn't done it. Even this failed to get me released – but at least the truth was out. I certainly wasn't going to go back to taking the blame.

It had taken me many months of investigation and interviews before I felt confident about running my first story about this highly controversial case. I prepared an updated submission for Derbyshire police, and on 27 January 1995 ran my exclusive article in the *Matlock Mercury*.

INNOCENT OR GUILTY?

The Home Secretary is to be asked to reopen the file on Stephen Downing, the teenager convicted of the Bakewell cemetery murder of Mrs Wendy Sewell in September 1973. A portfolio containing new evidence is to be presented to the authorities by Stephen's parents Ray and Juanita Downing in a bid to secure his freedom.

My report provided a detailed account of my investigations since the previous September, and highlighted a number of important factors that had not been made known to the jury until after they had reached their verdict. I was presenting our readers with some new facts, and challenged them to see what they could make of this fresh evidence. Would it throw some doubt on the murder conviction for them?

Calls came in thick and fast over the next few days. Most were supportive and offered praise for my efforts. In Matlock, several police officers smiled when they saw me and indicated I had put the cat among the pigeons. They also made it plain that head-quarters had now placed me on their black list. Stephen's response to the story was prompt.

```
Thank you for the copy of the Matlock Mercury. I
should like to express my sincere gratitude both
to you and your team for putting together an
excellent article. I understand from my mother
that it has sold 150 copies over and above the
normal circulation in the local shop. At least it
proves that a great many people are showing an
interest, even if it is only to see if they are
```

linked with it, as I suspect there will be a few
who are worried that their names might appear.

Following this first article we received calls from the usual local cranks, drunks or weirdos, but a few others seemed more sinister – and perhaps more credible. And then, remembering the attacks previously in the fire in the skip at the office, the brick through the window and lighted paper pushed through the letterbox, I warned the staff and the police about all the threats we received.

One in particular – and I can't be certain whether it was the same previous menacing caller – warned me to look under my car for a surprise parcel unless I stopped my investigations about Downing.

This was a bomb threat. Why would someone want to do such a thing? And was it just talk or was this for real? It was something I could not keep to myself, and when I told Kath she told me to go to the police station to report it. A senior officer at Matlock just grinned and shook his head in disbelief. A new young inspector advised everyone at the *Mercury* to check under our vehicles – just in case – and not to open any suspicious packages. 'If in doubt,' he said, 'call us.'

A few days later I was on my way back to the office from an interview in Cromford when I was halted by a queue of traffic heading back towards Matlock.

I could do little else but just sit there wondering what the hold-up was all about this time. As I was waiting, I noticed a police motorcyclist pull up alongside me. I wound down my window and asked him what the problem was. He said a possible explosive package had been discovered under a vehicle at the *Matlock Mercury* offices.

I told him who I was and that it could have been intended for me. He spluttered with shock and immediately said, 'Follow me.'

He put on his flashing blue lights and screaming siren and we travelled at speed back to the office on the wrong side of the road, with the officer frantically waving other people out of his way while he spoke to someone on his radio.

It was a bizarre experience, and while at times during my investigations I'd felt like I was part of some extraordinary soap opera, this was like something from a TV detective drama, dashing along on the wrong side of the road behind a police escort to a potentially major incident.

There wasn't time to think about any danger. I wasn't nervous at all – quite the contrary. I felt excited and stimulated, and my adrenaline levels were sky-high.

We finally entered a small cordoned-off area and I could see fingers pointing towards me as my car pulled into the side of the road. We got out, and the inspector pointed towards a car parked at the office. He asked whose it was. It was just a pool car, so this so-called bomber didn't appear to be targeting me directly this time.

As he radioed in to HQ, I looked around and then noticed a large cardboard box wedged under the rear wheels of the pool car. *Hang on a minute*, I thought, *that's not what I think it is, is it?*

I walked over to the car, despite the warnings being shouted towards me and, seemingly oblivious to danger, I hauled out this suspect package: the soggy remnants of a discarded fruit packing box that had simply blown down the road from the nearby market. It had happened before.

I heard someone mutter, 'Stupid boy,' like the character from *Dad's Army*. I wasn't sure whether it was aimed at me or this rather nervous police officer for causing chaos.

CHAPTER 15

THE SMOKING GUN

Information came to me from one of my contacts in Bakewell about John Marshall, the son of a prominent businessman, who was allegedly the father of Wendy Sewell's child.

I was told he was only about 19 when she became pregnant. His family owned Broughton's, an established elite outfitters and general store that served the gentry. They sold traditional country clothing, and even supplied uniforms to Lady Manners School.

My contacts believed the prospect of fathering an illegitimate child with an older, married woman in Bakewell at that time would have created a major scandal. It seems there was a determination to keep a lid on the whole affair, and John was shipped out of town, and later joined the army.

My informant, who went under the codename Port Vale, also mentioned the fact that five men from the area had been interviewed over the killing of Barbara Mayo, a young student from London found murdered close to the M1 at Chesterfield. This seemed an interesting coincidence with two young women – very similar in appearance – murdered, just three years and 12 miles apart. Was there a connection?

* * *

During January and February 1995 I presented two separate detailed submissions for the Home Office on behalf of Stephen Downing. I believed they contained new information that demanded some explanation. I said that I hoped to be able to prove reasonable doubt against Downing's conviction and trusted that, whatever the outcome, Downing may be considered for parole.

```
Dear Don,
Thanks for sending the copies of the submission.
I have read it several times so that I am familiar
with the contents. It puts across a very strong
argument to support and uphold my claim of
innocence. Hoping that your time-honoured efforts
will not have been in vain.
    Best regards, Stephen Downing.
```

I sighed heavily and put Stephen's letter aside, as I had the next edition of the paper to get out that day. We were running another major story about his case on the front page, based on my recent letter from him in Dorchester prison regarding the threats made to him by an unknown person in the cemetery. On 3 February 1995 the *Mercury* headline declared ADMITTED ATTACK TO PROTECT HIS SISTER.

The response to my report was just as overwhelming as the previous one. The phones didn't stop ringing with messages of support and information or requests to meet from people who thought they knew something.

An anonymous letter arrived ten days later, on 13 February. The writer claimed, 'Wendy was known to me and I had seen her prior to this incident date accompanied by a man in the wooded area, located down from the cremation Garden of Remembrance. This person was not Stephen Downing.'

She said that during this period she used to visit a farmer's wife in the Peak District, and her letter continued, 'She would quiz me if, or not, I knew anything about Wendy, who was apparently having a relationship with her husband. I did not know him to speak to but had, on occasions, seen Wendy with him in a van. It occurred to me on reading an article in a paper that a witness had come forward seeing a man run away. I believe he was blond-haired.'

A few weeks later, an anonymous phone call came in from a very frightened woman. It seemed that she was the writer of the anonymous letter, and she told me, 'Mr Red's wife became suspicious that he was becoming involved with a very attractive young woman from Bakewell. She said her name was Wendy Sewell. She asked me if I could keep an eye out and let her know if I saw them together. She thought Mr Red used to meet Wendy around the edges of the farm and wanted me to watch out for them as I rode around the lanes. I often used to see them together. Sometimes they were in a Land Rover, other times in the fields.'

'So what did you do?'

'Well, one day I saw them kissing. I think he saw me watching. You can imagine – I was a young girl in this situation. I was terrified after that. He kept giving me these stares when he saw me around the stables. I knew his secret. I didn't want to be involved any more.

'Quite a few local men used to come to the farm looking for work. He had this take it or leave it attitude towards them. I think most of them were frightened of him. There were some pretty heavy-duty looking friends used to come to the farm, too. I don't know who they were.'

My mind turned to Syd Oulsnam. Was he one of the local men employed by Mr Red at that time? They lived in neighbouring villages, so I thought it quite likely.

I asked the woman if she would be prepared to meet me. She refused point blank. She said she was far too scared of repercussions and didn't want to end up like Wendy.

* * *

There were so many fascinating aspects to this murder that I found difficult to comprehend. I wondered if Wendy's fingernail scrapings had ever been taken. If not, why not? What forensic data still existed? Was third-party blood found on the murder weapon?

Initial information given verbally by one of my police informants claimed that medical reports highlighted the fact that Wendy had suffered a broken shoulder during the attack, so it now seemed clear that she had put up a tremendous struggle to try to defend herself.

This vital information was not mentioned at trial, and again it would have contradicted Downing's alleged confession. It therefore seemed highly probable that her assailant would have been covered in blood, and I thought that with modern DNA techniques the police could match some to her real killer.

The police, though, constantly rejected any help or information, and quite incredibly constantly maintained that all the scene of crime exhibits, the paperwork and even the murder weapon had been 'burnt, lost and destroyed'.

My friendly police informants repeatedly claimed that this was all absolute rubbish, and confirmed the pips were lying again and just wanted to fob me off.

When I challenged the police about the victim's fingernail scrapings, I was quite bluntly told that they were never taken. One senior officer implied it was probably because her nails were too short. It turned out to be another lie.

My relationship with Derbyshire police throughout my many years of campaigning was frosty to say the least. And yet I remained determined to keep the boys in blue – and the Home Office – informed of my progress. With hindsight, however, this would prove to be a huge mistake, as I discovered that a few rotten apples in a barrel could easily contaminate the others.

I relied on a handful of loyal contacts, who like me believed in fair play and justice. Regrettably, I knew that some officers were working to a very different and opposing agenda. Keen to earn brownie points by proving their loyalty to police HQ, they constantly tried to discredit my efforts.

I feel that initially there was probably a feeling of embarrassment when I first started to make enquiries about this case, and some unease that I might expose a potentially deliberate police cover-up. I am sure that alarm bells started to ring loud and clear when I published some previously unknown facts and started interviewing key witnesses.

My first attempts to glean new information from the public proved a huge success, and I was overwhelmed by the response. It was as if the flood gates had suddenly opened, with people waiting for decades to tell their stories about this incident. Many people had simply lost faith with the local police force.

When I first arrived in Matlock in 1985, Derbyshire police were considered something of a joke locally. Just two years previously Chief Constable Alf Parrish was suspended following a county council investigation into police finances and the 'unauthorised' spending of thousands of pounds on the refurbishment of his private office at HQ.

Seventeen months later the then Home Secretary Douglas Hurd, in an unprecedented move, retired him in 'the interests of efficiency' after a career in the police spanning more than 30 years.

The deteriorating state of the force over which the new Chief Constable John Newing presided at the turn of the decade was first highlighted by Geoffrey Dear, Her Majesty's Inspector of Constabulary, in his annual report for 1990.

> *The bureaucratic requirements of the county council and the police committee are a major obstacle to the efficient management of the force. The county council's corporate strategy does not permit any realistic growth in police spending in real terms.*
>
> *This has meant a virtual standstill in developing the constabulary and its resources for the last eight years. The innovative spirit so evident in other forces inspected is translated, at best, into cheerful apathy in Derbyshire.*

Geoffrey Dear's criticisms prompted Chief Constable John Newing to admit in his own report of 1990 that community policing in Derbyshire was a 'myth'. Home Secretary Kenneth Baker joined in the condemnation. He described Dear's damning report on the Derbyshire Constabulary as 'among the worst ever on any police force'.

By mid-1991 the situation was even worse. Derbyshire police found itself facing the loss of its certificate of efficiency and John Newing evidently felt frustrated at having once again to defend his force.

He conceded, 'There is no doubt morale is worse now than it was 12 months ago. Morale is bound to be low. If the morale of this force is at the point it is alleged, then this report could be the thing that tips it over the brink.'

In 1993 Geoffrey Dear refused to grant Derbyshire police a certificate of efficiency. The same thing happened the following two years. The third refusal of a certificate in March 1995 was then accompanied by Home Office intervention; Minister David Maclean was forced to step in to announce emergency funding, and on a visit to Matlock he said, 'We have to remind ourselves of the past funding decisions. In a crucial period in the 1980s, when every other force was expanding, for whatever reason Derbyshire did not bid for more bobbies.'

This was the turbulent background against which journalists like me had to conduct relations with Derbyshire police. A force that held the dubious distinction of being the only one to lose its certificate of efficiency three times, in three consecutive years, was bound to be sensitive and defensive when approached by the press.

It might help to explain why Chief Constable John Newing and his assistant Don Dovaston proved such formidable opposition over the Downing case – which I always believed was in the public interest.

* * *

I received a call at the office one day from a man claiming to be an assistant to the curator at Derby Police Museum. He had a very strong Derbyshire accent and said, 'Eh up, youth, is it you that's looking for this murder weapon in the Downing case?'

I wondered if it was a huge wind-up. It was not the usual 'police speak'.

'The pickaxe handle?' I asked.

'Yes, that's it, that's the one. It's here. I'm looking at it right now. It's one of our prize exhibits. It's even got a brass plaque: "Stephen Downing, Bakewell cemetery murder, September 1973, victim Wendy Sewell".'

I was astonished. Then I wondered if it was just a hoax.

'Do you want to pick it up?' he asked.

'You're saying this pickaxe handle is in the Derby Police Museum?' I asked, still wondering if there had been a mix-up. 'I was told it had been burnt and destroyed.'

'No, mate, it's not been burnt. It's here. It looks a bit discoloured but it's one of our best displays. It's here all right. Been here for many years. We're quite proud of it. One of Derby and County's quickest convictions,' he said.

'Don't touch it,' I said excitedly, 'and please don't tell anyone else about it – and especially don't say you've spoken with me. I'll try to make some arrangements for collection. Many thanks.'

'No problem, mate,' he said. 'Just wanted to put you right.'

'Much obliged' I said, putting down the phone and doing a quick jig.

I sat down in disbelief. This was potentially crucial evidence and vital to any new appeal. Just like much of the prosecution paperwork, it had turned up despite continual claims from the force that all exhibits and documents relating to the case had been burnt, lost or destroyed.

I told Norman, Jackie and Sam, and enjoyed watching their equally surprised expressions.

Another informant rang from police HQ a few days later. I think he was a friend of the assistant curator. He told me there was a clear palm print on the heavily bloodstained wooden shaft that was certainly not Stephen Downing's.

He confirmed that, in addition, some blood was discovered on the handle, together with some hairs and fibres, but the most interesting fact was that none of it belonged to Stephen Downing or Wendy Sewell.

It clearly suggested the assailant might have cut himself during the attack. This was indeed compelling fresh evidence, and I was certain it had not been reported at the trial. I thought it could help eliminate Downing and possibly incriminate someone else with the use of modern DNA techniques. A breakthrough at last.

Just as I was about to jump for joy again, my contact warned that the palm print could prove to be a red herring. 'What do you mean?' I asked.

'It looks like it could belong to one of our plods. A PC who was left hanging about at the scene of crime was told to bag up all the bits and bring them back to the bobby shop. He probably picked up the whole lot in one and just did as he was told.'

I thought it was more reminiscent of the Keystone Cops. A young policeman left alone for hours on end in that cold, desolate cemetery, probably stamping his feet to keep warm in the darkness. I thought of potential cross-contamination and wondered if the bloody murder weapon had been placed in the same bag as Wendy's clothing. Vital clues could have been obliterated.

I already knew from paperwork leaked by other police contacts that the Home Office forensic scientist did not even attend the scene of crime, working and preparing his analysis from a base at least 25 miles away.

Friendly contacts within the force remained only too willing to feed occasional snippets of information through the system.

I had at least four very reliable informants, who remained supportive throughout my inquiry. Initially, most of my contact with police informants was via telephone calls and agreements to collect paperwork at arranged drop-off points. They were obviously worried about being spotted co-operating with me, as it could have led to possible prosecution, jail and at the least dismissal from the force for supplying a journalist with confidential information.

It was all very clandestine, and at times I felt like a spy infiltrating the system, trying to obtain snippets of information to help prove the establishment wrong. I knew that I had to protect my sources and that I could also face potential prosecution if I was caught.

Threats had already been made by the pips on several occasions, who claimed they already knew who was feeding me information and just wanted my confirmation.

This cat-and-mouse game went on for years, but gradually my contacts realised they could fully trust me. I met a couple of these guys as the case progressed because I think they were as keen to meet me as I was to understand their motives and thank them personally for their assistance.

I did, however, have to be extremely careful, as at any time this could have been a trap. It all added to the intrigue, and I don't think we could have continued unless there was trust on all sides.

I always believed in justice, and I knew that whatever paperwork I received was genuine and could therefore have been used in my defence as potential proof of an alleged conspiracy or cover-up, if necessary. To allow me to progress, I had to push all thoughts of danger out of my head in order to complete my enquiries – and I believed that being an outsider in the area allowed me to have a clearer perspective.

A little later that month I received another call from my police HQ contact to say that, contrary to what I had been told by Derbyshire police HQ just the previous month, fingernail scrapings were taken from the victim, and they had lain hidden in police vaults for 22 years.

'So you see, Don, what you were told was wrong. Many of the trial exhibits haven't been destroyed.'

I told him that Wendy's fingernail scrapings never appeared on the trial list of exhibits. Yet I had always thought it strange that none were taken from her, considering the brutality of the attack. Surely she could have scratched and clawed at her assailant? Once again, it was my hope that, with DNA technology, the scrapings and the murder weapon could be vital in linking Wendy to her attacker.

My informant rang back a few days later to add that records showed Downing's fingerprints definitely did not appear on the bloodstained shaft of the pickaxe handle, and there had been nothing obvious within Wendy's fingernail scrapings to link her to Downing.

My exclusive story in the *Matlock Mercury* ran with the heading DNA LINK: MURDER CLUES. The report encouraged the local force to use their high-tech DNA expertise to help eliminate people from their enquiries. I believed it could help to establish a clear and definite link to someone else – not to mention put the wind up any potential suspects.

The national press had now begun to show an interest in the Downing case. In particular, Frank Curran of the *Daily Star* regularly telephoned or met with me to keep abreast of any updates. I had contacted Frank when Ray Downing first got in touch with me the previous September.

As well as Frank, Allan Taylor and Brian Collins from Central Television and Rob Hollingworth from the *Sheffield Star* all began to conduct their own independent enquiries and faced similar hostility and threats from certain quarters.

Frank and Allan in particular helped to keep up the pressure. They interviewed the family, key witnesses, potential suspects, police officers and other interested parties. They agreed that there were too many inconsistencies in the original evidence to have produced a safe conviction.

The first major Downing story to hit the nationals was Frank Curran's front-page lead in the *Daily Star* in February 1995.

22 YEARS IN JAIL – BUT IS HE INNOCENT?

Love Cheat Wife's New Clues to Murder Case.

A cheating wife has given police clues which could prove a convicted killer who has served 22 years is innocent. The 'silent witness' says she knows Stephen Downing did not batter a woman in the cemetery.

The article went on to give details from one of the anonymous letters I had received earlier that month, and from other sources.

But it was Frank's second story the following week that really caused the muck to hit the proverbial fan. Picking up on my DNA article and talking to his own contacts within Derbyshire police, Frank Curran had another major page lead on the story on 13 February 1995.

TELL-TALE FINGERTIP SCRAPINGS COULD PROVE THAT STEPHEN DOWNING HAS BEEN WRONGLY JAILED FOR 22 YEARS.

Typist Mrs Wendy Sewell was murdered in Bakewell in 1973, but in her struggle scratched her attacker – his skin was

under her nails. Now the four suspects will be tested to see if their DNA matches. The *Daily Star* has discovered the scrapings have lain in police vaults for 22 years. But the evidence was never given in court. It would have cleared Stephen as his blood group did not match.

For some unexplained reason, gardener Stephen's defence counsel was not told of its existence. The *Daily Star* has discovered two other vital pieces of evidence, which point to a miscarriage of justice.

(a) Several fingerprints were found on the bloodstained murder weapon – a wooden shaft – but none were Stephen's.

(b) Experts told police that the killer was almost certainly right-handed. Stephen is left-handed.

Stephen, 39, has spent 22 years in prison and last night was still in Dorchester jail. Downing, then aged 17, with a reading age of 11, was arrested minutes after finding the body where he worked.

New suspects were recently named by a cheating wife who was in the cemetery with her lover when Wendy was killed. She wrote anonymously to a local paper telling how she saw Stephen arrive after Wendy was brutally attacked.

Frank went on to describe four men placed at or near the scene that day by the anonymous letter writer and others. He provided descriptions of Syd Oulsnam, Mr Red, Mr Orange and Mr Blue, and told of alleged sightings of them around the cemetery that day. He stopped short of naming them.

My telephone was red hot after the *Mercury* report – and then later with Frank's revelations in the *Daily Star*. Readers were checking in to compare notes and to see who was who. Names were offered to put faces to the four Frank had named as A, B, C and

D. Informants in Bakewell told me that these people were panicking. They had definitely recognised themselves in Frank's piece.

*   *   *

On the afternoon of 13 February there came yet another surprising call – from Syd Oulsnam. He thought he was the person described as Suspect A in the *Daily Star* report and asked, 'What does DNA mean?' He also demanded to know, apparently in all innocence, 'If my vehicle was involved, how could it link me with the pickaxe handle?'

I couldn't believe my luck. I explained, as best I could in layman's terms, the intricacies of DNA. I said that if Syd or anyone else had touched the murder weapon, or if the forensic evidence contained hairs or fibres from his vehicle, the police would be able to determine these facts.

Oulsnam was in turmoil. As in our last conversation, he at first denied ever being in the Bakewell area that day.

'I've told you, I was miles away,' he bleated. 'I already gave the police a statement telling them that I was nowhere near.'

I told him I had new witness statements from people on the estate who had seen his van up there that day, including two bus drivers, and reminded him that he even waved to one of them. What's more, several people had reportedly seen him in his van parked at the rear of the cemetery.

'I can tell you the registration number if you like, exactly where it was parked and for how long, plus I know exactly what you looked like in 1973. There's no doubt about it. It was definitely you, Syd. What's the point in lying about it?'

At first he continued to deny it.

'So, prove where you were, if you weren't at Bakewell cemetery, then.'

'It was a long time ago,' he replied weakly.

'With DNA and these new statements, I can probably prove where you were,' I told him.

He still denied it.

I put the pressure on by telling him, 'Look, Syd, eventually new DNA evidence is going to free Stephen Downing. Then there'll be murder and conspiracy charges brought against other people. It would be best for anyone who knows something to speak about it now.'

The mention of DNA had really got him on the run. 'Okay, I'll admit, I was parked up there, near the cemetery,' he said emotionally.

'What were you doing up there?' I asked, quite amazed by his admission – and half expecting him to just say cutting grass. I was staggered by his reply.

'I took Mr Red up there.'

My heart missed a beat. 'What time was this?' I asked.

'We got there about 12.30. He'd just come back from somewhere.'

'What happened then?'

'We waited around for a while near the gates. Then I drove to some waste ground at the back of the cemetery and parked up.'

'What were you doing there?'

'We were waiting. I had nothing to do with it!'

'Waiting? To do with what?' I asked.

'That murder. Wendy Sewell,' Oulsnam replied.

'Look, Syd, just tell me what happened. You could be in the frame for this at present. Let's help to clear your name.'

'I never got out of the van!' he insisted, in a panic.

'No, Syd. I'm not saying you did. Just tell me what Mr Red did.'

He paused. 'Mr Red went somewhere.'

'Where?'

'I don't know. Someone else was waiting for us.'

'Who?'

'I don't know his name. He was a friend of Mr Red.'

'Did Mr Red take anything with him from the van?'

'He took something from the back.'

'What?'

'I don't know.'

'What sort of things did you carry in the back?'

'Tools and suchlike.'

'Were there ever any pickaxe handles in the back of your van?'

'Yes, I think so. We had all sorts of odds and ends.'

'So when did you next see Mr Red?'

'I met up with him later in town.'

'Why didn't you wait for him?'

'I can't remember.'

I kept pushing him further. He was nearly in tears. 'Come on, Syd, try. This is very important.'

Eventually he replied, 'I remember hearing a shout or something, so I drove off.'

'What time?'

'About 1.20, I suppose.'

'Was Mr Red and this man meeting anyone else up there?'

'I don't know.'

'Was Wendy Sewell ever a girlfriend of Mr Red's?'

'Yes.'

'Do you know anything about Wendy and Mr Red having a row the night before?'

He was a bit vague, and paused before answering. He thought perhaps they had.

'I think he wanted to put something right.'

The call ended and for once I hoped the police had recorded my call. For weeks I'd been hearing strange noises and clicks on the office line and home phone. My staff and I were convinced that many of the calls coming into the paper were being monitored. We all deliberately said a few provocative key words just in case to try to drive the listeners crazy, but we were generally very careful about who we spoke to on the phone. I wondered if the police were monitoring everything.

I hadn't mentioned Mr Red's name at all. Oulsnam had volunteered that information. He'd now placed them both at the scene of crime, which also confirmed they'd given false alibis to the police.

Syd had seemingly confirmed a potential connection between Mr Red and Wendy, and news of a possible row the night before. I then registered a sudden mental note of extreme caution. Although Oulsnam's outburst seemed spontaneous, including a genuine expression of panic that he might have been identified within the *Daily Star*'s report as 'suspect A', his rhetoric appeared to be too cosy and convenient. I began to consider whether he had just added his 'Mr Red' allegation to test me, or to see if I was recording his conversation? He also refused to provide a written statement, which further added to my suspicions, and later, during a chat with Frank Curran, the author of the article, I found that Oulsnam had also contacted him, a few hours after he had spoken with me, to again confirm he was in Bakewell that day, but told Frank he had taken another (named) person to the area, at least an hour or more before the attack. It only enhanced my belief that he was a totally unreliable witness, who was definitely frightened of someone.

Other details began to fit into place. Jayne Atkins and her mother, Margaret Beebe, had both mentioned hearing a cry at around the same time as Syd. Ray Downing had seen Syd, shortly after 1.10 p.m., driving down the road away from the cemetery towards town.

I'd always assumed all this, but until then I had not known for sure. In addition, there was now confirmation of another man placed at the scene who was a friend of Mr Red.

5 February 1995

Dear Don,

It really is amazing the power the press has on people. I never would have thought for a minute that one of the four suspects would have come forward to tender evidence, perhaps even against his own friends. I find it equally hard to believe that the police have allowed vital evidence to remain in a vault for almost 22 years. It seems that they were desperate to secure a conviction and a fast one, with little regard for who shouldered the blame.

It has often been said that the truth will always prevail, and it now looks as if I am on that path.

It wasn't until the *Daily Star* took up my plight in a bid to establish my innocence that I began to have reservations about the kind of reception I would get from my fellow inmates. Any fears I had can certainly be laid to rest. This has become big news and a buzz of excitement ripples through the wing at mail call, with a number of eager lads jostling to be the next in line to read the following instalment in what has become Dorchester prison's very own soap opera.

Even staff are wishing me well in the fight to have the Home Secretary exercise a Royal

```
Prerogative of Mercy. The wealth of evidence
contained in the dossier would appear to offer the
Home Secretary little choice in what action he can
take. Whether or not Mr Howard will view it as a
case of Hobson's choice remains to be seen.
    Stephen Downing
```

Outside of my work on the *Mercury*, all my spare time was now taken up checking and rechecking official documents and old witness statements. I was also liaising with probation officers, Parole Board officials and civil servants at the Home Office.

I twice visited the CID at Matlock police station with anonymous letters and the envelopes in which they had arrived. I was also receiving generous support from many other quarters, including Stephen's childhood friend Richard Brailsford. He had tried to rally support for the campaign on several occasions over the past two decades.

Following my intervention on this case, Richard set about collecting more signatures for a petition calling for the release of Stephen and an official re-examination of the case.

Like me, he was to learn the dangers of meddling in this affair. He began to receive similar threatening telephone calls to his home and he was told by one anonymous caller that Stephen would be 'a dead man' if he was ever released.

Stephen wrote to me on 16 February 1995, full of concern for his friend and his own family.

```
Please excuse this letter being handwritten, only
I'm not really in the mood for typing after
hearing of the threats to you, Richard Brailsford
and his family, and also against me if I am
released. What is really bugging me is not knowing
```

if my family have also been receiving threats. It
is not something my mother would admit to me if
asked. Can you enlighten me?

  If my family is under threat too, do you think
the police will give them round-the-clock
protection and move them to a safe house? The last
thing I want is for one of them to answer the door
and take the full impact of a shotgun. I don't
want that to happen to anyone, not just my family.
I know that it sounds rather dramatic and something
you would come to expect in a film script, but I
am desperate to know that they are safe.

I was definitely followed on several occasions as I went about town during this period. Also, I often had an escort vehicle when I travelled across to Bakewell, or to Chesterfield to the printers.

I would sometimes have a chat with an innocent beat bobby about something completely trivial, just to see what happened. At times it all became quite comical, but I could easily lose my shadow, and I would then watch as they reached for their radio.

My informants mentioned the visit of CIB2, a police investigative unit who were particularly concerned with leaks, and told me they would have to go to ground for a few weeks, just in case. The drop zones became more important during this period to avoid recorded phone conversations and direct meetings, and to let the pips know that I knew I was being monitored.

Because of the potential dangers, I now decided to deal with the main investigation on my own. I didn't want any of my journalists' lives put at risk. I instructed my staff not to take any unnecessary chances and, in particular, not to meet anyone alone or after dark, and always to tell someone else where they were going. They were rules I was going to have to try to follow myself.

CHAPTER 16

GETTING TO KNOW STEPHEN DOWNING

It was not easy keeping in contact with Stephen Downing. There was always a considerable delay in exchanging information, and I knew all his calls and mail were being monitored. Some news therefore was related back to him in coded messages via his father in weekly telephone chats.

Although I wanted to concentrate on particular aspects of his original police interrogation and evidence, it became obvious that Stephen, at times, just wanted to pour his heart out. He was in the midst of a recurring nightmare, and at that time I probably represented his only lifeline.

He was a simple youth from a simple background. A young innocent thrown into a difficult and very dangerous adult world, and one that he had been forced to accept.

I pushed him again to write and explain about his early hours of detention in 1973 and received the following account:

```
I was led downstairs after giving my statement and
locked in one of the holding cells. My bed was a
large wooden bench about 6 by 3 feet. It had a
filthy blanket tossed over one corner and from the
smell of it I would say it hadn't been washed
since the day it was first put there. The only
```

other item in the cell was a toilet – a true
luxury for its day, as I was to learn later.

Even though I was fairly snug in this dimly lit
cell, sleep was impossible. At intervals of about
15 minutes I was asked if I was all right. I said
I was, and then Charlesworth and another PC came
in. They asked for a sample of pubic hair and head
hair. They told me they were being taken for
forensic analysis.

Soon after this I was taken back upstairs to the
same interview room. Fingernail scrapings were
then taken with the pointed blade of a surgical
knife. This operation was not without some pain
and discomfort – enough to cause me to pull my
fingers away. I was told it had to be done and to
keep still, but I think the sadistic sod took
great pleasure in my pain.

As each fingernail was scraped, the contents
were put into a separate envelope and labelled.
With the tips of my fingers still stinging and
spots of blood showing beneath my nails I was
returned to the cell. About another half an hour
went by and another two visits were made to make
sure I was okay.

The next interruption was again to take me away
from my cell and any hope of sleep. *Where to now?*
I wondered. But my question was soon answered. I
was bustled into a van and taken to Buxton police
headquarters. On my way out, I caught a brief
glimpse of the station clock and it was about 3
a.m. I was pushed out of the door to be met by the
cold and black of early morning. A yellow transit

van with black one-way windows waited at the kerb. I was flanked by two police officers and driven away to Buxton.

I think it took us about 20 minutes to get there. The Buxton police centre was brightly lit and seemed a hive of activity. I was beyond sleep now as I was taken to the counter and fingerprinted. A small sink was mounted on the wall to the side and I was told I could wash the ink off in that. After several attempts I gave up. My fingers seemed as black as when I had started. I was then taken along and put in a very large cell. The door slammed behind me and I was left there with my thoughts.

It was several days before I realised that I was not going to be let out, and when Wendy died it reduced the chances of the police finding out who was really responsible.

As I started to grow used to my surroundings I realised this cell was worse than the one at Bakewell. Although much cleaner, the only means of sleeping was on an angled concrete slab topped in wood and no more than two feet wide.

My dress boots were taken from me and I was asked if I had a tie or a belt. I hadn't either. I was then given a rub-down search. About ten minutes later I was disturbed again and was given a full examination by a doctor. Then I was left alone for a few minutes before some blankets were thrown at me – with apologies they didn't have any pillows.

The cell was freezing cold and I couldn't see any heating pipes or radiators. It must have been

hell in winter if it was this cold in September. I
counted seven blankets and folded two up as a
makeshift mattress to help take some of the
hardness out of the wooden bench. I used two more
as pillows and three to cover myself up. I don't
know how long I lay there before I fell asleep,
but it wasn't long. I woke to the sound of the
door being unlocked and a pint-sized mug of
lukewarm tea and a blue plastic plate with two
burnt slices of toast were thrust at me.

Time dragged slowly by. The door finally opened
and I asked if I could use the toilet. They showed
me where it was. I was told it was a good job
there were only two of us in the cells, otherwise
it would have meant a longer wait. I spent much of
the time pacing my cell like a caged animal. I had
not been asked to remove my boots when I returned
from the toilet, so at least my feet were warm. I
wrapped a blanket round my shoulders like a
Mexican poncho to keep my circulation going.

As I left my cell I was asked where my boots
were, and I told the sergeant I was wearing them.
He gave me a bit of an ear bashing about that, as
I was not allowed them in case I used the laces to
hang myself. So on returning to my cell they were
taken away again.

On the Friday I was to make my first appearance
before the magistrates at Bakewell Town Hall. I
was handcuffed and taken back to Bakewell police
station where I was put back in the same cell. I
thought my case was to be heard about ten o'clock
so, after being re-cuffed, I was marched 400 yards

through the streets of my hometown in full public view to the town hall. We sat through a few applications for extensions to pub licensing hours, then it was my turn.

Very little was said by the police or my solicitor Paul Dickinson, who had met me shortly before I left the police station. The magistrate turned out to be my former headmaster, Harry Schofield. Without any further ado, he then remanded me back to Risley Remand Centre for a week. The cuffs were put back on and I was then escorted through the streets again back to the cell at the police station.

My parents and sister, who had been present at my court appearance, were brought to my cell and locked up alongside me. We were allowed about an hour together before they had to leave. It was an emotional meeting and I cannot remember what was said, but I know they were supportive and wished me luck before they had to go.

The drive to the remand centre, near Warrington in Cheshire, took just under two hours. And when I got there it became obvious to me why anyone who has had the misfortune to spend time at Risley, even for just one night, will never forget the experience and will know how it became known as 'Grisly Risley'.

When we arrived at the reception area at the remand centre, I stood sandwiched between two police officers. A fat screw sat behind a high counter. One or two other particulars were taken. I was then ordered into another room and told to strip off. As I did my clothing was all noted on a property card before being tossed into a cardboard box.

Wrapped in a towel, I was given my prison number, 797501, and told to go to the stores for some clothing and then to go on to the bathhouse.

The kit I was given was not my size, but when I asked if it could be changed my request was denied. 'Nonce coming through,' bellowed one of the screws. Of course, the word meant nothing to me, but a few moments later a scream rang out from the bath area. I entered to find this guy standing in front of me naked and lobster red from head to toe.

I asked one of the others what had happened to him and I was told he was a 'nonce' and that he'd slipped getting into the bath. I was new to this kind of language, but I was told that a nonce was someone who had raped a woman or molested a child.

A scalding hot bath awaited each one that came through. The tap was left running so the bath overflowed and the water remained at the same excruciatingly high temperature.

If the nonces didn't like it they had the alternative choice of a hose-down, which consisted of a naked fire-hosing from a water jet so powerful that they couldn't stand up. The victims would 'dance', spending more time on their backsides because it was impossible to keep their footing on the slippery surface of the bathhouse.

It was hard to imagine the horrors Stephen had had to endure in prison. Treated as a sex offender and the brutal murderer of a young woman, he would have been considered the lowest of the low. An unwritten prison code forbade anyone from talking with him or befriending him. He would be ignored or antagonised as required. Fellow inmates might deliberately bump into him or verbally abuse him to try to trigger an adverse reaction. They would spit in his food or drink, or nudge his tray and generally make a nuisance of themselves. He was constantly on the lookout for any intimidation or attacks.

His account continued:

I was shown the scalding bath as a warning to behave, but an ordinary bath was reserved for me on that occasion. The threat was made, however – behave or you'll get the same treatment. I enjoyed the bath – my first since being taken into police custody. There hadn't even been any facilities provided for washing and shaving at Bakewell or Buxton.

After bathing, I dressed and collected my bedding along with a set of plastic cutlery, plate, bowl and mug. I was then put into a large holding cell with about 20 other blokes.

The walls were covered in graffiti and in places slices of bread had been stuck to them with knobs of margarine. From time to time, some of the occupants would spit on the floor, which was covered with dirty paper and fag ends.

After about two hours a screw appeared and read out some names – mine was one of them. We took it in turns to go before the doctor who asked if we

were well. That was the extent of our medical
examination. When the last man in our group came
out of the doctor's office, we were all taken to
the hospital. I found out there that I was
considered a suicide risk so I had to be kept in
the hospital where I could be watched every minute
of the day and night.

The ward had partitions throughout with two beds
in each section, making room for 24 beds in all.
But because of chronic overcrowding, several camp
beds had been erected in the centre of the ward,
so there were 52 of us sharing a space for half
that number.

The time passed quickly and soon Friday came
round. I was checked through reception and
told to get back into my own clothes before being
handed over to the police, who took me back
to Bakewell for my regular weekly court
appearance, which was followed by a visit from my
family.

I reminded them to ask for a hospital visit when
they came again. That way, we would not have to
try to talk through the mesh of a heavy wired
glass on a closed visit.

After travelling for thirteen weeks to the
magistrates' court, I was finally committed for
trial. This put an end to my weekly excursions.
However, my family began to visit me on the Friday
at Risley as well as on the Monday.

One of the worst nightmares I had while still on
weekly visits to the magistrates' court was to
pick up a dose of head lice.

```
    They gave me some shampoo from the sick bay but
it didn't help, and I had to have my long hair cut
off. They shaved my head. It had taken me over a
year to grow it long - and suddenly it was all
gone in just a few minutes. It was a sad day for
me.
```

Our regular discussions and correspondence provided a channel for Stephen to vent his feelings. I was gradually gaining his confidence and trying to look for any other information that might prove beneficial to his case. He continued:

```
My trial was at Nottingham Crown Court on 15
February 1974. To make it more convenient, they
transferred me to HMP Lincoln. I was again put in
a hospital. This time it had a single cell, number
13. I was there for two days and then moved to
number 9, which I shared with two other men who
were up on charges of murdering a prostitute. They
told me they strangled her for the money she owed
them.
    In court, I was asked how did I plea, and I told
them, 'Not guilty.'
    I remember very little of the trial itself,
except for the feeling of humiliation at being the
focal point of everything. Looking back, I didn't
feel the defence put up much of a fight.
    I was led downstairs to one of the cells to
await the verdict.
    The jury was out for less than an hour to
deliberate. I had lit a cigarette and only smoked
about half of it when the door opened and I was
```

told the jury were coming back. I sat in the rear
of the dock and the clerk told me to stand before
turning to the foreman. He asked him if he'd had
time to consider. He said he had and passed him a
piece of paper. The judge slowly unfolded it and
handed it back to the clerk. They had found me
guilty by a unanimous verdict.

They asked me if I wished to say anything before
sentence was passed. I was too numb with shock to
say anything. I think I said no and then just
shook my head.

Mr Justice Nield confirmed the verdict of the court, and explained
that he was unable to sentence him to anything other than a term
of imprisonment to be served at Her Majesty's Pleasure.

This sentence only applied to offenders under the age of 18
and technically had no time limit. Stephen, however, just wanted
to see his family and, as he was led to one of the holding cells
beneath the dock, his mother, father and sister greeted him and
reassured him he wouldn't be in for long – and that he should
never give up hope.

Twenty minutes later he was on his way back to Lincoln
prison, where he stayed for a couple of days before being transferred back to the remand centre at Risley to await the final decision as to where he would be sent to begin his sentence.

I knew these early experiences of prison life had affected him
badly. Being locked up for 20-plus hours a day must have been
absolutely horrific for Stephen. He immediately missed his loving
family and warm, carefree environment, especially given how
immature for his age he'd been. He faced dangers at every turn
and was forced to mix with many violent, devious and calculating criminals.

He struggled to fully understand his predicament and always thought he would be cleared after changing his statement so soon after being forced into making a false confession.

He was not streetwise at all, and he had no experience of violence or severe bullying, retribution or punishment for something he hadn't done. He kept expecting to wake up and realise that it was just a horrible nightmare – but when the cold facts of reality finally set in, he knew he was on his own, and he had no idea how he would ever get out of prison.

He found great difficulty in coming to terms with his new situation, but said that, eventually, he just learned to cope.

*   *   *

Stephen Downing's prison career was a crazy itinerary of frightening venues. He had been to at least ten different prisons since September 1974, including high-security establishments at Wakefield, Gartree, Nottingham and later Dartmoor. He even saw Moors murderer Ian Brady at Gartree from just a few feet away in the exercise yard.

His prison summary made for depressing reading. It confirmed his state of mind and limited intelligence in the early years. It also confirmed the horror he had experienced as a child-like youth of 17.

His first prison report from Swinfen Hall, where Stephen arrived in May 1974, was typical. It described him as a dull, lifeless and emotionally immature young man, who never displayed any feelings but could be stubborn at times. On arrival he had been at a loss, moving around like someone in a dream.

It said he would not speak unless approached, and even then would only answer in monosyllables. He had eventually found a comfortable niche and since then had been content to remain in the background, not making any real attempt to improve himself or to make use of the facilities offered.

His work effort was poor and he continued to give the impression he was on another level, oblivious to what was going on around him. He was polite and friendly enough in his dealings with staff, though with little to offer by way of conversation. His continued denial of guilt for the offence precluded him from gaining true insight. Overall, he made little progress, though he was better able to cope generally.

His Parole Board reports were excellent. Often he was described as a 'model prisoner', but time and time again his unwavering protestation of innocence was considered the one major obstacle preventing his release or transfer to more open prison conditions.

His casework officer's report from 1994 was a typical example:

> *Downing has done over 20 years in custody, I believe due to his denial of the offence. Until he admits to the offence, it is impossible for anyone to comment on his attitude to the offence or degree of remorse shown.*
>
> *Downing's behaviour has been exemplary. He shows good moral standards that would be commendable in a normal social environment. He is friendly and communicative to both staff and other inmates. I find no abnormalities in his attitude towards women. He has a respectable outlook. No concerns have been voiced and his attitude towards women has been commendable.*

Downing's prison reports confirmed that it took him a few years to settle before he learned to accept his lot and make use of the time available. I thought he deep down always maintained the belief that the cavalry would eventually arrive to help clear his name, as any innocent person locked away under those circumstances would probably admit. Without a belief in justice, what hope is there for anyone?

Throughout the years Stephen made several applications for his case to be heard by the Parole Board, but it was always rejected. And as his legal team confirmed, 'he was deemed unsuitable for treatment due to his continual denial'.

It seemed that unless he admitted to the murder and sexual assault, and agreed to attend treatment programmes, he would not be judged to have shown any remorse whatsoever, and consequently would still be considered a potential danger to the public. It was a ludicrous catch-22 position that could never be resolved.

In 1990, Stephen was reported as being 'mature and well-balanced'. By 1993, however, at the same establishment, he was considered 'out of touch with the real world'.

He wrote:

> Reporting staff are now saying that I am immature. Yet in 1990 I was considered mature. Presumably these observations are made by the same reporting staff. I don't think it is unfair to say that I am out of touch with the real world – especially when one considers the length of time I have been away.

I considered that this man had been locked away for decades. He had spent all his adolescent years and the prime of his life in jail, and yet the authorities had the audacity to describe him as 'out of touch'. Most people under those conditions would have become stark raving mad by then.

*   *   *

While his latest parole report was being considered, Stephen and some other inmates at the Verne prison at Portland were questioned over alleged obscene telephone calls to a female member of staff out of hours. This happened in late 1994, shortly after I began my investigations into his case. While enquiries were being made, Stephen was transferred to Dorchester prison.

Dorset CID, reputedly acting on reports from an anonymous source, made extensive enquiries. Many of the calls were said to have come from a phone not generally available to prisoners, and were made after lock-up. The police even claimed to have recorded some of the conversations.

When I learned that Stephen was one of a number of prisoners under suspicion, I contacted the senior investigating officer to intervene, as I was sceptical of their motives so soon after beginning my own enquiries.

I challenged them as to who this alleged anonymous source was, but was advised that Downing was just one of several people questioned – in his case because his original offence was described as a 'sex attack'.

When it became quite obvious that Stephen did not have access to the phone in question, and had always been locked up when calls were made, the inquiry was suddenly dropped. He didn't receive any explanation or apology, but mud sticks, and this accusation came at a critical time, just as his biannual parole review was in process. Stephen wrote to me in despair on 22 January.

```
I was pleased to read of the progress that you are
making. I don't want to dash anyone's hopes of
success but can't help feeling that the whole
thing will be a wet squib. With all this now
coming on top of me, I can't help wondering if I
```

will ever get out. I feel that I am eventually
going to be told that the Parole Board thinks I
should go back into the category B system and go
through the whole lot yet again. I'm sorry for
being so depressed.

CHAPTER 17

FACE TO FACE AT LAST

Negotiating the bureaucratic red tape to finally meet Stephen proved extremely frustrating. It took many weeks before I finally obtained permission and was able to set out on the long haul to Dorchester late in the afternoon of 22 February 1995.

It was a dreadful journey. It was bitterly cold and the day deteriorated rapidly into heavy rain, sleet and then a thick, swirling fog, which reduced visibility to almost nil and caused me to miss my turn-off on the motorway. I eventually arrived at my hotel around midnight.

At two o'clock the following afternoon I reported to the visitors' block. The waiting room was like hell on earth, packed to overflowing. When all the visitors were asked to register and hand in their visiting orders (VOs), one of the warders said, 'You're that reporter bloke, aren't you?'

Word got around fast. 'Yes,' I replied. 'I'm here to see Stephen Downing. It's all been arranged.'

'Not with those, you're not,' came the gruff reply. The prison officer was pointing to the package of goodies I had brought down with me from Stephen's family and friends. 'You'll have to leave them all here,' he said. 'Put them in a locker if you like, but they can't go in.'

I had gone through each and every item on the telephone with prison officials several days previously and been given permission to take them in. I tried to explain, but quickly realised it was like talking to a plank. He said, 'You don't have to go in, you know? Nobody will bother if you don't turn up. He'll understand.'

'What's the point in obtaining permission when you refuse it at the last minute?' I asked. The officer looked at me as if he was auditioning for the part of the Straw Man in *The Wizard of Oz*.

'All visitors come with me,' he shouted out into the packed office. The babble of conversation reached fever pitch as dozens of people poured out to join the assembled group and walk up the slight incline towards two very large wooden gates. The prison looked like a medieval castle standing on top of a hill.

I let the others go first and then began to follow. 'And just where do you think you're going?' the officer bellowed.

I replied angrily, 'I've got a VO to see someone. You've just checked it. Remember?'

'You'll go nowhere until I say. Stay there and I'll go and check. He might not want to see you.'

I was getting nowhere fast. 'And what about these papers? Stephen has to see them,' I shouted.

I watched the large group of visitors go up the hill and disappear through the gates. I had been told I would be allowed a minimum of 20 minutes and a maximum of an hour for the visit. I kept checking my watch and paced back and forth in frustration.

It was 2.20 as I re-entered the waiting room and a woman suddenly appeared from behind the counter. 'Can I help you, dear?' she asked. 'Are you visiting someone?'

'Yes, but I was told to wait here,' I replied.

'I should ignore that! Go up to the gate – they've probably forgotten all about you.'

'Yes, I think you're right,' I replied. So, once again, I marched up the hill towards the gates. I banged on the outer studded door.

Finally, a small half door within the main door opened and a big, burly officer popped his head out. 'Yes?' he shouted. His mouth was full of food and he sprayed half-digested fragments all over me. He had a meat pie in his hand.

'I'm here to see a prisoner,' I replied wearily.

'You're too late and you need a VO,' came the answer as bits of food continued to shower the area.

He was about to shut the door and disappear when I shoved the bundle of papers at his chest to stop him. 'I have a VO. I was told to wait by ...' I crouched down slightly and saw the same officer I'd seen about half an hour before. 'I was told to wait by him,' I said, pointing.

The man seemed to be grinning and turned away to hide his face. He too was eating something. 'Come in, let's have a look. Who is it you're wanting to visit?' he asked.

'Downing – Stephen Downing,' I said, emphasising the surname.

The officer studied the VO and checked his watch. 'You should have been here at two o'clock.'

'I was here well before two o'clock. I think you'll find the VO was stamped before two,' I replied. I was getting very annoyed but knew I had to keep my temper in check.

'Come through, but you'll have to wait here. I'll check.' I was invited into a small courtyard sandwiched between the main gate and another heavy-duty security gate about ten metres away.

The officer then disappeared into an office, lifted the phone and dialled a number. He put his pie down and turned his back. I could only hear snatches of the conversation. I then heard him say, 'Just a minute.' He turned and asked me, 'Can you come back tomorrow or next Monday?'

'No, I can't!' I replied, 'I've come a hell of a long way. The visit was booked in. The VO's been stamped. Do I take it you're refusing me admission? It will make a bloody good story for the nationals.'

The officer's face remained devoid of any emotion. I heard him tell his SO that I might make trouble. 'Wait here, please,' he demanded.

'Can I see Mr Downing, please?'

'Look, just wait here.'

I must have waited another five minutes before I finally heard the keys in another security door rattle, and then the SO appeared with two other warders. 'Mr Hale? Come through, please. In here. No papers. No notebooks. No tape recorders. No pens, no pencils, no rulers – nothing. Do you understand the terms?'

I nodded, then he added, 'Do you agree to a strip search?'

I could hardly believe my ears. I was being treated like a terrorist. It was undoubtedly another delaying tactic and a humiliating sample of the prison life Stephen had endured countless times, but I realised that if I wanted to see Stephen I would have to agree to their demands.

'If necessary,' I replied. 'But what the hell is going on?'

'Put your clothes on the chair; shoes, keys, watch and coins in the tray. Down to your undies, please, sir.'

Reluctantly, I began to undress and gave the officers their brief moment of triumph. Three other warders crowded into the doorway and sniggered. 'Right, get dressed, sir. Nothing goes in or out. Hands on the table at all times. You will sit facing the prisoner and nothing is to be exchanged. Do you understand?'

I felt quite cold and quickly dressed. I said nothing, but in my rush to get dressed I 'accidentally' swept the first warder's half-eaten meat pie onto the floor. As it hit the deck, I then trod on it and swivelled my foot to make sure it was truly flattened.

'Oops, I'm so sorry about that,' I said. It was a small but very worthwhile victory. The look I got from that big, fat, greasy warder was meant to terrify me, but it had quite the opposite effect.

Time was precious now. As I dashed outside I wondered just how much was left of it for my visit. 'How long have I got?' I queried.

The SO glanced at his watch and then at the whingeing warder who looked for all the world as if he'd lost a close relative.

'Half an hour probably,' he said as he opened the other gate. The officer opened the final door into the visiting room and the first person I saw was Stephen, patiently waiting for me. It was a defining moment. After months of phone calls and letters, we finally met face to face.

He looked calm and well. I wish I could have said the same for myself. I was a bag of nerves, and I was not quite sure what to expect. I had imagined a slightly larger person, and perhaps someone not quite as friendly.

The room was ever so noisy and packed with other visitors and families, but Stephen seemed quite at home in this semi-hostile environment. Kids were running about here and there, and there was a constant flow back and forth to the refreshment bar. I found it extremely difficult to concentrate, and I also felt claustrophobic, despite the large room.

I was ordered to sit directly opposite him. His back was towards the entrance and the tea bar. People were bobbing about behind him and a few annoying kids kept brushing past me and disturbing my train of thought.

Stephen, though, seemed very calm and relaxed, and amazingly he showed no animosity whatsoever towards the system that was responsible for his predicament. I found it hard to understand this – especially after he'd spent more than two decades behind bars. I felt sure I would have displayed some anger, and perhaps some bitterness towards this unforgiving and unsympathetic system.

He looked ready and eager to spill all. I think he had been genuinely looking forward to my visit, and I knew that, thanks to his location in Dorchester, it was very difficult for his family to visit. Apart from his legal team, I was the first proper visitor he had seen in ages.

My head was full of questions, but as I had not been allowed to take anything in I had to rely on my memory. I didn't want to rush it, so I thought a gentle chat would be the best way to start, asking him first about his daily duties. I wanted him to feel quite comfortable before asking the more important questions.

As we began to talk, I noticed three warders positioned around the table in a triangle a few paces away. They would obviously be able to hear every word. No one else had any people looking on.

It was an awkward atmosphere, but this was the best we could do. I was hungry and thirsty, and I noticed the refreshment counter in the far corner of the room. A few seconds later an enormous prisoner suddenly appeared at the table, towering over everyone. 'Tea, coffee, cold drinks, any food?' he asked.

'That sounds good,' I replied. But as soon as I said it I felt a slight kick to my shin, and noticed Stephen had his mouth cupped by his hands as if he was trying to whisper something to me. He was shaking his head slightly. I got the message. 'No, it's all right. No for now.'

The huge prisoner muttered something then moved away and started cleaning some of the empty tables. I asked Stephen, 'Is there something wrong?'

'That's old Billy. He's an odd one. He's in for poisoning,' Stephen said.

We both laughed. The three warders remained expressionless.

I was conscious our time was limited. 'Stephen,' I began, 'I've read everything you've sent to me. However, I want to ask you a bit more about the confession you made. Can we start at the beginning? It's about your time in the cemetery.'

He sighed, but then gave a full account of everything that happened in the cemetery and when he volunteered to help the police. It was obvious the memories were still quite painful for him despite the passage of time. I particularly wanted to check the circumstances of his so-called confession.

Stephen explained, 'The police asked me to give an account, so I did. I was interrupted at intervals by a police officer in a suit – I think this might have been Younger, I don't remember, who prompted me by saying that such and such a thing sounded better, or it meant the same thing. I'll give you an example. I told the officer that I watched her. He stopped me and said, "You followed her with your eyes?"

'I said, "Yes."

'He said, "Okay, so you followed her. Go on …"

'And this got written down as "I followed her". I protested when it was read back to me, but they said it meant the same as watching her. I foolishly accepted this.

'It allowed them to manipulate my statement to their own advantage. So, yes, they did put words into my mouth, and yes, they did change my statement. I didn't sign or initial any of the alterations. I only signed it at the end.'

'In biro?'

'Yes.'

'And they wrote it in pencil?'

'Yes,' said Stephen with a wry smile.

I glanced at the warders. They now appeared to have dropped their guard and seemed interested in what he was saying. Stephen also seemed comfortable, and then a loud bell sounded. Several visitors stood up to leave.

'Is that for us?' I asked, believing my half-hour plus was up.

'Not unless you want to leave, sir,' came the reply. I looked up. The warder added, 'You can have another 30 minutes.'

'Let's talk about your boots, Stephen,' I said. 'Your mother seems to think you changed your boots at lunchtime when you went back home for a few minutes.'

Stephen replied, 'I was wearing my best dress boots when I left the cemetery. They are dark blue in colour, with a leather sole. I put them on in the morning by mistake and decided to change into my working boots.'

Stephen then gestured over his shoulder, adding, 'My best boots are in my stored property locker here. My father asked the police a couple of weeks later if they wanted them for forensic testing. They said no.

'Yet, if what they said was true and I attacked Wendy Sewell before I left the cemetery, I would have had blood on them. When I went back to the cemetery I was wearing my working boots.

'I had blood on them because I was wearing them when I found Wendy. They were the ones that went off for forensic testing.' He laughed. The police had checked the wrong boots.

The bell finally sounded. I thanked him for his cooperation and pledged to continue with my investigations. Outside, the officer who saw his meat pie destroyed gave me a final glare before I went through the gates and marched back towards town. It was one of many similar prison visits I was to make over the next few years.

Getting out of Dorchester jail was certainly much easier than entering, and once that final large metal gate clanged shut behind me I felt relieved to be finally heading home.

I was mentally and physically drained, and wasn't looking forward to the long drive back to Derbyshire, especially with a swirling, gusty wind and driving rain that hammered against my windscreen for hours on end. But it did at least give me some time to replay our conversation back – time and time again – in my mind, while negotiating the endless motorway miles.

I couldn't fault any of his replies. He was neither hesitant nor evasive, and answered everything as best he could. I had been surprised that he had quite a dry sense of humour, sharing with me some of the antics of his regular routine.

I would soon be able to see my wife and children. Stephen, however, had already been denied any hope of a family or a normal life. He had adapted well over the years to the regimented prison life, and never seemed rattled despite being so closely watched. He'd told me, 'You soon get used to this constant scrutiny.'

My headlights finally illuminated the M1 turn-off sign for Matlock, but as I spotted an onward sign for Bakewell, my satisfaction at meeting Stephen soon turned to anger. Had he just been a convenient scapegoat in some bizarre conspiracy?

I was always surprised by the number of people who kept repeating the phrase 'he was serving time for someone else' or 'for something he didn't do'. It became a constant source of annoyance.

I wondered just how many people in authority at that time had, for whatever reason, misinterpreted or misrepresented the facts, or even ignored vital evidence. I was frustrated by my own slow progress, but remained determined to push ahead and find the answers to so many anomalies.

*　　*　　*

On my return to Matlock I was given a list of all the messages that had come in during my absence. Each was said to contain fresh evidence crucial to my investigations, but as per usual many were from an assortment of the usual local cranks and weirdos. There was little new.

One note, however, proved worthy of some interest. It was from a local medium who claimed to have worked on several police cases relating to murders and missing children. She said she had just visited Bakewell cemetery and had gone into a trance, allegedly reliving the murder sequence.

She concluded that the victim had been stripped and then choked with some sort of ligature that she believed was her tights. She claimed to have felt the texture.

It was interesting, but when I considered her remarks I wondered if she had simply read about much of the case just recently. Perhaps she had spoken with some people who had inside knowledge. Her remarks about the alleged choking brought back some horrific memories of the mortuary photographs and the extensive signs of bruising about poor Wendy's neck.

I also remembered Ray Downing's description of Wendy on her final bus ride into work. He said she had been wearing tights underneath ankle socks, yet I saw no reference to tights in the police notes, the trial papers or even in the forensic reports – but they were clearly shown in the scene of crime photographs. In addition, there was no reference at that time to Wendy's purse, shopping basket, handbag and any other personal possessions.

My police informant believed the tights went missing, so didn't appear on the scene of crime exhibits – despite appearing on the photographs.

The medium's adventures gave me another good splash in the *Matlock Mercury*. BEYOND THE GRAVE CLUES announced the headline that week. I considered it might give folk something else to worry about.

I later received some compelling information from my informant Port Vale about the murder weapon. When I asked him if it contained a BUDC mark – Bakewell Urban District Council – as all tools were supposed to have been security stamped, the answer was *no*. So the chances were that it did *not* come from the council store. Ray Downing also confirmed that private detective Robert Ervin had checked the same thing with the council many years before. The inventory confirmed there should have been six handles in the store. A quick check confirmed that the number tallied. All six were there, and all six contained the vital BUDC stamp, yet the murder weapon didn't. No reference to this anomaly was ever made at trial.

CHAPTER 18

JUST BECAUSE YOU'RE PARANOID DOESN'T MEAN THEY'RE NOT AFTER YOU

Each time I went out, whether on foot or by car, I thought I was being followed. Whenever I drove any distance in the car, suddenly another vehicle would appear, following close behind. I recalled trips across to our publishers in Chesterfield when I felt I was being followed. There had certainly seemed to be one or two cars on my tail directly after leaving the office, and sometimes late at night, when the dazzling headlights kept a constant distance.

Whether day or night, it kept happening. It seemed to go on for months – or did it? Were the threats finally hitting home? Was it affecting my judgement? And who would be following me, the cops or villains? Both sections appeared hostile. I regularly took the advice of the 'friendly' detective inspector to check under my car each time before moving off.

Unexpected or strange parcels were opened very carefully. Trips to Chesterfield, Wirksworth or Ashbourne, and visits to other witnesses, were restricted and kept strictly confidential. It was all done on a need-to-know basis. Only a few people were informed of my appointments.

Interviews about the Downing case were only to be conducted by me, and I kept asking staff if they had heard any unusual clicks on their telephones either at home or at work. One night, at home, I received a phone call at about nine o'clock.

The caller just said, 'Chelsea, ten minutes.' This was one of a number of prearranged call signs. The meeting place was only a short walk away.

At the agreed point, I looked around. It was quiet and there seemed to be no one else about. I leant against the car park wall opposite the Edgefold Social Club and waited. A hand suddenly grabbed my shoulder. I almost jumped a mile. 'Bloody hell! I've just lost another two lives,' I said.

'Sorry, mate. It's all a bit hush-hush at the minute. I couldn't take any risks. It's more than my job's worth to be seen talking with you at the moment.' My contact was a good community bobby.

'Why, what's up? Are your lads following me?' I asked.

'No, I don't think so. But last week you gave me a car number that might be of interest.'

It was the number plate of a car I felt sure was following me.

'It's either Special Branch, MI5 or the "Invisible Men", a couple of guys working with CIB2 – you know, the Complaints Investigation Bureau that doesn't exist?' he said. 'The car's registered to a special government departmental pool.

'These guys are Premier League. It's worse than the Kremlin in here at the moment. The word is they're interested in some of the people you are interested in. What's more, in your submission you mentioned some potential links to the Barbara Mayo case.'

'Is there a connection?' I asked.

'Not that I'm aware. But there's something funny going on. New faces, London accents ... be careful, mate.'

'So, they think there is some connection?' I insisted.

'I simply don't know. But it was high profile at the time. And now there's a sudden revival of interest from HQ. There's also a reluctance to reopen your man's file,' he added.

'So what about my two spooks?' I asked, referring to the guys in the car I believed had been following me.

'I think you blew their cover.' He laughed.

I watched him disappear over to the far side of the car park and past the lido, back into town.

*   *   *

I'd already received a tip-off from a key contact at Derbyshire police HQ in Ripley that several top-secret documents had been forwarded from the Home Office containing confidential information about the Wendy Sewell case and other similar murders. The main file was marked 'Jigsaw Murders', and contained details of other unsolved killings in Derbyshire and neighbouring counties going back more than 30 years.

My contact said a Home Office coordinator had been appointed to oversee developments, under the control of a commander from CIB2, a new special operations and intelligence unit based at Scotland Yard.

The mention of CIB2 was enough to strike fear into the hearts of many hardened police officers. Local beat bobbies compared them to the Gestapo. Their job was to police the police, and their reputation was that of a rough, tough, unorthodox and ruthless group who were a law unto themselves, rather like the Special Branch of old. It was said they would stop at nothing to investigate some alleged misdemeanour.

Part of their role was to monitor any potential appeal cases and to examine any complaints against individual officers, and to plug any leaks. Journalists were therefore in their spotlight. Were they monitoring my phone? Or was I just being paranoid?

*   *   *

I contacted Stephen's lawyer for a catch-up about appeal prospects and to find out the likelihood of any release on parole. I knew Stephen had already enjoyed a successful home visit to Bakewell in March 1994, and had previously obtained occasional weekend leave to meet with his parents in Weymouth, with all visits under escort.

I also knew that any application for consideration of release via the appeal courts would have to be routed through the government's Criminal Cases Unit (C3), which specifically dealt with claims of miscarriages of justice.

He did not, however, give me much encouragement about tackling an appeal. On the contrary. He warned that my direct involvement could in fact jeopardise Stephen's chances of parole and even his release.

I took his meaning. It was not uncommon for prisoners who upset the applecart to find their status suddenly take a dive. I knew things would probably get a lot worse before they got better.

My earliest contact with the Home Office suggested Stephen's file had been passed around like a hot potato for years. They seemed to hold the belief that no one in prison is ever innocent. Denial of a serious offence was considered just an excuse and meant the inmate was potentially more dangerous.

Despite fighting Stephen's corner as hard as I could, I often wondered if I was up to the task. The family had tried in vain for more than two decades to have their claims heard, but I began to question whether it needed someone more than a local newspaper editor to investigate Stephen's case and to sustain this daunting job.

Although I was an experienced journalist, this miscarriage-of-justice business was a whole new ball game for me. I hadn't realised just how intense it would be, and how emotionally involved I would become.

I regularly became so frustrated and angry about what had happened, and the fact Stephen had been simply locked away and forgotten. I wondered how many other people had been detained in similar circumstances.

The fact that I was trying to find sufficient fresh evidence to help quash his conviction put a great deal of pressure on me. I think my reputation and position also put a great deal of expectation on me. Much of it was probably my own fault for taking on such a gigantic task, but at times it felt like my world was caving in.

I found it very difficult to cope with everything. My family life and personal commitments were important to me, but trying to be a good dad plus running a busy media outlet and then trying to solve a murder mystery all became too much at times.

There were many times when I thought about giving up, but as I had started this latest campaign I needed to see it through. If Stephen was guilty and it could be proven, then so be it, but what if he was innocent? From what I had seen so far there was a great deal of material that had not been shown to the court, and more information was coming in all the time to support his claims.

I also knew that he could be in his seventies before being considered for release at this stage. His family had refused to give up – and they had been campaigning for 20 years longer than me.

During the quiet hours of the night, my brain kept demanding to know just who I was to be able to take on the police, the Home Office and the government. What difference could I make to an open-and-shut case that the police refused to respond to?

I had repetitive nightmares about being trapped in a cave while pot-holing. It was something I had never done in my life before, but it all seemed so real and dramatic, being asked by a shadowy figure to look for someone in a dark, narrow cave that became smaller and smaller. As I pulled my way along, the walls and ceiling became much tighter and impossible to navigate, until eventually I became stuck. I could neither go forward nor back. I was trapped in a claustrophobic nightmare.

My health throughout this whole saga was a constant worry. If the baddies didn't bump me off, then perhaps the medics would. The job was hard enough without all this extra stress, and I was working day and night to keep pace with everything. It was certainly taking its toll on me, and I was finding it difficult to eat and sleep.

* * *

One of my first conversations with the Home Office in March gave me that extra impetus to keep going.

Some pompous desk jockey in the Criminal Cases Unit kept telling me in his plummy tones, 'Downing is in the Verne prison. He's been saying he's innocent for years. Nobody really cares, nobody's in the least bit interested in him. He's just one of many who continually say they're innocent. They're all the same. I don't know why you bother. He's just a nobody.'

I couldn't believe my ears. I was furious and told him so. 'Look, first of all he's not at the Verne, he's been at Dorchester for several months. Secondly, there is new evidence to support his claims of innocence. And finally, I care. For more than 20 years he's been saying he's innocent. Does that not tell you something?'

The man finally lowered his tone. He obviously wasn't used to being spoken to like that. He said, '797501, Downing, Stephen. He is in the Verne. The records clearly show this.'

'Then your records are wrong,' I replied heatedly.

'I don't think so, sir,' he argued.

'Yes, I think you will find they are ... sir.'

'I can tell you exactly where he is, where he's been since 1973 and how long he's stayed at each establishment. I have all his records to hand.'

'Then I suggest you get them updated. I can assure you that he is in Dorchester prison.'

'No, sir, the Verne.'

'Dorchester,' I repeated.

'Why do you keep saying Dorchester, sir?'

'Because I went to see him last week. I can give you the visiting order reference number, time and date.'

He suddenly went very quiet. I could hear some mumbling, then shouting in the background. 'Well, thank you for the information. I'll make enquiries.'

The man sounded very self-important. He refused to give his name. 'Just before you go,' I persisted, 'you claim to be thorough with your records. Tell me, what was Mr Downing's sentence?' I asked.

'Oh, that's easy.' The note of confidence was creeping back into his voice. 'Mr Downing was convicted in February 1974 at Nottingham Crown Court. He was given a mandatory life sentence and ordered to be detained at the Queen's Pleasure.'

'And was there any recommendation of tariff given?'

'Yes, they recommended a minimum tariff of 17 years.'

'Really, 17 years? So, he should be out by now, then?'

He hesitated, realising he had been led into a trap. 'Seventeen years ... hmmm ... hang on a minute ... I'm sure it says seventeen years ... that's strange.'

'Yes, you are quite correct. By rights he should have been out about five years ago. So why is he still inside?'

I could hear him shuffling papers. Then his composure returned. 'Of course, he's what we call an IDOM – In Denial of

Murder. If they don't admit to their crime they're pushed back down the queue.'

'But what if he's innocent? He's hardly likely to admit to something he didn't do. What if he never changes his plea?'

'Innocent?' he almost spat out the word. 'They're all innocent, aren't they? That's what keeps journalists like you in business.'

If he had not been miles away on the end of a phone, I am sure I would have given him a piece of my mind.

Stephen certainly would have preferred to have been at the Verne, as he told me in a letter dated 13 March.

```
Thank you for your most recent letters and the
books that accompanied them. What a pity we are
having such wonderful weather. I hanker after the
walks I used to be able to take at the Verne and
now I'm stuck indoors and behind bars, though
hopefully not for much longer.
```

On 27 March 1995 I received a letter from the Home Office stating the grounds on which the Home Secretary could refer Stephen's case back to the Court of Appeal.

```
The Home Secretary would not normally consider it
right to exercise this power of reference unless
presented with new evidence, or a new
consideration of substance that has not been
before the courts and which appears to cast doubt
on the safety of the conviction.
   We will be looking to see whether the
representations disclose grounds on which it would
be appropriate for the Home Secretary to take any
action. It may be necessary to make further
```

```
enquiries into the conviction. Although the
enquiries will be carried out as quickly as
possible, this may take a little more time.
    We understand that Derbyshire Constabulary are
not actively looking at the allegations made in
your case, but will do so if our consideration of
the case reveals any matters that require further
investigation.
```

I was appalled by the pathetic response from half-hearted officials at the Home Office. It was totally dismissive of my submission and ignored my claims of fresh evidence and the many anomalies and contradictions within the original case notes.

Stephen Downing changed his lawyer in the late spring of 1995 and I was soon introduced to his new barrister, John Atkins. He was very able, confident and enthusiastic. He helped convert my original findings into an acceptable legal submission. John was also keen to look into the possibility of an appeal. Several threats of legal action by his firm eventually persuaded Derbyshire Constabulary to release important paperwork and exhibits, including the murder weapon – the pickaxe handle – following my earlier conversation with the assistant curator at Derby Police Museum.

*   *   *

I'm sure my colleagues at the *Mercury* believed I was completely paranoid at times. Yet they were not the ones to have already faced potential death several times. My mind kept recalling the late night at the office when I received a hoax call about a fire.

It led to a horrific lorry chase, as I drove in terror while a huge metal monster chased me across topsy-turvy moorland roads, banging into the rear of my car as it tried to push me off the road and into oblivion.

I had a most fortunate escape that time from my pursuer, with only quick thinking and luck on my side in the form of an empty field to thank for my survival. Every time I went anywhere near that same place again, I recalled this dramatic episode in my mind and the knowledge that only an instinctive, split-second decision saved my life.

As for paranoia, here was clear evidence of at least one desperate attack. I then began to study the other facts. When I'd dived out of the way of a car at Darley Dale while out jogging one dark night, I was sure the car was trying to run me down – but there could have been some doubt about the driver's intention. And although I took the bomb threats seriously, together with clicks on the phone and other vehicles following me, plus several attacks on the office, my mind kept returning to this very frightening lorry chase.

I had experienced my first, and I hopefully my last, high-speed chase for the highest stakes possible – my own life. And I believed there was now no room whatsoever for doubt.

Someone was definitely trying to kill me.

CHAPTER 19

WALKING IN ROBERT ERVIN'S SHADOW

As I looked through the shelves of our new Downing filing system at the *Matlock Mercury*, now full of dusty old papers and folders, the name of investigator Robert Ervin kept appearing. I found Ervin's involvement extremely interesting. Unfortunately, he had died in about 1984 – some ten years before I began my own enquiries. He spent many years studying the Downing case, working on and off for the family for a decade after Stephen's conviction.

He was a former member of the army's Special Investigation Branch. He was convinced that Stephen was innocent, and in 1980 he helped to compile a new appeal proposal to William Whitelaw, the Home Secretary. He also contacted the former West Derbyshire MP Matthew Parris.

Ervin produced medical evidence to confirm Stephen's learning difficulties at the time of the murder. He always felt that Stephen's naivety was not fully explored at trial.

Despite Ervin's optimism when interviewed by the *Mercury* in the summer of 1980, he later heard that the Home Secretary refused to accept any new grounds for an appeal. I quickly realised that I was walking in Robert Ervin's shadow, though while he had been dealing with matters that were relatively fresh in the minds of locals, I was working some ten-plus years later, when the trail was distinctly colder. He had come so close, but could I go that step further and finally prove Stephen's innocence? I was determined to finish the job Ervin had started, and if I was to do so I knew it was vital to track down his case notes, if they still existed.

I managed to locate his widow, but she could offer little assistance and suggested I contact Bobby Vince, a former colleague of Ervin's, who often worked with him on the case. I later found out that he too had passed away. His neighbours told me his elderly sister was still alive and lived near Rotherham. Her name was Constance Riley.

I realised there was only a tenuous link to Ervin and wondered if she would be of any help. But then I thought about my own parents, and their reluctance to throw anything out.

Constance Riley lived at a large, detached property with a long driveway. As I pressed the old brass bell, I listened carefully and could hear an elderly voice shout, 'I'm coming! I'm coming!' A well-dressed lady opened the door. She had half-rimmed spectacles and long white hair tied back neatly in a bun.

I pulled out my press ID card and gave her a brief explanation for my visit. 'An editor?' she said, sounding surprised. 'Yes, call me Connie. Come on in. I'm Bobby's sister. Well, I'm actually his baby sister.' She seemed a live wire.

'I'm 76 and still rocking,' she said. 'I can still sing, dance and play music.'

I followed her into her sitting room, and we sat down on an old velvet sofa. I told her about Stephen's case, and about the work her brother did with Ervin.

'Poor Bobby. He had his life in the army. I think he'd been everywhere – just like that reporter Kate Adie. Wherever he went there was trouble,' she said, laughing.

I told her it was essential to try to find some new evidence for Stephen's case. 'This could really help, Connie,' I said. 'I'm trying to find any paperwork linked to your brother or Robert Ervin.'

She looked puzzled and replied, 'I think most things were thrown out when Ethel – that was Bobby's wife – died. I think Mr Ervin had problems too. A dicky ticker. But some things did come here. Bobby was an amateur sleuth.'

I sat up in anticipation. 'What sort of things?' I asked.

'Some papers and files. Some old army stuff. Mostly junk. But you don't like throwing things out, do you?'

'And where are they now?' I enquired.

She struggled to her feet and waved her stick. 'In there, I'll show you.' She pushed me into another room. It was piled high with all sorts of household rubbish. Connie led me over to the sideboard, pointed to the piles of files and papers, and sat down at her piano. 'Here, this is all Bobby's stuff. You have a look and I'll play you some music. Any requests?'

I nearly asked her if she could play 'Far Away', but instead said, 'No, not really.' I was too engrossed in rummaging through everything.

Every now and again she would stop playing to ask for my opinion of her performance.

'Wonderful, excellent!' I replied.

After trawling through for some time I was beginning to get a bit despondent, but then I finally saw it, sticking out from near the bottom of a pile. It was a dog-eared, yellowing file marked 'Downing Appeal'. They were very old papers and typed carbon copies, all very faint and some I couldn't read.

I found two other files about the case, and pulled them out. I then returned to the sitting room. 'Have you found anything?' Connie asked.

'Yes, thanks, these papers could be very interesting. I wonder if I could borrow them? I'll return them after copying them.'

She walked across and gripped my hand. 'I don't want them back. Keep them. I'm sure Bobby wouldn't mind. You were on the same side, after all. You've given me some company and I don't get much. And I've had a chance to show off my piano playing.'

'Wonderful, Connie. I've enjoyed your music and your company too. It was excellent. I'll be in touch.'

'You old smoothie,' she chuckled as she showed me out.

*   *   *

I examined the files in more detail the following day. Much of the paperwork I had already seen before. I was halfway through the second file when I found an interesting copy of Robert Ervin's letter from 1979 to South Yorkshire Police asking for information on any other unsolved murders with a similar background. It was very faint, and I could hardly make out the exact date. I found no sign of any reply.

Ervin's notes mentioned the Barbara Mayo murder case, and he seemed to be querying whether there was any military connection. This could be due to the fact that the victim was allegedly hitch-hiking and on her way to collect a car after it had broken down somewhere near the army barracks at Catterick along the A1.

There were also references to the murder of Jackie Ansell-Lamb. Both women had been murdered within a few months of each other in 1970. Wendy Sewell was killed just three years later – and just twelve miles from where Mayo's body was found close to the M1 motorway near Chesterfield, with Jackie Ansell-Lamb's body discovered near Knutsford, in Cheshire. Within his notes he also gave details of the many similarities between these two 1970 murders and that of Wendy Sewell. He also implied that the police believed the first two murders may have been linked.

In addition, Ervin's scribbled notes claimed that five men from the Bakewell area had been quizzed by police about the Barbara Mayo murder. He included a reference to Mr Red and another person, and believed both were former associates of Wendy Sewell.

These new facts were dynamite. It was a treasure chest packed with witness statements, notes and supporting documents, and they all added to similar rumours from Ray Downing and town gossips about Mr Red, and information supplied in general from my Bakewell police contact.

One article in the folder from 1970 asked:

HAVE YOU SEEN THIS MAN OR THIS TYPE OF CAR?

If you have seen a man who looks like this driving a Morris 1000 estate car, the Mayo Murder team wants to hear from you.

The article said that Detective Chief Superintendent Charles Palmer of Scotland Yard urgently required information about this car driven by a man aged between 25 and 30 of medium build, with mousy-coloured hair brushed back with a quiff at the front, who was seen giving a lift to a girl closely resembling Barbara Mayo and dressed in very similar clothes. It was accompanied by a photofit picture of the man they wished to interview and a picture of the suspect's car.

As I continued to thumb my way through Ervin's old files, I noticed another reference to the Mayo case. It was the *Derbyshire Times* front page from Friday, 28 September 1973 – just two weeks after the murder of Wendy Sewell.

MAYO CASE STILL UNSOLVED.

Retried chief to continue hunt for killer.

The detective who hunted the killer of Londoner Barbara Mayo for 11 months retired from Z Division of the Metropolitan Police at the weekend. But Chief Supt Charles Palmer vowed to his colleagues before he left, 'I'll still find the strangler.'

The Chief Superintendent began his hunt for the killer three years ago when he was seconded to Derbyshire CID to lead the murder hunt – one of the costliest ever undertaken by the county force. But 11 months and thousands of man-hours later, Chief Supt Palmer was taken off the case and returned to London. It was the first murder case in which he failed to find the killer. Before he retired, he took photostat copies of the entire Mayo file and intends searching through them until he discovers the vital clue which might send the killer to jail.

I was certain Ervin was drawing connections between the murders of Wendy Sewell, Barbara Mayo and Jackie Ansell-Lamb. Within Ervin's dusty box of historic press cuttings there were also some copies of old, confidential police reports that mentioned details of the attack on Wendy Sewell, suggesting it may have been committed by two people and that the person who landed the fatal blows was probably right handed. Stephen Downing batted left handed.

As I rummaged further, I found an extremely important document relating to the alleged threat made to Stephen in the cemetery when he found Wendy.

It was a letter dated 22 February 1974 from Ervin to Stephen's solicitors. It described how, during a prison visit Ray had made that day to his son, Stephen told him about the mystery man who had threatened him shortly after he found Wendy. He told his father exactly what the man had said and what he was wearing, giving an almost identical account to the one given to me just a few weeks earlier.

Here was positive confirmation that Stephen's lawyers had definitely been told of the threat made in the cemetery against his sister, a few days after he had been convicted. This also confirmed what Stephen had said, although his reasons for keeping quiet up until then were not fully explained in Ervin's note.

Another dust-coloured folder revealed advice from Stephen's counsel, Mr Dennis Barker QC, dated 5 March 1974. It showed that Barker felt Stephen had left it too late to tell the story of the mystery man who made the threat.

> *Mr Dickenson [Stephen's original solicitor] saw Mr Downing on a number of occasions, on not one of which did Mr Downing make any mention of this happening. Nor did he to his father on any visit, nor to any of the psychiatrists, nor to myself or junior counsel in consultation.*
>
> *Moreover, he made no mention of it in the witness box, though he had ample opportunity to do so. In my opinion no Court of Appeal will allow this 'fresh evidence' or explanation to be given on appeal – and even if they did, they would pay no attention to it.*

I had already seen Stephen's reports and spoken to him about some key aspects of his case, including the reasons for keeping the news of the threats to him secret for five months. He and his younger sister, Christine, were close and he obviously felt protective towards her. He would not have wanted to put her at risk in any way by talking about the man who threatened him. Stephen's counsel Dennis Barker didn't find this a plausible excuse, however, and advised against going for an appeal. I believed it was another serious error by his legal team.

Turning to Stephen's confession, he acknowledged that, 'The Crown's case rested in large measure on oral admissions and a written statement made by the accused to the police.' He then, quite amazingly, and incorrectly in my opinion, repeated his assertion made at trial a month previously that there had been 'no impropriety' on the part of the police in obtaining this confession.

He then added, 'Mr Downing could not and did not give any real reason why he made such admissions.'

What?

I compared the trial notes with Barker's opinion and realised he had made numerous mistakes, failing to understand the true defence evidence and neglecting to challenge many of the prosecution claims in court. It seemed that Barker had totally forgotten, or ignored, Stephen's pre-trial statement, later surprisingly highlighted by the judge during his summing up rather than by Barker as part of a legitimate cross-examination, that Stephen was 'tired, hungry, my back hurt, and I was only just able to keep awake'.

I also wondered why Barker had also forgotten to challenge the fact, even though the judge reminded him and the rest of those in court, that Stephen had previously said, 'Mr Younger put his hand on my shoulder twice to wake me up.'

Additional justifiable claims indicated that bets were also being taken by officers that someone would make him confess. And from reading the trial transcript, it was also obvious – even though it was left to the judge himself to point it out – that Stephen had said, 'I signed the written statement. It was untrue. I made it because they said they would question me all night if necessary and I did not realise Wendy was very badly hurt. My statement was read out to me. I was told to make it, that is the impression – it was not of my own free will.'

I felt extreme anger as I read Barker's opinion notes, and could not understand his lack of challenge at trial to many of the prosecution claims. In addition, I kept wondering why the judge, and not him, had highlighted some potentially compelling arguments within Downing's statement, including:

> *The questioning had gone on at the station for eight or nine hours. As the hours wore by this young man became tired and you may have little hesitation in concluding that if a suspect is falling asleep and having to be shaken, it is no time to continue interrogation.*

The judge had even commented:

> *That is bordering, you may think, on oppression if he is not given food and the rest of it … what was put, you see, there was this condition of tiredness … one officer had said, 'Admit it. We know you've done it.' Another said, 'You will be questioned all night.'*

I continued reading Barker's letter of advice against appeal, and unbelievably he later claimed the judge's summing up had been 'impeccable'. I most certainly did not, but he certainly did a much better job than Barker.

If it was so impeccable, why was there was no mention of the vital and contradictory psychological reports, the differing forensic analysis and the fact that Downing had a limited mental ability?

There was also no challenge to the contents and timings of various witnesses who could perhaps have supported Stephen's alibi, and no detailed criticism of the scene-of-crime exhibits, lack of fingerprints on the murder weapon, and the knowledge of a third person's palm print, hairs and fibres.

Within a bundle of original trial papers I came across an 8-page 'chronological report' giving the alleged dates, times and events leading to the Wendy Sewell murder, that had been compiled by Downing's defence team. Unfortunately, it was riddled with errors, anomalies, omissions and inaccuracies. Barker could have challenged a failure to identify an angry man at Wendy Sewell's office, the reason for her early bus ride, why workmen at the crime scene didn't first call for an ambulance rather than the police; and rejected a chance to cross-examine several key witnesses with contrasting statements.

There was no mention of the woman in a salmon pink top coat and her dog, who had spoken with Stephen less than an hour before the attack on Mrs Sewell, and the fact he had been off sick for a couple of days. She had been another defenceless young woman – so why didn't his lawyers query at trial as to why he hadn't attacked her at the same isolated spot?

Downing's barrister failed to cross-check, examine and clarify several witness statements, which could also have helped determine the precise time of the attack on Wendy. Charlie Carman's statement in particular with regards to Downing and Mr Orange was full of anomalies. It should have been fully established as to who saw who, when and where. This could have confirmed Downing's alleged alibi.

So many opportunities to challenge the prosecution's circumstantial evidence were either missed or totally ignored. Other witnesses could have been called in his defence – including the ambulance driver and even PC Ball, who attended the scene of crime – and they could have given more explanation about the extent of bloodstaining to their uniforms.

I concluded that Barker did a very poor job on Stephen's behalf, and I regretted the fact that, like other key individuals in the case, he was no longer alive to answer some difficult questions.

Ervin also discovered some additional facts about the 'running man' and, like me, was desperate to find out who he was and seemed amazed that the police made no attempt to trace him.

One policeman confirmed he interviewed a long-haired youth from Lady Manners School. His notes stated, 'He was tall, fair and athletically built – and worked in the same cemetery for a few weeks just before Downing started his job there. He looked remarkably like the person identified by Mrs Louisa Hadfield.' However, there was no mention of what this youth actually said.

Another of Ervin's memos, dated 1 January 1974, revealed how he learned that a Peter Wheeler had heard that a man had been seen running from the direction of the cemetery by Louisa Hadfield, and that she said George Paling had also seen this man leaning over a wall saying, '"God, what have I done!" or words to that effect'. It seemed to confirm my belief about Paling, that he had 'watered down' his evidence to distance himself from this person, and perhaps increased the probability that Paling knew who he was, and that he in turn knew Paling.

Hadfield reported the 'running man' to the police within days of the attack, and they also interviewed Paling on the night of the attack, yet Ervin only heard about this from neighbours three months later.

Ervin subsequently obtained his own statements from Hadfield and Paling. They broadly fitted with Paling's account given to the police and Hadfield's account later given to me.

However, on closer scrutiny, they also contained some very interesting new facts. Paling's evidence read out at trial stated that he had seen the running man at around 1.10 p.m., but he told Ervin, 'It could have been nearer 1.30 p.m.,' while repeating his claim that 'the man was really exerting himself ... and he was definitely in a hell of a hurry'. This time difference was vitally important. It could have supported Downing's claims of innocence as he was seen leaving the scene at 1.08 p.m., with the running man spotted just two minutes later. I wondered if Paling was persuaded by the police to revise his timings based on their assumptions about that day and after interviewing Stephen.

Louisa Hadfield gave Ervin a more detailed description of the running man's clothing, adding that he wore 'brown boots and a jeans-type jacket like those in the war, and a battle-dress-type belt'.

She also said, 'The man was running very fast. I was worried about this and went to the police on the following Saturday and made a statement.' She hadn't told me about his footwear, or the style of his denim jacket, but my visit was at least ten years after Ervin's – and more than twenty years since the murder.

Hadfield gave Ervin a very convincing description of what really happened when she reported the matter. She said, 'The policeman, Ernie Charlesworth, said, "I don't think it's relevant. I think it's just somebody got caught in someone else's bed" – or words like that.

'Charlesworth said, "I suppose you know we have someone for the murder?" – something like that. I got the impression that I was wasting their time.'

There were many scrawled notes from other potential witnesses with the registration numbers of cars parked near the cemetery on that day. It was all hauntingly similar to my own experiences. The numbers were still visible, together with dates, descriptions and a reference claiming 'All given to police but rejected'.

Another compelling note then caught my eye. It was written on a torn-out piece of paper from a book. One particular man's name, Mr Red, was ringed in biro with the comment 'Sheep Sale, Shropshire?' It highlighted the fact that two sheep sales were held in Shropshire that day, at different venues.

Suddenly, my mind was in complete tandem with Ervin's. Mr Red's alibi relied on his claim that he attended a sheep sale, but did he actually go? And if so, which one did he attend, and how did he get there and back? I could see Ervin's logic. If he went at all, did Mr Red go to the early sale – and still have time to get back and meet Wendy?

This was incredible news and the very first time that I had ever seen any reference to two sales at different venues, and wondered how this might have affected the original investigation and trial.

Ervin's witness statements, from Mrs Gibson, Mrs Sheldon and Mrs Beebe, also mirrored much of my own work. Mrs Beebe's said:

> *The police came around but the kids were asleep, and they didn't even bother to take a statement. I was told later that the children had been taken out of school to show the police where they'd seen the lady on the graves. The police claimed this was impossible and the children couldn't have seen anything, as she wasn't on the graves until the workmen were present. They claimed the victim Wendy Sewell had stood up and fell forward across the graves – this would have been 1.20 at the earliest – and the children would have been back at school by then, and therefore couldn't have seen anything.*

The police of course were very much mistaken, as the attack must have happened long before 1.20 p.m., for Downing and the other workmen only arrived to see the aftermath of the attack on

Wendy Sewell when she had moved across to the graves where they witnessed her fall.

Mrs Beebe told Ervin of the threats she had received, echoing exactly what she told me 21 years later. There were other jottings from Ervin and copies of handwritten, anonymous notes referring to sightings from children in the cemetery at lunchtime on the day of the attack.

These notes claimed the children had been playing among the gravestones when they were suddenly frightened by something quite extraordinary and fled in panic. Here again was further proof the police had been made aware of the claims by children in the cemetery of seeing something, but had dismissed them as 'figments of childish imagination'.

As I read through the final pages from Ervin's files, I was shocked by what I discovered. It was a key section from the prosecution's medical report on Wendy Sewell. It confirmed:

Mrs Sewell suffered several lacerations to the skull. She was also found to have a broken shoulder following a violent struggle with her assailant.

This latter point alone completely contradicted the prosecution case. It now looked highly likely the police had just compiled a script for Downing to sign based on their limited estimations at that time.

His supposed confession made no mention of any struggle, and I immediately knew I had stumbled across a real gem. I contacted John Atkins to advise him of my findings.

As I was talking, one of my reporters said there was a call for me on the other line. It was from one of my most reliable informants. He said he had some vital news and asked me for an urgent meeting.

CHAPTER 20

CLANDESTINE MEETINGS

The following day I drove to a pub at Monsal Head. I went into the bar and bought two halves of best bitter. I then sat down outside at one of the picnic benches and waited for my contact to arrive. He was a constant source of valuable information. He parked up and strode across to meet me. Even in plain clothes he still looked like police.

I smiled and said, 'Dave, loosen up. It's a wonder you're not wearing your helmet.' He was obviously nervous about meeting me in public, and kept looking round. 'Look, you're having a quiet drink,' I insisted. 'Relax!'

He scowled at me and moaned, 'Your face is all over the nick at the moment.'

'Yes, I thought it might be. So is that why you have dragged me out here? Tell me something I don't know.'

'Do you know Mr Orange has a record? He went to prison just before the World Cup. He missed the final.' Dave gave the distinct impression it was more of a crime to have missed the World Cup victory than to get sent down.

'He was at school with your Mr Red. We had a report about Mr Red back in 1973. Apparently, he was questioned over the Barbara Mayo case in 1970, along with four other men from Bakewell. Two of them were his associates.'

'Yes, thanks Dave,' I said. 'Mr Orange has admitted some of this before, but I would certainly welcome anything else from official police reports.'

I told him I had just located some other prize documents from another key informant – without actually disclosing it was from Robert Ervin's historic files.

Dave then handed me some copies of police paperwork from 1973 and early 1974, which were slightly different to those of the private investigator.

'So what else have you got?' I asked. 'Any copies of important interviews?'

'Only about Mr Red, and a summary and timeline of some vital interrogations, but I have some other news for you,' he said excitedly. 'Mr Red was interrogated for two days at Chesterfield – I have all the details – but eventually they had to let him go. No forensics match. He was pulled in for questioning over Wendy Sewell's murder within hours of the attack. He had a good alibi, though, his uncle. He said he was with him at a sheep sale somewhere.'

I thought about telling him about Ervin's notes and the claim that there were two sheep sales held that day in Shropshire, but then decided to keep my powder dry.

Dave seemed anxious yet eager to continue. 'This is the most important news,' he said. 'This is further to the information that I gave you a while ago. There was another inquiry in 1979. I don't know all the details. Mind you, you were right. Downing's prints were not on the "bloody" murder weapon – but it looks as if there was a clear palm print. There may also have been hairs and fibres, and a third blood sample.'

'And who does that belong to?' I asked.

'Now, there's a real mystery. As I told you before, it could even have been one of our guys. It was a real cock-up. And I don't believe the hairs and fibres were ever checked as they too didn't link to your man Downing, so were probably discarded.'

He was referring to the probability of cross-contamination at the scene of crime. I had previously been informed that all the prime exhibits – including the murder weapon and items of clothing – may have been bagged together in error by an inexperienced bobby left alone.

Dave was still nervous, stopping to look around again before he continued, 'Now, Don, this is a real gem. The victim definitely put up a fight. She suffered a broken shoulder ... and, keep this to yourself for a few days, it looks like she was badly kicked as well as beaten, and most likely by someone wearing "winkle-pickers".'

This confirmed what I had been briefed by my police contact some time before, and only just discovered in Ervin's file – that within the police medical notes it is acknowledged that Wendy must have put up a violent struggle against her attacker.

This additional confirmation about Wendy's defensive battle again totally contradicted Stephen's original confession on which his conviction was based. There was no mention in any official reports of any kicking or a struggle, and Stephen was definitely wearing his dress boots – not winkle-pickers. What's more, he never even owned a pair.

*　　*　　*

Later that day I met up with my friend Allan Taylor from Central TV. Like me, he was annoyed by PC Ernie Charlesworth's claims that Stephen had been responsible for other childish pranks.

He said, 'I've been researching Wendy Sewell. She was no angel. Fell out with her husband and fell in with everyone else, it seems. Anyway, I went to see the father of her child, John

Marshall. He tried to deny everything at first. He was sweating a bit, but then admitted it.'

Allan grinned. 'I've also been putting a bit of pressure on Syd Oulsnam. He's reluctant to talk to reporters ever since he phoned you. It seems Mr Orange and Syd Oulsnam have reported you, me and Frank Curran to Bakewell police for harassment. They've apparently told them that reporters keep hounding them.'

'Really,' I said. 'It was Syd who phoned me. It will be interesting to see what they have told them.'

Allan added, 'I'm following up on Louisa Hadfield's running man too. I'm going to speak to Mr Blue next week.'

Some time later Allan confirmed he had spoken to him. Allan arrived unannounced and said Mr Blue was 'shaking like a leaf' at being confronted again by Louisa Hadfield's testimony. Allan said that, following his visit, Mr Blue then took several weeks off work on sick leave.

*   *   *

I was busy writing up the main headings for the paper when I heard someone tapping on the back door. I opened it and was confronted by a very large woman in her early thirties. She almost filled the doorway. She had a child's arm gripped in each hand, and they were crying and whimpering by her side.

'Are you that Don Hale?' she asked.

'Yes,' I replied. 'How can I help you?'

'I've got some news for you about your murder case.'

'Would you like to come inside?'

'No. A friend of mine wants to meet you urgently – and it's strictly private. You know what I mean? No cameras, no tapes.'

'Who is this friend? Where do they want to meet me? What information do they have?'

'Look, I don't know the details,' she said, 'It's a woman, though. The back of Somerfield supermarket, three o'clock tomorrow afternoon. Okay?'

'Yes, fine,' I replied.

As I waited in the car park the next day, I was beginning to think it might be a set-up, when I was suddenly prodded hard in my side. A woman in her mid-fifties who looked like a hippy and had rings in her nose, ears and eyebrows was staring at me.

'So you're that editor bloke, then?' she asked.

'Yes, I'm Don Hale. I understand you have some information?'

'I've got this friend who's keen to meet you at Flash Dam. He has some interesting news,' she explained.

A meeting in another isolated spot. My thoughts drifted back to the lorry chase, about practising the advice I'd preached to my staff about not going for any meetings in out-of-the-way places alone. She asked, 'Does the name Mr Red mean anything to you? And a sheep sale?'

'Tell me more.'

'Don't know a great deal. Crabby, he calls himself. He used to be a male nurse. Seems to know about your case, something from the early seventies. He says he's prepared to meet you if you're interested.'

'How much?' I asked.

'No money. He's bad with AIDS. Money isn't his thing. Take a few cans of lager if you must. He's just trying to survive,' she said, grabbing her bags.

'Okay, I'll be there,' I agreed once again.

*   *   *

Reaching the dam the next day, I parked on the road. It was only a short walk up a steep grassy bank. The area had been deserted for years. I could see a man sitting on the bank throwing stones into the water. 'Crabby?' I asked. The man didn't even turn his head to acknowledge my presence.

'So, the newspaper man?' he said.

'Your friend said you had some information,' I replied.

He remained silent. Crabby looked like he'd been living rough for some time. He was in his late fifties with short-cropped hair. He was unshaven and wore a badly torn grey jacket and a red and white checked T-shirt with grubby jeans and mucky boots. He seemed painfully thin and his cheeks were hollowed. He had a ring in each ear lobe.

I could hear him wheezing. I offered one of the cans of lager I had brought with me. He snatched it without even looking at the label. He pulled open the top and drank half the contents down in one.

'You know Bakewell?' he asked.

'Reasonably well,' I replied.

The man rose to his feet. 'Well, that Wendy Sewell murder that's been in the papers again. I know who did it.'

'Really,' I said.

'I know it wasn't that lad who got caught.'

He now had my attention. 'And have you any proof?' I asked hopefully. I kept turning round to make sure no one else was likely to appear. I wanted to be on my guard, just in case.

He crushed the can and flung it into the shallow stagnant water. He walked a few yards along the bank, then sat down again. He grabbed another can and began to gulp down its contents as if it were last orders.

'I had a good job once as a medic in a nursing home near Sheffield. It was also a sort of hospice for the terminally ill. Got

AIDS though, didn't I, through my own stupid fault. It's only a matter of time.'

He seemed despondent, but I was determined to try to get him to talk more. 'Would you make a statement?' I asked.

'No fucking statements! Anyway, I won't be round long enough for it to make any difference.'

I said, 'Your friend thought it could help get Downing out of jail.'

'Perhaps it will. I know Dolly – the woman you spoke to – from the road. She lost her son. He would have been about the same age as your man. Poor sod.

'Twenty-two bloody years inside for someone else. It was only when Dolly showed me an old cutting that I put two and two together and realised it was connected with one of my former patients. Dolly wanted me to tell you.

'I worked at this hospice place for about six years. We used to get all sorts. Money can't buy your health. I used to work nights, mainly. I used to nick a few things – drugs, like. Soft stuff, mainly, but then I got hooked. They often turned a blind eye as no one wanted to work this graveyard shift. This would be about the early seventies. I would look after the old sods who had cancer. Put one or two out of their misery. They begged me,' he explained, as if asking for absolution.

'One patient was a farmer from north Derbyshire. He seemed okay, but quickly deteriorated. Cancer of the liver. Very advanced. He was odd at first, kept himself to himself and didn't have many visitors.

'Gradually, he began to talk and open up. The pain was terrible. He found difficulty in sleeping at night. He'd talk to me and then ramble on for hours about all sorts. All rubbish mostly, but then he kept shouting something about a murder.

'He shouted it out several times one night and I had to call for assistance to help calm him down. He mentioned a Wendy, then Mr Red, then murder again. Had her head smashed in or something. At first I thought perhaps he'd done it.

'The next day, when he'd settled down, I asked him about it and he wanted to know what he'd said. Later, his nephew visited, and I could see him talking and they were pointing towards me.

'The following night the same thing happened. I thought he'd probably read about this murder. He got wound up, but later when the drugs took hold he became more lucid. He would shout out, "No, I won't tell lies. Stop it. It was murder."

'Certainly, whoever he had been talking about had threatened him and made his life a misery. He still seemed terrified of whoever it was. His only visitors seemed to be the nephew and a woman.

'The lad came every two or three days. I overheard them talking. He would stay for an hour or so and sometimes he would read to him before he fell asleep. I kept trying to talk with the nephew after his visits. About a week later the old man suddenly grabbed my arm and told me to sit down. It was in the early hours and he was restless. I bribed him a bit. I said, "You tell me about this murder and I'll give you something to help you relax." He was going to get it anyway.

'This guy finally explained that in 1973 he was asked to lie for a relative. He'd gone to a sheep sale somewhere with a couple of friends. He only mentioned a name once. Anyway, when the group returned, this man, Mr Red, was waiting for them.

'He was in a right state. He threatened them and forced them to agree to give him an alibi. He said the man had a vicious temper and they all reluctantly agreed. They were told an excuse that Mr Red had knocked over an old lady in his Land Rover. He said he had been drunk. It was all rubbish. The uncle told me it was the same day as the Bakewell murder in 1973. He knew the victim was Mr Red's girlfriend.'

Crabby now seemed quite emotional. 'It was only a month or so later when the old man died. The next day the young nephew came and collected his things and arranged for the funeral. He said he would put things right, and gave me a tenner for looking after his uncle.'

I was fascinated by this meeting, but I was uncertain as to how credible it was or whether any of it could be used as evidence. The old man had died, and Crabby, by the sound of him, wasn't too far behind. Without any statement it was fairly worthless, although I knew it could provide some interesting background information – and again it added doubt to Mr Red's alibi.

It seemed the old farmer wanted to get this off his chest but didn't want any of his own relatives to become involved or be threatened after he had gone. When I asked Crabby if he knew why Wendy had been attacked, he said, 'I think she had become some sort of liability and wouldn't keep her mouth shut.'

I stretched my arms to relieve the stiffness and began to thank Crabby for his time and trouble. 'Hey, where are you going? You've not heard the rest yet,' he said.

'The rest?' I asked. 'What else can there be?'

'Your murder case may be linked to some others.'

'You must be joking,' I replied.

Crabby stood up and explained, 'The nephew wanted to go to the police and believed Mr Red was responsible for the Sewell murder, but he wouldn't let him until he'd passed away.'

He continued, 'There was another man, now dead, who was a pal of Mr Red at the time. He was strong and well built, in his late twenties, who was very fit and had the look of an ex-boxer. He had lightish hair and a quiff. Both were apparently questioned over that Barbara Mayo murder a few years before.'

As soon as Crabby mentioned the quiff, I remembered a reference to it in some old newspaper cuttings within Ervin's notes. Police were supposedly looking for a man with a quiff in 1970 after the Barbara Mayo murder. Then I thought of the reference to Wendy being kicked by winkle-pickers. This Teddy Boy hairstyle and footwear could fit together, I reasoned.

Crabby relieved himself in the grass. He said he had wanted to tell his story before. We had been talking for about an hour, and it was getting very cold. His eyes were watering. I thanked him but remained uncertain as to how any of it could be used, and whether it was just another elaborate hoax.

CHAPTER 21

BATTLING BUREAUCRACY

Despite many months of debate and resubmitting paper after paper, I finally received a devastating letter from the Parliamentary Secretary of State, Tim Kirkhope. Dated 29 November 1995, it was sent in response to my submissions in January and February, addressed to MP Patrick McLoughlin.

> I have looked very carefully at what you, Mr
> Downing senior and Mr Hale have said about Stephen
> Downing's case and the various documents, which
> have been submitted to us. I have to say at the
> outset that I have not found anything in these
> representations that provides grounds for the Home
> Secretary to refer the case.
>
> As you will appreciate, the points raised in the
> representations have been considered, or could
> have been considered, by the courts already. I am
> sorry, for I know this will be a disappointment to
> you and Mr Downing's family.

Disappointment? I was absolutely gutted. After more than a year's hard slog it all seemed to have come to nothing. Yet another dead end. As I studied his response in more detail, though, it became quite obvious he had failed to read or understand the sheer complexity of this case.

His initial knockback and his eagerness to gloss over much of my submission was the first of many similar setbacks over the next few years, but once again it made me all the more determined to keep going and find the key evidence to help overturn Stephen Downing's conviction.

I sent a strong letter back to Mr Kirkhope pointing out the many errors with his analysis and enclosed some further paperwork to help clarify my claims. A few weeks later I was told that, due to this latest submission, the minister would look again at some of the facts presented. Patrick McLoughlin MP and I were also given an open invitation to visit the Home Office again. Some progress at last, perhaps?

1 January 1996

Dear Don,

First, I should like to wish you, your family, and all at the *Mercury* a very Happy New Year.

I am looking forward to the outcome of the Parole Board's recommendations and whether or not the Secretary of State will agree to their decision. I also live in hope that it will not be long before you are able to publish an exclusive ahead of any story another paper may print. Before I close I would like to say a special thank you to you for all the support and hard work you have put into fighting the case on behalf of my family and myself. I hope that you are keeping well, and that the year ahead will be a good one for you.

Stephen Downing

However, my overall optimism soon proved premature when another devastating letter addressed to Patrick McLoughlin arrived in early January 1996 from Ann Widdecombe, the new Minister of State at the Home Office, in relation to Downing's parole review.

Dear Patrick,

Thank you for your letter of 30 November about Stephen Downing, a mandatory life-sentence prisoner. I am aware of your interest in the case and your previous contact with my predecessor Michael Forsyth.

When he wrote to you on 5 July, he told you that psychological and psychiatric reports were being prepared. These have been received and disclosed for Downing, who has made written representations to the Parole Board. The board will consider his case in early January.

At this stage, I cannot give you any guarantee as to when Mr Downing can expect the final decision on his review. This will obviously depend on the nature of the Board's recommendation.

For example, any Parole Board recommendation for a lifer's transfer to open conditions requires approval at ministerial level. I can assure you, however, that following the Board's decision, all necessary action will be carried out expeditiously in this case.

Yours, Ann Widdecombe

A week or so later, yet another disappointing – but this time half-expected – letter arrived, this time from the Lifer Group at HM Prison Service, confirming, 'On the evidence available to the panel, the Parole Board considered implausible Mr Downing's protestations of innocence in respect of the offence, which had a sexual motive. The panel noted that throughout his sentence Mr Downing has, as a result of his protestations of innocence, undertaken no work directly related to the offence.'

Attached were copies of reports from Home Office psychiatrist Dr Rowton-Lee:

> *Staff who knew Downing best took the view that his behaviour inside in recent years has been impeccable.*
>
> *Stephen Downing was a hardworking man, choosing his companions carefully. He behaved and presented himself in such a way that movement to open conditions seemed to be appropriate after 21 years imprisonment. I too took this view.*
>
> *However, one problem remained, which was denial of the offence after initially admitting it. My view, nonetheless, was that he should progress to category D conditions for a continuing assessment of his safety for release. He has continued at interview to present well, and it was difficult to fit this man with the profile of somebody who behaved in such a way.*

Julia Long, a psychologist at HMP Verne, also added her weight to a growing team of experienced staff who were quite unable or unwilling to accept his claims of innocence. Her report, dated September 1995, acknowledged Stephen's excellent pattern of behaviour, but confirmed that she too remained concerned simply because of the denial aspect.

Shortly after making a confession, Downing retracted it and has steadfastly denied his involvement in the offence since then. In conclusion, any assessment of risk is difficult where the person is in denial of the offence.

The circumstances surrounding Downing's offence are well documented in Home Office summary and in several subsequent reports. He claims there is fresh evidence that might at some point in the future form grounds for an appeal.

I understand too that Downing has attracted a number of favourable reports indicating that he is a model prisoner as evidenced by his behaviour on the wing and observations of his interaction with both staff and inmates.

On each of our earlier interviews, he was courteous and co-operative and always punctual for appointment. However, his continual denial rendered fruitless any attempt at offence-focused work.

In light of the lack of evidence-focused work and his persistent denial, it is my considered opinion that Downing is not an acceptable risk for release at this time.

This refusal of Stephen's basic human rights became a constant and major bone of contention, and it was eventually decided after consultation with his QC, Edward Fitzgerald, that a submission was required for presentation to the European Court of Human Rights.

The Home Office had consistently refused Downing, and others, an oral hearing with the Parole Board due to his denial, and consequently the prison psychologists used this same denial aspect as serious grounds for concern over his supposed mental state. Their logic included the belief that a prisoner was potentially more of a danger to the public if they refused to admit to their guilt. It was simply catch-22.

At Downing's trial in 1974 the judge ordered him to be detained 'at Her Majesty's Pleasure', a sentence only applicable to juveniles, with a recommended tariff of 17 years. The Home Secretary was now the only person who had the power to intervene and determine a potential release date.

Stephen had served almost 23 years, some 6 years over his recommended tariff already. If he had lied and said he was guilty, he could have walked free then. But as he consistently maintained his innocence he had to stay in jail. Due to his denial, Stephen, and in fact any other prisoner who remained in denial of the offence for which they had been convicted, were automatically denied access to the Parole Board. Each prisoner therefore had to appoint someone to present a case to this authority on their behalf.

It seemed a disgraceful legal anomaly, and Edward Fitzgerald was one of the few men in the UK both willing and able to try to address it.

Dear Don,

The main purpose of writing is to ask if you would like to be called to give evidence at my Parole Board tribunal in November. I have received copies of most of the reports. It is hoped for your part you will be able to shed light on the case as you see it from your own investigations. Hope something comes out of it by the end of the year. After all, we have been waiting too long for a breakthrough.

Best wishes, Stephen Downing

* * *

The European Court, which met in Strasbourg, studied Stephen Downing's case and declared the Home Secretary's power to hold young criminals 'at Her Majesty's Pleasure' was illegal.

The European Court declared that the British Government were in breach of Article 5 of the Human Rights Convention, and it was expected that courts could have three options:

To release Stephen Downing on licence.
To state the reasons why he is still being detained and to
    determine category classification.
To confirm a date for his eventual release.

In real terms it meant the government now had to permit Stephen Downing, and every other prisoner in the UK who had served time beyond their recommended tariff, the basic human right to have an oral hearing with the Parole Board. It particularly applied to prisoners like Stephen, who were 'in denial of murder' (IDOM). The case attracted the attention of the national press, but it had no bearing whatsoever on Stephen's separate appeal against his conviction.

I later received a copy letter from a senior civil servant at the Criminal Cases Unit (C3) within the Home Office, stating:

```
The government are committed to ensuring that
those who are convicted of this uniquely heinous
crime of murder are punished appropriately. The
Home Secretary is disappointed that the European
Court of Human Rights has found the current
procedure for deciding on the releases of juvenile
murderers - which has been in place since 1908 and
which has worked well - breaches the European
Convention on Human Rights.
```

> However, the judgment does not affect the Home
> Secretary's power to set the tariff, the maximum
> period to be served for the purposes of
> retribution and deterrence, for juvenile
> murderers.

It seemed obvious the government would not accept this new ruling without a fight. And, sure enough, Stephen's lawyers had to go to the High Court to overcome the government's objections to the ruling and win the right to challenge the government through a judicial review.

*   *   *

Throughout 1996 I worked very closely with Stephen's legal team, but it seemed we were now facing the daunting task of battling against the British government on two major fronts.

I still believed the most probable escape route for Stephen – apart from a rope ladder – was via the Court of Appeal. It was through this system of review that his lawyers could argue the case and help prove that the original conviction was unsafe. Stephen's barrister John Atkins travelled to Derbyshire to view the scene of crime at Bakewell, and to meet Stephen's family for the first time. He stayed at our house in Matlock.

I ran a story describing how the opinion of scientific experts would be needed to help free Stephen. Many readers offered money. One, who wanted to remain anonymous, even promised £50,000.

I told John Atkins about this incredible generosity but, although he was both amazed and very grateful, he was confident our application for funds from the Legal Aid Board would be successful.

He was right. And much to the dismay of Derbyshire police, who did everything possible to try to discredit me, my reports and the need for further examination of key exhibits, we secured £13,000 to help fight the case.

It ensured that we could now pay for some of the country's top forensic, photographic and police-procedure experts to assess the original scene of crime evidence, Downing's clothing and the murder weapon, and to help counter many of the prosecution claims presented at trial.

*   *   *

Sam Fay, my deputy, became very ill and had to attend Whitworth Hospital for tests. His appearances at the office became less frequent and eventually I brought in Marcus Edwards, an enthusiastic and ambitious sixth-form schoolboy, to join our team as a part-time reporter.

Sam made the odd visit to the office, but unfortunately he was becoming weaker each day. He still retained an interest in Stephen's case but his concentration was waning, and it was evident he needed all his strength to fight his own desperate battle. Shortly afterwards he was admitted to the local hospital on a semi-permanent basis.

Then came a further blow. Jackie Dunn, one of my young journalists, announced she was looking for pastures new. I was gutted because Jackie had been an absolute rock to me. She was always so enthusiastic and inquisitive, and at times she had kept me going despite many hardships and setbacks. It was understandable that she would want to leave, of course, as she wanted to progress in journalism and the *Mercury* was a small newspaper in a small town.

Jackie had put in a tremendous amount of background work on the case, particularly in the early days, when she spent hours sifting through the archives at the County Council and sourcing press cuttings about the 1973 murder. She was also very good at debating some of the many anomalies my research threw up and in analysing witness statements – in particular with regards to Jayne Atkins, a key witness at the first appeal.

* * *

As the campaign to give Stephen Downing justice began to develop and national publicity increased, I suddenly discovered that Stephen had been transferred unexpectedly – seemingly overnight – from Dorchester to the bleak and positively remote Dartmoor prison, which now made it virtually impossible for anyone to visit him, including me.

It seemed Stephen had been given the impossible option to either tell me to get lost or to admit to his guilt after 20-plus years, and if he refused he would be shipped out to some God-forsaken place as quickly as possible.

Dartmoor was an isolated, run-down, historic jail that had once housed Napoleonic prisoners. He was put on a special wing with all the other 'trouble-makers and fellow prisoners in denial'. According to Stephen, half of its windows were either missing or broken, and it was freezing cold for much of the time, with little or no heating. He was asked to take part in a sex offenders' course, but naturally refused. I was also prohibited from seeing him there due to my role as a journalist.

I wondered if the ongoing row with the Home Secretary over the European Court ruling had inspired this unexpected and unnecessary move.

His first letter, dated 29 June 1996, told of some of the horrors of this latest detention centre – long before the winter chill set in.

                                    HM Prison, Dartmoor,
                                    Yelverton, Devon.

Dear Don,
I thought you would like a few words from me? I
have gone down with a cold again. The cell is quite
spacious though sparsely furnished. There is no
light switch on the inside so lights are turned off
at 11 p.m. I have had to wedge closed one of the
windows - but even that doesn't ward off the bitter
cold. I am typing this with my denim jacket on.
It's just as well a donkey jacket is part of the
clothing issue, as I might have to start wearing
that too. All outgoing letters are censored and all
phone calls monitored. The regime here is very much
different from other places I have been to.
    Best wishes, Stephen Downing

From Stephen's correspondence and his chats with his family on
the phone, it seemed that he was still clinging to the hope of
another transfer out to a more modern facility with education
options.

                                    14 October 1996

Dear Don,
As much as I appreciate all that everyone is
trying to do for me, the mere mention of any other
establishment is likely to have the Allocations
Unit considering it as a possibility. I have
already had to write, pleading with them to send
me to Littlehey rather than anywhere else.

```
It is true that I would be closer to home if I
was at Nottingham, but that is a Category B prison
and would be a step backwards for me in terms of
progression through the system.
   The reason I feel so strongly about Littlehey is
that they offer education seven days per week and
part of the curriculum includes law and chemistry,
which I would like to study. I know of no other
prison which offers those. At the end of the day I
am the one stuck behind bars, so I want my
incarceration to be as comfortable as possible.
   Stephen Downing
```

After delays and deferments, Stephen Downing's human rights case finally returned to the High Court on 1 November where, regrettably, they dismissed his application for a judicial-review challenge against the Parole Board from the previous January and decided not to recommend him for release, and also refused to allow a transfer to more open conditions.

The judges claimed that although his right now existed following a ruling by the European Court of Human Rights, at the time the Board considered his case he, along with other mandatory life prisoners, was not entitled to an oral hearing. Disappointment once again.

Downing's legal challenge via the European Court system was like playing bat and ball with the British government, and it all became rather complicated and confusing over a relatively simple issue. It hinged on the fact that his legal team believed Stephen had been denied his basic human right of being allowed to represent himself at a Parole Board hearing because he remained in denial of the offence he was first charged with. It also included a challenge to his excess tariff time.

Towards the end of 1996 the knock-backs from the Home Office and the Parole Board seemed to have had a devastating and debilitating effect on Stephen. I had never known him quite so down and depressed. I was getting very worried that he might even consider harming himself, and each subsequent letter seemed to indicate that he was becoming more and more despondent. It must have been an absolute nightmare for him. There was no light showing for him at the end of a depressingly long tunnel.

2 November 1996

> This will be my fifth Christmas without a visit
> from my family. It's supposed to be prison policy
> to promote family ties. If it wasn't for my
> family, I would withdraw any attempts of an
> appeal, and say, 'You've kept me this long, you
> can keep me for the rest of my life.'

A few days later he sent me another desperate letter. It was obvious the thought of spending another Christmas on his own was playing on his mind.

10 November 1996

> I am appreciative of our local MP, Mr McLoughlin's
> concern for my welfare. I am wondering if I might
> be able to call on his assistance to help me
> obtain a transfer before Christmas. With only a
> few weeks left my chances seem rather slim, hence
> the need for all the help I can get. It is grossly
> unfair for my family to be treated in this way. I

should hardly call this promoting a family policy.
I will be writing to my barrister John Atkins to
see if he can assist. I'm sorry to feel so
despondent, but you get that way when the Home
Office is not content with just having its pound
of flesh.

CHAPTER 22

THE TEA AND CAKES DEPARTMENT

During the early part of 1997, thankfully, the tide finally began to turn, and it turned so rapidly and quite unexpectedly that it soon gave Stephen some cause for optimism regarding the appeal against his conviction.

I helped submit yet another updated report to the Home Office via John Atkins. And with the boost of legal-aid funding we pressed ahead for an extensive review of all the forensic and photographic evidence, plus a thorough examination of police procedures. The revised findings could then be resubmitted as fresh evidence.

We expected the funding to take some time, but amazingly it was approved within weeks and the Legal Aid Board readily endorsed a welcome full grant towards essential casework expenses.

Forensic expert Russell Stockdale – a chartered biologist and a former principal scientist at the Home Office Forensic Science Service, and an independent scientific consultant to the legal profession – examined Downing's bloodstained clothing, work boots, personal items and the murder weapon. He drew many of the same conclusions made by Dr G.E. Moss more than 20 years previously, who disputed the findings of the prosecution's forensic scientist Mr Lee. He wrote:

*I am not able to agree with Mr Lee's pronouncement that the
blood on Downing's clothing was inconsistent with his simply
having found and turned over the body. Downing's
instructions at trial and which have remained consistent since
then were that he had found Mrs Sewell lying on the footpath
when he returned to the cemetery. In conclusion, I must record
provisional reservations about the scientific evidence which
was tendered at trial.*

Geoffrey Oxlee, a founder member of the Society of Expert
Witnesses and an imagery analyst for over 40 years, wrote a
report highlighting the 'unsatisfactory' forensic investigation and
recording of crime imagery at the scene, which no one was ever
able to explain. He also suggested that Wendy's clothing may
have been taken off before she was attacked, again contradicting
Stephen's account in his confession statement.

The experts' reports added further credibility to Stephen's
claims of innocence, and his conviction was looking more desperate by the minute. John Atkins was delighted and decided the
time was now right to consider an application for Leave to
Appeal. He hoped this could be approved as early as March.

The next few weeks and months, however, would be a roller-
coaster of emotions. On 18 January 1997, I received a letter from
Stephen confirming he had just been moved from his hell-hole at
Dartmoor to Littlehey Prison near Cambridge. I thought my
pressure on the MP and Home Office had finally paid off.

Soon after reading about Stephen's welcome transfer out of
Dartmoor came the inevitable bad news that I had been dreading.
In early February Sam Fay died. His family had told us to expect
the worst but it was still a major shock. Sam's final days were spent
at Whitworth Hospital, the local care unit, which together we'd
campaigned to save many years before. He had given me some

early advice about Stephen's case and later expressed his appreciation of my efforts in the latter stages of my investigation.

*   *   *

In the Spring of 1997, C3, the specialist Home Office department dealing with Stephen's case and other alleged miscarriages of justice, was rather hastily disbanded, and all parties were suddenly informed that the new Criminal Cases Review Commission (CCRC) would take over all of the outstanding cases with immediate effect.

It always seemed barmy to me that the government should only have a relatively small, specialised section looking at alleged miscarriages of justice. I had dealt with C3 since 1994 and in my opinion it was just a sham operation seemingly controlled by Oxbridge-educated people who were employed to fob people off.

It was mission impossible to get anyone to listen to anything new. Behind the scenes it employed many more of these hard-nosed doubters who, in addition to being poor record keepers, were also rude, arrogant and totally uninterested in anything that might dare to challenge the British justice system and the establishment.

It was all scripted, and in their eyes there were no innocent people in prison. How could there be? All convictions were correct, as all defendants had been given a fair trial, and if anything was wrong with the procedure it was put down to the jury. How wrong could they be?

I presented at least half-a-dozen updated submissions on behalf of Stephen Downing before the CCRC finally came into being. Indeed, I was one of just a few key players and justice campaigners who had actually pushed for a new independent review body to be established.

I had even been asked by the Prime Minister and senior Whitehall officials to give my views on what was wrong with the current methods of review – and asked how they could be improved. My experiences as a prison visitor were also noted.

My reports were controversial, but my early encounters with C3 were often rather comical. They probably thought I could be easily fobbed off by some rather grand old ladies who fronted this old-fashioned review board.

My preliminary reports were only reviewed due to sheer persistence by the 'tea and cakes' department, who at times invited me to London for a cosy chat about 'all this fuss'. I had spoken on the telephone with a Ms Williams, a rather genial-sounding lady in her sixties with a strong Welsh accent who told me she was originally from Cardiff, and kept repeating how she was now looking forward to retirement.

When I arranged to see her, I was asked to attend an office within the Home Office, where she would run though my findings with colleagues. On attending, I was shown into a quaint and rather musty-smelling old room with lots of dark wood panelling and a small, high window.

Ms Williams entered and introduced herself. She seemed pleased to see me after months of talking with her on the telephone and corresponding through letters. She was followed by two other ladies of a similar age. They all shuffled into large old-fashioned armchairs purposely laid out for them, and I sat directly opposite with a small table to my left, which I thought was probably for the contents of my briefcase.

I was just about to pull out my files when another lady suddenly entered through a large creaking swing door and came towards me pushing a tea trolley containing the department's best china plates, together with strawberry jam and what looked like homemade scones.

'Lovely,' said Ms Williams, adding, 'Shall I be mother?' while pouring the tea. The ladies chatted among themselves about how wonderful the scones appeared, and how they all loved a really good cup of strong tea.

I showed them copies of my submissions and we chatted about many important aspects of the case. One of them appeared to be constantly nodding off slightly, while another was knitting. She said it helped her to concentrate.

Later, they thanked me for coming 'all that way' and said they'd get back to me. I heard nothing, though, for ages despite umpteen phone calls to Ms Williams's office. Eventually, after six months, I was invited back and faced a similar pantomime experience. They said they still found it difficult to understand why I was 'campaigning for a murderer'.

I visited the Home Office, and other governmental review departments, several more times before I was officially notified that the Criminal Cases Review Commission (CCRC) – to be based in Birmingham – would take over all existing case work.

Some time later I received a greetings card from Ms Williams, who by then had retired and was back in Cardiff. She wished me well in my endeavours and claimed her hands had been tied by the system.

In March 1997 Stephen's case was one of the first to be considered by this new authority, the CCRC. He was quickly allocated a case-file reference number and I received a polite note to confirm that, after nearly four years of hard slog with C3, the Home Office had quite simply run out of time to re-examine his case.

My initial concern was that, after years of negotiation and submissions with the Home Office and C3, we were suddenly back to square one. My additional concern over the transfer of documents from London proved justified when I was informed by the CCRC that much of my paperwork and updated submissions were mislaid in transit somewhere on the M1.

I had horrific visions of my files spilling out onto the hard shoulder or disappearing into grass verges. I wondered, *How on earth could secure data become lost in transit?*

My experiences of dealing with these inefficient bureaucrats meant that I had already become quite accustomed to expecting the worst. I always said C3 was a joke from start to finish – at the expense of numerous innocent prisoners.

I instructed the CCRC that, in view of the circumstances, I would call down to see them and personally hand over copies of my files to ensure there was no further delay or loss of essential paperwork. They seemed rather taken aback by my stance, but within days I travelled to their new offices in the centre of Birmingham with several boxes full of updated paperwork.

When I started to deal with them, I quickly realised I was embarking upon another soul-destroying and frustrating journey, submitting and resubmitting paperwork that had been systematically checked and rechecked countless times before. It was a very slow process. The need to perpetually repeat everything with so many new and different people increased my workload to an unprecedented level.

On top of this, I suddenly had my parents' unexpected health problems to contend with. Kath and I travelled up to Manchester most weekends to help with shopping, gardening and odd jobs for both sets of parents. My mother in particular had been in deteriorating health for years, but now, it seemed, she was racing downhill.

Often she couldn't even remember who I was. It was like chatting with a stranger. She was suffering from Alzheimer's disease and had additional problems eating and drinking. She spent time in hospital and often, when she came home, she was unable to look after herself or my father, who had his own serious medical problems, including Parkinson's disease.

They had always been there when I needed them. Their constant slide was a shock and a bitter blow. It left me devastated.

CHAPTER 23

THE COVER-UP

A welcome bonus came during the summer of 1997, when I received a surprise call from a newspaper colleague who advised me that a key witness might be willing to come forward to support Stephen Downing's claims of innocence. The most surprising factor was that this new witness was a retired former detective who had served for nearly 30 years on the Derbyshire force, a large part of which he spent based at Bakewell.

He said he had been in charge of a re-investigation into the Wendy Sewell murder in 1979, and needed to see me urgently.

My colleague had met the man – whom I will call Rodney Jones – at a funeral, and I thought that perhaps the graveyard location, plus the fact he had met someone from the *Mercury* group, had finally pricked his conscience.

This Rodney Jones was apparently vastly experienced and had once worked in Liverpool with Derbyshire police's deputy, Don Dovaston. He had been reading about the progress of the case in the papers and admitted he'd had something on his mind for years, and now felt compelled to meet with me and talk about his findings.

I was suspicious, of course. Why would an ex-detective suddenly want to offer me confidential information after more than 20 years of silence? I sat back for a few moments, then picked up the receiver. *What the hell*, I thought. *I've nothing to lose.* I dialled the number and, after a few short rings, Jones answered.

When I told him who I was, he began to sound rather nervous. He refused to talk on the phone but, after some persuasion, agreed to meet me the following day in confidence at my office at 11 a.m.

He arrived on time, with his coat collar half-turned up and a shifty look in his eyes. He gave me the false name we had agreed. He seemed obsessed with not being seen coming into the office, although he parked his large blue Volvo right outside. I ushered him straight through to my private office.

'You're not to record this,' he said immediately.

'No, nothing will be recorded,' I reassured him, 'but it would be helpful if I could take some notes.'

'No notes,' snapped Jones. 'Let's just talk things through first.'

I studied the man very carefully. He was tall but heavy-set. He was sweating even before the interview had started. Jones had only recently retired from the force and was terrified of losing his pension if he spoke to the press. He was also concerned about breaching the Official Secrets Act.

I did my best to calm him down, gave him a cup of coffee – three sugars, as requested – and agreed a special code to preserve his anonymity on future visits.

I set about trying to coax out of him the real reason for his visit, all the time attempting to conceal my excitement that I might at last be nearing a breakthrough. I wondered what vital piece of information he might have.

Jones explained, 'I joined the force in 1962, but I left a few years later when I became disenchanted. I became a publican, but soon realised that police work was in my blood and returned to join the old Derby and County force at Buxton about November 1971.

'I was in CID there for about five years, then went to Matlock, then Clay Cross. Two years after that, I was transferred to the police house near Taddington, then on to Bakewell.

'I arrived at Bakewell about two months after the Wendy Sewell murder. I didn't think there was anything out of the ordinary about the case, but wasn't told too much about it.

'During autumn 1979 I was working late in CID at Bakewell police station when I was asked to see someone who apparently wanted a word in private. This person, whose name I believe was Steven Martin, was a young man who I believe said that he owned a florist's shop near Ripley.

'He said he lived with his father near the shop. He made mention of his uncle who was related to Mr Red and lived at a farm over towards Tideswell. The uncle was understood to have bred fighting cocks.

'This uncle had confided in Mr Martin and told him that Mr Red and another man had forced him to give them an alibi stating that he had been with them on that day in 1973. He wanted people to tell lies for him so there would be no connection with the murder.'

Jones paused for a breather. He was still looking round nervously all the time. He kept saying that he hoped no one else from the office had seen him. I still wasn't quite sure whether he was genuine, a crank or a police spy determined to either derail my campaign or just find out more about my progress. He still seemed very much ex-cop.

When he mentioned the name of the young man interviewed, I instantly recalled Robert Ervin's files and Crabby's comments at Flash Dam some two years previously. I thought that some further missing pieces of the jigsaw were coming together at last.

Crabby had mentioned a similar young man who had often visited his dying uncle in the hospice where Crabby worked. It now seemed that Jones and Crabby were talking about the same people.

'The uncle was sworn to secrecy by Mr Red, but he was dying and he felt he had to tell his nephew, this Steven Martin,' continued Jones. 'When his uncle died just a couple of weeks later, Martin felt he had to tell the police. He thought something should be done. That was the reason he came to the police station – he told me the whole story.'

Jones now seemed upset, and I thought I could see a tear forming in his eye. 'Steven Martin had always thought Mr Red had been to a sheep sale,' he went on. 'He was devastated when he found out the truth.

'I can't remember if he told me the names of the other people who corroborated the alibi. They were responsible people, though, farmers who had gone to buy sheep, all relatives of Mr Red. I think their statements were checked. This nephew was in his mid-twenties then and lived at home. I saw him again several times and even went to his house a couple of times.

'I applied for a copy of the prosecution file on the Sewell murder, and it arrived within a couple of days. I took it home to read and study.

'There was a statement from a detective constable, but I noticed something that didn't tally. I continued to acquaint myself with the facts.

'There was a disputed witness statement by a man from Buxton, but I was beginning to get really worried now. There appeared to be some major flaws in this case. I noticed about a dozen statements from officers *who did not exist*. They were neither signed nor dated. There were other statements from officers who clearly had not taken the details. I queried one particular statement taken by an officer, which had his name and number on it. When I checked it with him, he denied any knowledge of it. He said it was all rubbish. He said not only had he not signed it, but he hadn't written it.

'He's an inspector now, but he was too scared to do anything about it then. He told me to leave well alone and that they'd obviously made a mistake. It was no mistake though. It was all part of a cover-up.'

He continued, 'I then had a surprise visit from a detective superintendent from Buxton, Tom Naylor. He just barged into my office and began making threats. He pressed me against a wall. He had his arm locked against my throat. I was almost choking. He said he hoped I didn't think I was going to get Stephen Downing out of jail.

'He said the shit would certainly hit the fan if I did, and added that the press had better not find out about all this. I later found out that all the lads at Buxton called him Creeping Jesus.

'He would suddenly appear behind them without their hearing his approach. He told me that I had to interview Mr Red with a detective sergeant, and then interview other witnesses. I said I didn't go along with that, but I was told in no uncertain manner that that was the way I had to play it.

'Mr Red came down to the police station at Bakewell with his solicitor at about 7 p.m. a few nights later. As instructed, I interviewed him with a detective sergeant. Mr Red was really wetting himself. He was soaked in sweat and shaking like a leaf.

'He was shaking so much he couldn't even light a cigarette. He constantly denied ever knowing the Sewell woman. He said he wasn't sure whether he'd made the trip to the sheep sale and claimed he couldn't remember now, but he did say there were about four people who went there by car, whom he named.

'I was then instructed by Naylor to interview suspects, then witnesses. I was unhappy about this and decided to put his request in the last paragraph of my report.

'Normal procedure would be to pull everyone in at the same time and interview them separately, so that suspects and witnesses didn't have time to compare notes and get their stories straight.'

Within a day or two, Jones said he was given one of the biggest rollickings of his life by another senior officer at Buxton. 'He told me there was no need to put these comments in my report,' said Jones. 'I thought my future was on the line. But I heard nothing more. I saw Mr Martin again later, but he was not very happy with the outcome.'

Jones concluded, 'I gave a two- or three-page report to the divisional commander, but again I heard nothing more. I retired in 1990, and I've been wanting to get this off my chest for a while. I think Downing is innocent.'

Jones was obviously still feeling uncomfortable about telling his story to a journalist, and kept demanding assurances that he was not being recorded and that his name would not be mentioned in any reports.

His tale, however, was ringing very loud alarm bells with me, and I needed to check my notes with Crabby and his comments about a 'friendly copper', and other information claiming a high-ranking superintendent had helped to support Mr Red's alibi. Was this superintendent Tom Naylor, the same one who had threatened Jones? The grey areas were suddenly becoming much clearer.

I thanked Jones for his information. He still wanted to know whether he could give his story to the authorities without losing his pension. I didn't know and I didn't want to be accused of tainting a witness, so I suggested he should contact an independent solicitor for advice. He left the office, saying he would be in touch again.

Meanwhile, I made enquiries about Detective Superintendent Tom Naylor. One of my informants passed me a letter written by

Naylor to police HQ on 1 February 1982, in which he explained he had interviewed Ray Downing in September 1981, in response to a letter received by the chief constable from Ray. Naylor wrote:

Mr Downing gave a long history of the case and his reasons for believing that his son was innocent. A great many of the matters he raised had been dealt with in the initial inquiry. His main points were that he considered Mr Red, a former associate of the deceased, may have been responsible for the murder.

Where possible, having regard to the length of time which has lapsed since the murder, I have found an answer to each of the points Mr Downing senior has raised. Mr Red was apparently eliminated from the inquiry during the initial stages of the investigation.

On Saturday, 30 January 1982, I saw Mr Downing at Matlock police station. I discussed the various matters he had raised and advised him of the outcome.

So it appeared that Naylor eliminated Mr Red from the inquiry in 1982, with no mention of him being originally interviewed in 1973 and then again in 1979, nor anything about the claim that his alibi for the day of the attack had been challenged at that time. This information could have proved vital to Stephen Downing's chances of an appeal in 1980. It was clearly suppressed, and his defence team were unaware of any such interviews or claims of false alibis.

*   *   *

True to his word, Rodney Jones returned to the office several days later. He once again entered in a cloak-and-dagger manner through the back door, using his agreed assumed name. As soon as he was alone with me he continued his story.

'I believe the uncle made a death-bed confession to his nephew,' claimed Jones in one breath. 'The nephew was very disappointed by the reaction of the police and eventually disappeared.'

I was puzzled by his comment. 'Disappeared? What do you mean?'

It all seemed very suspicious. A young businessman, who still lived at home with his parents, had simply vanished off the face of the earth.

Where had this witness gone to?

Jones didn't know. He said he used to live in Ripley but had mysteriously vanished not long after giving his statement. Jones said he was placed on the missing persons list for nearly two decades, and he thought he might have gone to somewhere in the Brighton area – but claimed all enquiries to try to trace him had failed.

'Nothing was ever heard from him again,' said Jones.

'So nothing more happened?' I queried.

Jones paused and then reluctantly admitted, 'Martin's statement was filed away. Without the lad it was impossible to progress.'

'So the police just let Mr Red off the hook?' I asked.

'That's why I came to you,' said Jones. 'I thought you would know what to do.'

'It's a bit late,' I said. 'It's from 1980 – will you at least give me a written statement?'

'No, no – definitely not!' said Jones.

'Well, if you won't give it to me, give it to Downing's solicitor or someone else. Even the Commissioner for Oaths or the Criminal Cases Review Commission,' I urged.

'And my pension? What about my pension? It's a lot to risk.'

I felt two emotions simultaneously. Sympathy for a brave man who thought he was risking everything, and anger that he wouldn't put things in writing. In the end anger and frustration triumphed over sympathy. 'Then why bother coming to me if you haven't got the guts?' I demanded.

'I'll think about it. I'll be in touch,' replied Jones as he left the office.

The following day Jones telephoned me and agreed to visit a solicitor in London to discuss his position regarding his pension and the Official Secrets Act. After that meeting he was reassured enough to give a statement directly to the Criminal Cases Review Commission.

It was later alleged that the original file containing Jones's allegations from 1979 was only produced by Derbyshire police following a marathon legal struggle involving High Court demands from Stephen's defence team.

Finally, the police were forced to corroborate all these details – but at a price. John Atkins said the police made him agree that all the evidence relating to Rodney Jones's interrogation of Mr Red, which the police had at first denied even existed, could not be shown to me or even discussed with me.

John was furious, but I told him not to worry. I had already spoken with Jones on several occasions and I believed that I knew the probable contents of the file. As long as Jones's statements became part of the new defence evidence, I didn't really mind.

CHAPTER 24

MULTIPLE MURDERS

The Home Office contacted me in the summer of 1997 and asked me to submit an urgent and updated report directly to them about any alleged links I had identified between the Wendy Sewell murder in 1973 and two other similar killings from 1970, namely those of Barbara Mayo and Jackie Ansell-Lamb.

The latter victim had been discovered lying face down and half-naked close to Macclesfield in Cheshire, just a few months before Mayo's body was found close to Junction 29 of the M1 at Chesterfield – which was only about 12 miles from Bakewell. Derbyshire police had already linked these two earlier cases and I was hoping they could now review my evidence and join up the dots.

The many old newspaper cuttings collated by Robert Ervin had shown me that Barbara Mayo and Wendy Sewell were strikingly similar in appearance. Both were young, attractive women who looked fit and healthy, with long dark hair. The victims had all been found half-naked and been brutally battered about the head in frenzied attacks, and it now seemed that they had all had personal effects stolen.

I had my own notes about these allegations, some information from police informants and also copies of press reports from the time, but Robert Ervin provided the real key. His knowledge of the full circumstances and background to the 1970 murders proved invaluable.

Wendy Sewell was found in almost identical circumstances to Jackie Ansell-Lamb, and both cases attracted numerous anonymous letters. One of the most unusual coincidences, however, concerned the claim that at least four men from the Bakewell area had been questioned over both the Mayo and Sewell murders. And, more importantly, according to a reliable police informant two out of these four had also been ex-boyfriends of Mrs Sewell.

My police contact had previously confirmed that Mr Red was definitely one of the men questioned.

The police at that time were, however, looking for a fair-haired man with a quiff driving a Morris Minor Traveller. I recalled that Crabby had mentioned a friend of Mr Red's who sounded similar, with a quiff and Teddy Boy looks. I wondered if he wore 'winkle-pickers' too.

Mayo and Ansell-Lamb had both been strangled, and I said in my report that although the post-mortem report made no direct mention of Wendy being strangled, the mortuary photographs indicated severe bruising to the victim's neck.

I questioned the apparent disappearance of her tights and personal items. I began to wonder if it was the same killer of all three young women, who may have removed some items as bizarre trophies.

My report was despatched in haste with attachments as requested and, quite amazingly, just a few weeks later – and almost three years after my first submission to Derbyshire Chief Constable John Newing – the county force suddenly organised a press conference to announce they were reopening the Barbara Mayo murder case after nearly 30 years. And even more surprisingly, the officer taking charge of this press conference and banging the drum for police efficiency was Don Dovaston, who had always been so dismissive of any new evidence in the Downing case, believing it was all cut and dried.

I could hardly believe my luck. I thought perhaps they had taken notice of the submissions I'd handed to them some two years earlier about potential links to other similar murders of young women and to my recent revised presentations to the Home Office.

I expected an urgent call from the police incident room asking me over for further talks, and I waited patiently for another press conference to say they were now looking into possible connections with the murder of Wendy Sewell. I thought perhaps Stephen Downing might even be released much sooner than I anticipated.

Nothing happened.

As that week's *Mercury* deadline was fast approaching, and as I had still not received any word from the police, I decided to take the initiative.

The front page of the Mercury of 25 September 1997 appeared with the strap line: 'Bakewell murder links to Mayo case', with the main front-page story devoted to the similarities in both crimes. Under the headline FINGERPRINTS OF A KILLER appeared pictures of Barbara Mayo and Wendy Sewell. Side by side, the physical resemblance was striking.

As the paper hit the streets, I made a call to the police incident room and outlined my lead story for that week. I got through to a senior officer, who seemed genuinely surprised to hear of a possible Sewell connection, and said I might hear from them again. He did, however, add that I should not hold my breath.

Several more days passed before my long-awaited call from the Mayo incident room came. 'Are you available for an interview?' they asked.

'Yes, tomorrow afternoon or Friday?'

'No, I mean now,' came the reply.

'Well, yes, I suppose so,' I said, taken aback by the sudden urgency.

'Wait where you are, then. We'll be there in 20 minutes.' Sure enough, less than half an hour later two detectives arrived at the *Matlock Mercury* offices on Bakewell Road, having raced over the moors from Chesterfield. It seemed they were deployed by CIB2, the secretive team that didn't really exist known with a certain degree of sarcasm by fellow officers as the Invisible Men.

They seemed more like undertakers than policemen. I showed them copies of my recent submissions to the Home Office, local MP Patrick McLoughlin and the Criminal Cases Review Commission, all of which highlighted possible connections with the other cases, particularly between the Mayo and Sewell murders.

They were astounded and told me categorically that the first they'd heard of any potential links was when my front-page article had appeared that week. The men spent about an hour going over my files.

When they came to the name of Mr Red and the other close associate of Wendy's, their jaws dropped. Although I had always named all possible suspects and anyone connected with the victim in my official submissions, I had been very careful never to mention any names in my press reports.

Until that moment, the officers had been totally unaware that Mr Red, and at least one other man linked to Wendy Sewell, had been questioned over her murder.

'Why do these names surprise you so much?' I asked.

They confirmed Mr Red was one of the men from Bakewell questioned over the Barbara Mayo murder – something I had already been told by a police contact some two years previously – but they were shocked to find he had such strong connections with Wendy Sewell.

One of the officers said, 'In my book to be interviewed over one murder is unusual, but to be interviewed over two is too much of a coincidence.'

I explained that I had given this same basic information they now had to the chief constable's office back in January 1995. I said that I believed Assistant Chief Constable Don Dovaston – the man now leading the re-opened Mayo investigation – must have been well aware of it.

Eventually, the detectives took away copies of the relevant paperwork and drove off. Later that day I received a phone call from Central Television's newsroom. They had read the front page of the *Mercury* and wanted to know if there were any updates on the Downing case worth running in their evening news bulletin.

I told them that two detectives had just visited me from the Mayo murder investigation team and had taken away documents that referred to links to the murder of Wendy Sewell.

Two hours later a producer from Central got back to me and said the police had flatly denied visiting me and added that they had no intention of doing so. I could hardly believe my ears. I went over the details of the visit again and said it had taken place in the reception office of the *Mercury* with witnesses. The two detectives' names and their ID were listed in the visitors' book. Both men had signed in, and I had verified their credentials. The producer basically called me a liar and put the phone down.

Unfortunately, my old reporter pal Allan Taylor, who had been such a supporter of my campaign to free Stephen, had left Central by this time, and no one else really took up the case with as much enthusiasm.

Perhaps there was a reason they were called the Invisible Men after all.

*   *   *

When the police euphoria about re-opening the Barbara Mayo case began to fade, Derbyshire police ran their own headlines in their *Upbeat* in-house magazine, with a page-one splash WE NEVER GIVE UP!, and added that DNA could now help solve this 27-year old murder mystery. It carried an almost identical sub-heading to my own front page of the *Mercury* – from some eight months before.

More than four years later, however, after spending a small fortune on man-hours, technology, fruitless searches throughout the world and a multitude of further interviews and the re-examination of evidence, the operation was suddenly scaled down.

The real killer of Barbara Mayo, Jackie Ansell-Lamb and no doubt Wendy Sewell too remained at large. And Assistant Chief Constable Don Dovaston suddenly announced his early retirement.

About nine months later, Derbyshire police also confirmed the pending retirement of controversial chief constable John Newing. He was officially retired from service on 31 December 2000, and, very unexpectedly given his years of complete silence, he indicated in a final interview live on BBC Radio Derby that Derbyshire police had made a sudden and dramatic shift in their position on the Stephen Downing case, with Newing claiming, 'Downing should not be in jail,' adding, 'When he is cleared, the case should be re-opened.'

This was to be the first ever admission by a senior Derbyshire police officer that Downing was innocent, and that the real killer behind this and possibly the two other similar unsolved murders could still be out there somewhere.

CHAPTER 25

THE NATIONAL INTEREST

My regular correspondence with Stephen Downing continued, though his letters started to come a little less frequently. I soon learned why, as his letters began to arrive in handwritten form.

2 September 1997

I have had to hand in my typewriter after being
told I am not allowed it after no less than 5
years - and some 7 months of which have been spent
in here. After submitting a complaint to the
governor, I was told I could have my mechanical
one handed in on a visit. I believe it all began
when John Atkins asked if he might be permitted to
see me again in the afternoon. He was told no.
John had phoned the prison and was told by the
Lifer Governor that he could see me. I am sure it
was one of the Wing SOs who refused and was
niggled at getting his decision overruled.

   Next, I was told I could no longer have any
letter-headed paper, even though I showed them the
invoice. I am still awaiting a reply to my
complaint. I would also like the strike removed.

```
   Given the recent way I have been treated, I am
washing my hands of helping the prison do anything
for charity. I do hope there will be news of a
major development soon, particularly to say there
will be an appeal. I would also like bail to be
granted, as I want to be with my family.
```

From the other side of the frosted glass screen at the *Mercury* office, one of the girls announced, 'It's Emma Burman from the BBC at Birmingham.'

Having seen some rapid progress with the new expert witness statements, ex-detective Rodney Jones's admission and a case review under way by the CCRC at Birmingham, it was a good time for the media beyond the *Matlock Mercury* to start taking an interest.

I also heard from Rachel Bowering, the producer for the BBC's regional investigative programme *Midlands Report*, who wanted to review the case for a proposed documentary programme, which would be called *Murder in the Graveyard*.

I was told the programme would be shown on 5 February 1998, and initially just throughout the Midlands region, which meant many parts of our own circulation area in the Hope Valley, South Yorkshire and even certain parts of North Derbyshire would miss out. However, the news of another important media investigation was welcomed by Stephen.

```
Thank you for the additional papers and account of
my case. I am most grateful for all the time you
have put in to aiding my case along. Hopefully,
something positive will come out of it. I am not
quite sure how the BBC is going to manage this
without my account of events. Even if they allowed
```

me out for a couple of days on a temporary
licence, I would not cause the Home Office or
prison any concern. As from this Saturday, I will
be able to function as a listener affiliated to
the Samaritans but will not get my ID card and
badge until after the full six weeks training.

As you rightly say, this year looks like it
could be of interest. Given the knowledge of the
BBC programme being put together, I think the CCRC
will hold back until it has been shown. I was
pleased to hear the lawyers should have their
legal submission ready for the CCRC this month.

As the date of the broadcast approached, Rachel asked me to
attend the TV transmission and take part in a live radio phone-in
programme immediately afterwards.

I travelled across with my young trainee reporter Marcus
Edwards, and we watched the broadcast in the studio manager's
office. This was the first time I had actually seen it. I was nervous
about the phone-in afterwards, but fortunately my anxiety was
unnecessary. By the time we entered the radio studio the switch-
board was lit up like a Christmas tree with hundreds of people
eager to offer messages of support. Everyone in the Midlands
seemed to want their say over this matter.

Ray and Nita were also on the line somewhere and had been
listening to the programme. Stephen's barrister John Atkins was
in the BBC's Exeter studio and a representative from the CCRC
was on hand to talk in general terms. Derbyshire police, however,
refused to take part.

17 February 1998

Dear Don,

I am pleased to say that I was given a private
screening of the video last week. I was really
impressed with the way it was put together and
highly delighted with what everyone said. It's not
surprising it made quite an impact. Two members of
staff who watched it said it was powerful stuff
and said it was difficult to treat someone when
you know they're innocent.

    Best wishes, Stephen Downing.

And again on 22 February 1998.

It was most heartwarming to read the two
letters published in last week's *Matlock Mercury*
of the public support. My case officer said he
was interested watching the video. I had a
wonderful visit today from my family and they
told me the commissioner had also seen the
video.

The documentary was eventually broadcast to the entire nation
on BBC2 in September 1998. During the week leading up the
broadcast, it seemed that nearly everyone and his dog wanted to
claim an interview with me to find out more information about
Downing's appeal prospects and additional background information to the case. *The Times* newspaper featured the case and
compared it with some of the major miscarriages of the century.
Reporter Danny McGrory claimed, 'The Downing File has
re-opened 25 years too late.'

And at the end of September 1998 I received a call from Matthew Parris, the former MP who was now a columnist with *The Times*. We had been friends and acquaintances for years.

I reminded him of a previous call I'd made to him some years ago when I first asked about his involvement with the Downing case. Parris was the MP for West Derbyshire when I first arrived at the *Mercury*. He resigned his seat in 1987, with Tory colleague Patrick McLoughlin taking over from him. I was both surprised and disappointed by his initial reactions at that time, but I was certain he had now read McGrory's story and seen the BBC2 documentary. I considered the powerful combination had pricked his conscience, persuading him to write an honest account of his actions from the early seventies.

In October 1998 Parris's article was published, in which he described Ray and Nita coming to him for help when he was MP in the seventies and Stephen had been in prison for five years. He wrote very honestly about how he'd done the proper thing, but not necessarily the *right* thing.

The truth is, I didn't work very hard on it. I could maintain that I did all that was possible – and on paper that is true. It is also true that however much effort one had put into supporting Mr and Mrs Downing's struggle, it would probably have made no difference at the time.

Oh yes, I can justify my actions to you without difficulty. But you have no window into my thoughts. I have. So I will always know that, underneath, I wrote Stephen off right at the start. If I had really listened: If I had really followed up, if I had gone beyond the call of duty, and if I had then concluded that Mr and Mrs Downing were right, then I would have fought their corner however hopeless the fight – and who knows how that might have helped. I did not do so.

Matthew also wrote to Stephen personally on 21 October 1998.

Dear Mr Downing,

Thanks for your letter to the editor of The Times.
I am sorry they did not publish it. It was a good
clear letter. I do talk with Don Hale from time to
time and he keeps me in touch. But I have told Don
and must say the same to you that it is best for
me to keep out of this now. I do not want to jump
on the bandwagon so late on. As you know, I wish
you well. As I said in my article, I do not think
there was anything that could be done in those
early years after your conviction - and even if I
had made more of a fuss, I am sure I would have
failed until new evidence came forward as it now
has, but I am sorry that I did not at least try,
and repeat those apologies to you personally.

Matthew Parris, The Times Room,

House of Commons

Despite Matthew's honest appraisal and the swelling support in
the national press, however, it was to be a further two years before
the CCRC finally announced their recommendations.

CHAPTER 26

THE WAITING GAME

I had been in regular contact with Commissioner Barry Capon ever since my initial submission and supporting documents to the CCRC.

My hope was that Stephen's case would be rapidly referred to the Court of Appeal on the grounds that his conviction was unsafe. In addition, I was also working hard with Downing's legal team to secure his potential release on licence via other methods, including the European Court and the Parole Board, as he had by then already served more than 24 years in jail for a murder he said he did not commit – more than 7 years beyond his recommended tariff date.

However, progress with the CCRC seemed to grind to a halt in the middle of 1999 – more than two years after they had first been shown all my files and submissions for consideration.

It was all extremely frustrating and resulted in MP Patrick McLoughlin raising the matter in the House of Commons.

More than 15 months later, however, Patrick and I would still be asking the same questions, and once again we faced a blank response from the CCRC commissioner.

*   *   *

The visits to my parents' home in Manchester increased around this time. My mother and father were both having severe health probems, and the 120 mile-plus round trip at the end of a long, hard week was affecting my own health too. My mother was eventually taken back into hospital for more tests, as she had great difficulty eating. I hoped she would soon recover and regain her strength. It was not to be. Following a brief spell in North Manchester Hospital, she died suddenly.

As I was recovering from the family tragedy, I heard that, completely out of the blue, Steven Martin had contacted Stephen Downing – nearly four years after I'd met with Crabby, who had first mentioned this elusive nephew. And it was now more than two years since Rodney Jones claimed Martin had raised serious doubts about Mr Red's alibi in 1979 but then vanished shortly afterwards.

Martin claimed he didn't know he was on any missing persons list, as he'd been travelling the world. He returned to the UK in 1999, and when he re-applied for a new driving licence his name was highlighted by the authorities as a person of interest. His details were then forwarded to the CCRC.

He was happy to confirm many of the details told by Jones. He then gave a statement in support of Stephen and also wrote to him in prison. His letter confirmed:

```
I have recently been approached by the Criminal
Cases Review Commission who I'm sure you are aware
are reviewing your case. I gave some information
22 years ago. I wasn't aware that it related to
your case until a police inspector came to visit
me. He impressed on me at the time how convinced
he was that you have been serving time for someone
else's offence.
```

During the early part of 2000 I was travelling to Manchester and back most weekends to visit my father, who now resided in a care home in south Manchester. I spent time reading to him or updating him on developments about the case. My mother's unexpected death had broken his heart, and one day I received an urgent call from my brother to say our father too had died very suddenly. This was just a few days after my last visit, when he had looked and seemed much better and, according to staff at the home, he had even joined in with another resident's birthday party the night before and had a little dance.

Within 12 months I had lost not only my parents, but two of my best friends and most ardent supporters. The shock of losing them both hit me very hard. For several weeks I was a total wreck. My own health had deteriorated, and I hardly had the strength to continue. I found it hard to concentrate on anything and had to take some time off work. It was a huge shock.

My dad was always interested in my work and particularly the Downing case, and during each visit he always wanted to know the latest news. My life seemed so empty with no parents to call for a catch-up. My family rallied around me, but grief is such a hard thing to bear.

*   *   *

One of the most frustrating aspects about the CCRC's investigation was the speed of their inquiry and their reluctance to accept any fresh evidence provided by a number of key sources.

There was also a constant demand for me to reveal my sources, which of course I refused, as the police had always seemed determined to discover and expose any officers who were helping me with my enquiries.

Quite often, many months after submitting paperwork they'd

requested, they would ask me to supply the same details again, claiming they had not seen them before.

Barry Capon also caused much frustration and criticism within the media by falsely promising to me and others that the Downing decision would be taken in June, July, August and then eventually September.

He also told the MP Patrick McLoughlin and the BBC that he would not be looking into the possibility that others may be responsible.

If that was his policy, I queried, why then were he and his team still looking into that precise aspect? He was still hounding me for more facts about certain individuals, and he was still interviewing potential suspects and their associates.

This new and unexpected area of investigation intrigued a whole new section of supporters and added more credibility to Downing's claims of innocence.

I was pleased the commissioner had at least taken note of some strange anomalies within this case, yet I remained concerned at his failure to understand several other important factors. Indeed, when he wrote to me following reports in the *Mail on Sunday* and *The Times*, he claimed it was 'news to him'.

I replied stating that he should have been aware of the information in the reports, as he and his colleagues had been told about them on at least three previous occasions, and I even included copies of earlier correspondence to corroborate these facts. My junior reporters were better acquainted with the facts than he was.

Part of the fresh evidence now included a compelling statement from Rodney Jones and his own key witness Steven Martin, along with Jayne Atkins and other local informants.

Several potentially important witnesses approached me first, and by arrangement I forwarded their details to the CCRC to provide direct and untainted evidence. One witness was a local woman whose mother was a good friend of Wendy Sewell. She claimed her mother said that 'Wendy always had an eye for the men', and recalled that on the day of the attack Wendy appeared bubbly and quite happy.

She said she was not frightened of anything and was definitely 'on her way to meet someone she knew on the day she was attacked'. She also confirmed Wendy was in a hurry, and said that afternoon when her mother heard about the attack she had tried to tell the police – but said they were not interested.

Her new witness statement confirmed, 'Wendy was happy – and I thought that maybe she wanted to put right an argument. She was definitely not in fear of anyone and was looking forward to the meeting.'

Her statement again confirmed my theory that Wendy did have a pre-arranged meeting with someone she knew. This may also have been the man who visited Wendy's office in Bakewell earlier that day, as reported by her boss, John Osmaston.

A second witness also came forward at a much later stage and gave his evidence to the CCRC. He was a relative of the one of the workmen present that day with Downing who had seen Wendy staggering among the gravestones.

He claimed, 'The workmen watched as the young woman staggered to her feet on the gravestones, tottered and then fell heavily, banging her head against a gravestone.'

He said his relative criticised his fellow workmen for not trying to help her, and watched as Wendy moved, waving her arms about in panic and trying to prevent anyone from helping her. He said they later regretted their actions, believing that if an ambulance had been sought immediately Wendy might still be alive today.

* * *

Following my debates with the CCRC, Syd Oulsnam – a vital witness but not a suspect, in my opinion – claimed to Commissioner Barry Capon that he had never spoken to me. Capon queried this with me, even though I had sent details of all my phone calls and meetings with Oulsnam to him.

I said if I had never spoken to him, why had he reported me to the police in 1995, along with a couple of other journalists, for harassment, even though he had actually phoned me?

Capon also challenged me about the claim that Wendy Sewell had no children. He said it was stated at trial that the Sewells had no children. I told him that I had made that very same point in 1995. She did have a child, but it was out of wedlock. The father of the child was not David Sewell, but was said to be local man John Marshall, with whom she had had an affair. Capon remained unconvinced and demanded I produce a birth certificate.

I then contacted one of my correspondents in Bakewell. She was of a similar age to Wendy at the time of her murder, and by sheer coincidence she had been in the same maternity ward in the local Cottage Hospital just a few weeks after her, when she had her own baby.

She was friendly with Wendy, and also knew her mother. In such a small town it was impossible to keep secrets. Their babies were delivered by the same midwife. She gave me enough detail to warrant a trip to Bakewell register office, and within minutes I was able to obtain a copy of the birth certificate, which contained no mention of the father.

I quickly faxed the birth certificate to Barry Capon. I also sent him a brief letter, and tried to avoid any sarcasm when I added, 'Please find one birth certificate for Wendy's child – out of wedlock – as promised. I trust this will be sufficient to prove at least one affair?'

*   *   *

A short time later I received another unexpected call from Syd Oulsnam. I had not spoken to him for several years, since he had phoned me in a panic about DNA evidence. He claimed he had just received a letter from Barry Capon, stating that I had given evidence against him. In all my dealings with the authorities I had always assumed and been assured of anonymity and confidentiality. Now it appeared my evidence had been leaked to an associate of a potential suspect.

I hastily agreed to meet him. I took along young Marcus Edwards, just in case there was any funny business. Oulsnam was waiting in his van. He finally admitted to the CCRC that, as I had already confirmed, he had been driving his van on the day of the attack and parked on the waste land at Burton Edge, near the back of the cemetery … but now he was changing the story as told to me in 1995 big time, claiming he was alone and not with Mr Red.

Ever since his first phone call to me, Oulsnam had told police he had never been anywhere near the cemetery that day, let alone given Mr Red a lift there. In his original police statement in 1973 he also denied being anywhere near Bakewell, so this was further proof of his deception.

When I asked him if Wendy was Mr Red's girlfriend, he replied, 'No, that was all finished a couple of years before.' I knew that previously he'd told police that they had never had a relationship – so here again was another blatant lie. Oulsnam did confirm that Mr Red had been interviewed several times about this murder and another.

He also told me he had copied the letter from the CCRC and given it to Mr Red. I thought, *Thanks, Barry Capon – advance notice to two key individuals.* It was a real spoke in the wheels of justice. Oulsnam took pleasure in showing me the letter from the CCRC. I was staggered and could hardly believe my eyes.

Oulsnam then made a rather unusual comment, quite out of the blue, about Mr Orange. He told me Mr Orange and Mr Red had been at school together. He said they had been friends. It was a fact that I already knew, but I couldn't help wondering if he was trying to deflect some blame onto Mr Orange, or trying to deliberately implicate him in some way.

The following day I complained to my union, the National Union of Journalists (NUJ). They were equally horrified by the possible consequences of Capon's action in blowing my cover. He had been made aware of previous threats to my life, yet here he was writing to all and sundry, saying I had given evidence against them.

On 25 August I wrote a letter to Capon setting out my concerns, expressing fears for my personal safety and that of my colleagues.

At first he seemed to ignore my main complaint and simply replied:

```
I appreciate and understand why you are reluctant
to reveal your sources within the police force.

    However, I wonder if you would be able to speak
to each of the officers concerned to ask them if
they are willing to contact me. Their approaches
will be treated in confidence. When you have done
that could you please tell me and let me know how
many officers you have spoken to.
```

This continual implication that I was somehow obstructing their investigation was coupled with a similar warning from the police that I was not helping Stephen's case or myself by failing to reveal the names of my informants. For good measure they would often drop a hint that obstruction could warrant a two-year stretch inside. It was a risk I was prepared to take.

I knew my police informants were as determined as me to put right a wrong, and I would do whatever I could to protect them. Their threats were like a red rag to a bull and inspired me even more in my efforts to get to the truth.

Eventually, I received a somewhat half-hearted apology from Barry Capon, in which he remained oblivious to any potential dangers.

I should perhaps say in response to your protest that I had always assumed that what you were telling me was available for me to use in any further enquiries.

I have mentioned your name to others whom you say told you that they have changed their evidence over the years, since I believed that by doing so they might be willing to confirm to me, rather than deny it, not knowing that I had been told otherwise by you.

As you will appreciate, I need to hear it from them and not as hearsay from you. It was never my intention to put you in any danger or difficulty, and I apologise if you feel this has happened.

* * *

In the middle of June 2000, after four years and many tens of thousands of pounds, the European Court finally announced a legal landmark ruling confirming that Stephen, and indeed any other prisoner throughout the UK, who was in denial of an offence was entitled to an oral hearing with the Parole Board. It was an extraordinary legal victory spearheaded by Stephen's QC

Ed Fitzgerald, and a huge embarrassment for the British government.

The ruling ended decades of legal absurdity. I had twice before attended the Board hearings on Stephen's behalf to present his case. On other occasions it was left to his legal representatives to provide support details.

It had all been nonsense and a complete waste of time, because although his prison records often told of his good behaviour and even called him a 'model prisoner' at times, he was always refused access to the Board due to his continual denial of his offence, which meant he and many others like him were considered too dangerous to be released simply because they refused to admit to something they hadn't done.

The ruling would still need to be implemented in British law, but to help compensate for his trauma over the years Stephen was awarded an out-of-court payment of 500 euros, plus costs. It was a surprise yet welcome result, which eventually proved the spark to light the political and legal touch-paper. In addition, it finally woke up the national press and boosted his appeal process.

My visits to the Downing household had become less frequent, but we still kept in touch several times a week by telephone. Stephen also phoned them as often as he could for any direct updates, as everyone was on tenterhooks as the provisional date approached for the CCRC to make their decision.

The day before the scheduled announcement I went to see Ray and Nita to talk through what was likely to happen. None of us dared contemplate another rejection, but following my contact with Barry Capon, the police and Stephen's legal team, I felt confident of at least getting a referral.

I was still working flat out with the CCRC, right up to the last few days, and answering query after query that had already been answered before, which would probably make little or no difference to the outcome, but this organisation was very picky and particular, and always needed a couple more examples of hard evidence from my key sources.

Nita shook like a leaf as she tried to pour out the tea and had to ask Ray for help. 'I just can't settle,' she said. 'My nerves are shot. Every time that blessed phone rings I don't know if it will be Stephen, the press or some government official with news.'

Ray too looked shaky. He said he'd had to step up his tablets for a range of medical problems and had cancelled some taxi bookings so he could be on hand.

They kept asking for my opinion, but I could only explain what I knew. I didn't know for certain when precisely or how the decision from the CCRC would be announced. 'Look, I will let you know as soon as I hear – and will you do the same, please?' I asked the pair. 'You might hear before me, or at least Stephen could be informed first. He should be told first, out of common decency.'

They both stood up and gave me a huge hug. Tears were streaming down Nita's face, and Ray was also very emotional. 'Thanks for everything Don,' Ray said as I headed for the back door.

'No problem, but it's not over yet, Ray. Let's remain optimistic and just keep our fingers crossed.'

On 13 June 2000 I ran a headline in the *Matlock Mercury* outlining the latest episode of this ongoing soap saga – ANXIOUS WAIT FOR DOWNING'S PARENTS – and I provided a detailed update on developments.

* * *

By now the case was attracting unprecedented publicity. Daniel McGrory wrote again in *The Times* – almost two years after his original report – that Downing's case was one of the great miscarriages of justice of the century. His article sparked an immediate media frenzy. Much of the blame for the delay in announcing the decision was directed towards Barry Capon, who perhaps had misled the media pack once too often.

National newspapers like the *Daily Express*, the *Independent*, the *Guardian* and *Mail on Sunday* published pieces, though the labelling of the victim in some corners of the national media as the Bakewell Tart certainly wasn't to a lot of people's taste, mine included. I hated the label, which had nothing to do with me, though I took plenty of stick for it anyway. It was easier for the national media to use a label like that when they didn't have to live locally.

Television wasn't to be left out of the national coverage, with *Channel 4 News* visiting the *Mercury* offices and the scene of crime during late August and broadcasting a report on the case. And interest wasn't just confined to these shores. TV crews from all over the globe were now contacting our offices for updates.

Stephen welcomed the attention, and there was some optimism in his correspondence, even if his experiences meant his outlook was firmly grounded in a weary kind of realism.

29 August 2000

Dear Don,

As you can imagine, I am well pleased with all the publicity and have nothing but support from all the inmates. I would like camera crews to go to Jack Straw and ask him what he proposes to do. I am sure that being put in such a compromising situation will force him to make a positive move or face severe ridicule.

> I have written to my solicitor about my mail
> being delayed. One letter postmarked 4 August was
> not given to me until 22 August. I have made
> efforts to complain but my applications have been
> returned by the same member of staff.
>
> I understand you are making good headway
> with your own investigations. I also hear you
> uncovered details of the love child's birth
> certificate. I now understand it is likely to be
> October before the CCRC make their decision, but
> you only have to look back to them saying it would
> be July. I take little notice of such empty
> promises.
>
> I want to propose release on licence and
> consideration of transfer to open conditions as an
> alternative. I am still no closer to getting my
> own computer for legal and educational studies but
> hope the solicitor will be granted legal aid to
> take a judicial review against the prison.
>
> Best wishes, Stephen Downing

The period of wait was hard to bear. Both my office and mobile phone rang continuously from nearly every national in the country, and from abroad.

It was almost impossible to phone out as there were so many inward calls, much to the disgust of my advertising staff, who were struggling to collect their copy. It seemed everyone now wanted a slice of the drama – and exclusive interviews with either me or the Downing family.

At times it felt hard to think or breathe with all this constant attention, and amidst all this chaos my team and I still had to turn out a newspaper.

Genuine visitors to the office had to fight their way through a pack of journalists, who were trying to hang onto every word that anyone said. It was sheer bedlam for days on end.

*　　*　　*

Having endured an interminable and frustrating wait for the CCRC to finally address Stephen's case, and having applied as much pressure as I was able to through the *Mercury* and the national media, not to mention the help of the likes of MP Patrick McLoughlin, who once again applied pressure in Parliament, it looked like a new date was now on the cards, as Stephen confirmed in his letter to me.

19 October 2000

I had a letter today from my solicitor who tells me the CCRC have set 13 November to preside over my case. Barry Capon said they may come to a decision or they could call for further disclosures of documents or investigations. One can only wait and see what the outcome will be.

I couldn't call Stephen, and many of his calls out of prison were blocked. He was on lock-down for much of the time and not allowed to communicate with anyone, as they didn't want him talking to the press. From quick chats to his parents I understood that he was only allowed the odd very brief call home – which was closely monitored – but he spent much of his time waiting frustratingly in his cell, with his bags packed, just in case of any immediate release.

CHAPTER 27

THE LONGEST DAY

Monday, 13 November 2000 was one of the longest days I have ever known. And, once again, it was to bring disappointment.

I made several calls to the CCRC's press office in Birmingham throughout the day, and my phone never stopped ringing with other media enquiries. It seemed the world was waiting for this crucial announcement.

However, after many painstaking hours of waiting and pacing the floor, I was finally told that the decision wouldn't be confirmed until the following day – as the CCRC needed to advise the victim's relatives first.

Throughout this lengthy legal process the CCRC had shown little or no regard for the thoughts and feelings of Stephen and his family and supporters, and now they conveniently used this latest shield as a further excuse for delays. I'd found it frustrating that when Jack Straw was the shadow Home Secretary he and his team were supportive of open government and critical of Tory Home Secretary Michael Howard over this issue. One of his team had even said they would 'move heaven and earth to force an investigation of his case'. But with Labour in power it had been the same red tape and bureaucracy. The CCRC had spent over three and a half years looking at the facts and now they needed yet more time?

We were advised that the decision would be made at 3 p.m. the following day. Surely they couldn't let us all down again.

The next day was incredible. Dozens of specialist camper-van-type vehicles carrying the very latest satellite dishes and hi-tech equipment lined Firs Parade in Matlock, adjacent to the new *Mercury* offices. Our phones rang and rang. Sky News arrived, then the BBC and ITN. All the main players were camped in our small, first-floor editorial office.

I had no idea how or when the announcement would be made. All I could do was sit and wait. It was hard to resist telling the reception staff not to put through any unnecessary calls. I was waiting for the most important call of my life.

The office crackled with nervous anticipation. We jumped every time the phone rang. No one could concentrate. Talk was very strained. It felt like the clock had stopped: 2.30 p.m. came, 2.40, and still nothing. Who was going to tell me about the decision? I fully expected Barry Capon to make contact, or perhaps Downing's legal team.

Stephen was waiting at Littlehey. He had been packed and ready for a couple of days in case they let him go straight away. I doubted that, as I was convinced he would still need a bail hearing – unless the Home Secretary intervened to allow his release on licence.

At 2.58 my phone rang. It was Patrick McLoughlin. He was almost breathless as he asked, 'Have you heard the decision?'

'No, Patrick,' I replied, puzzled. 'They said I would be notified by 3, and probably by fax.'

I was hoping he wouldn't block the line in case the commissioner was trying to get through and, at first, I didn't realise he already knew the decision.

'You've done it!' he exclaimed. 'You must be so pleased. Downing's case is to be referred to the Court of Appeal. Go to the fax and you should have the official press release any moment.'

He may have said something else. I can't quite remember. He was ecstatic – and I was too, even if my mind had gone blank. All the TV cameras had recorded the call and my reaction. I felt shattered and emotionally drained. All these years of hard work had finally proved worthwhile.

There was a tear in my eye as I read the official statement, words that I had hoped and dreamed to say one day, but never dared indulge them too much. But here they were at last: 'The Criminal Cases Review Commission has referred the conviction of Mr Stephen Leslie Downing to the Court of Appeal.' It felt so good to say them aloud.

As much as my team and I were celebrating the news of Stephen's referral back to the Court of Appeal, along with what seemed like most of the world's press, I wondered if, when or how he had been given the news.

As crazy as it might seem, I was blocked by the authorities from visiting Stephen or having any direct verbal communication with him. All his calls were made to his parents' home in Bakewell, so it was several days, perhaps even a week later, before I eventually learned of his reaction from his parents.

From what they told me, it seems Stephen had been marched down to a senior screw's office by two prison officers, who implied he was in trouble.

He had heard the echoing footsteps along the empty corridor long before realising they were heading for his cell. Two well-built warders entered and escorted him after an exhausting day at work.

All the way, he wondered what he had done wrong, and in silence he hastily tucked his shirt in and made himself look respectable. It was a worrying and seemingly endless march through a series of locked gates before he finally reached his destination.

The senior screw surprisingly welcomed Stephen and quickly dismissed his military-style escort, later telling him they were old school and that unfortunately he had inherited them. The talk was that this officer was one of a new breed of fast-track senior men with Home Office experience.

He told Stephen he had read his file before saying, 'You have been in prison for over 25 years for a murder you didn't commit – a young woman in your home town?'

Stephen told him, 'Yes, sir. I didn't do it!'

The officer then explained that many others now shared his belief, and that it was the governor who had asked him to speak with him. He asked Downing if he knew that the CCRC had been studying his file.

'Yes, sir, for several years now,' he replied.

'Quite,' he acknowledged. He then grabbed a large brown envelope from his desk and handed it to Stephen, telling him, 'This could change your life. Take it back to your cell, read it carefully and your solicitor will be in touch very soon.'

He added that he thought someone was probably pulling strings for him at the highest level, and indicated that he was becoming an embarrassment in the prison system.

Ray told me that Stephen's evening meal was waiting for him on a metal tray when he arrived back to his cell. He said that although he ignored his food, he tried to put his brain into gear.

The more Stephen considered the conversation with the senior officer, the more his head spun. He suddenly felt very heavy. He was completely exhausted.

Stephen's mind wandered as he recalled his career as a backward 17-year-old working his way through some of Britain's toughest establishments. The years of anguish and torment had certainly taken their toll, and at the age of 43 he now looked about 10 years older. He was stocky and overweight, and he suffered with stress, angina and nerves. He had spent practically all his life in one institution or another.

Stephen kept remembering his trial, and the steep steps up from the dark, damp former death cell under the dock at Nottingham Crown Court. Many others had made that same journey before facing a last dance at the end of a rope. Downing knew that if he had been convicted of that murder just a few years earlier, he too might have seen the judge put on that fearsome black cap.

The expectation was almost overwhelming. He felt cold and wet from sweating. He pushed his food tray aside and studied the large brown envelope. It was labelled 'Private and Confidential', with his name, prison number and current detention address.

Stephen opened it very slowly and very carefully but with trepidation. He knew it was now or never. He didn't want to contemplate losing again – and spending the rest of his life behind bars for something he hadn't done.

His father, Ray, admitted he was concerned for Stephen and wondered if he could survive another rejection and potential humiliation. Stephen's hands shook as he opened the document and pulled out the contents. He knew he was the longest serving prisoner detained at Her Majesty's Pleasure.

There was a brief letter addressed to him from his solicitor and the CCRC. He quickly read it but struggled to understand its true meaning. It mentioned a report, attached. He pulled at the paperclip and hastily thumbed through the paperwork.

After reading the final pages, 'Conclusion and Recommendation', he stared back at them again and again. It seemed so unbelievable after all this time that his case was finally to be referred back to the Court of Appeal.

Following a chat many years later, Stephen tried to recall this historic moment. 'I can't remember all the exact details, but I know I was shocked when I realised my referral had finally been granted, as it could have gone either way. Obviously, it was very pleasing to know that it did go the right way.

'I remember sharing my letter with some mates in prison. Quite a few had been backing me, and we were all really happy with the outcome – but I think I was far happier than they were! I was just so thrilled to receive some good news for a change after all those years.'

*   *   *

On Wednesday, 15 November 2000, the day after the decision, practically every national newspaper in Britain ran the news of Stephen Downing's referral on their front pages – with many more continuing for days afterwards until the Sunday papers came out, and then it all began again.

Derbyshire police, for once, had very little to say. A police spokesman said the force would have to consider reopening the murder case if the appeal found Stephen was not responsible for Wendy Sewell's murder. He added, 'We can't discuss evidence in public, although others can. It's all subject to the appeal.'

As I'd found throughout this campaign, it was easy to forget there was another victim in this case who was unable to defend herself, and on 16 November I received a letter from someone in Ontario, Canada, who provided a timely reminder.

Malcolm Benyon was Wendy's cousin. I was moved by his sentiments. He spoke of her as a 'young, fun-loving person'. He said her parents loved her and were very proud of her, saying she had no brothers or sisters to defend her. Although he praised my tenacity and the faith of the Downing family, he was angered by some national press headlines and believed Wendy could have been saved if help had been called sooner.

CHAPTER 28

FACE TO FACE AGAIN

With the case now referred back to the Court of Appeal, there was still one pressing question to address: when would Stephen return back home to his family? The Downing family and poor Stephen remained in limbo. We all knew he was still on standby, and I hoped that for once the Home Office would show some respect and sympathy and allow him out on leave at least.

On 26 November I went to see Stephen in prison at Littlehey. I wanted to see him face to face again, without the need for any censorship.

At first the prison refused my visiting order – but then suddenly rescinded their decision. I was told it was the governor's last week or so.

Over the past few weeks I had been working closely with a number of major newspapers and had helped negotiate a deal for Stephen's parents to receive some payment for exclusive interviews. It helped towards their campaign costs over the years.

As I had been working quite closely with journo friend Nick Pryer from the *Mail on Sunday*, and knew that he wanted to meet Stephen, I included his name on the application. No one apart from me, Stephen's family and a few close friends had ever seen or spoken with him in jail.

I think I must have provided the only opportunity to see Stephen in prison, as I am sure that any direct application for a press interview would have been rejected. He was still on lockdown for much of this time, but as I had seen him several times before the prison knew about my role in his appeal with the CCRC.

Nick wanted to try to obtain a new and exclusive photograph inside, together with a taped interview in which he could record Stephen's thoughts and feelings following the referral. He put a very small and discreet camera in his pocket, in addition to a miniature tape recorder.

I was waved through security at the prison, and when I said that Nick was with me he too was allowed through the gates. We had our visiting orders stamped and underwent a very basic search, putting our valuables into a small tray. Within a few moments we were taken through to the visiting area. We had been given a table at the far end of the room, well away from anyone else. No guard was allocated.

Stephen entered with a broad smile, but he looked pale and drawn and was obviously stressed. We all shook hands and I introduced him to Nick, and explained what he intended to do. He had been made aware of some things from his parents during a rushed visit and calls home, including a special deal with the *Mail on Sunday* that would benefit his parents.

Initially, we spoke about all sorts of things, including how he had coped over the past few weeks, the problems he had had phoning out, and the fact that the prison had put him on standby with all his belongings packed and ready to go.

Stephen said, 'It seems strange, but for years I have not had to worry about any clothes. My mother told me that I needed to buy a suit, as I will have to appear in court and can't just turn up in jeans and a T-shirt. I have been looking through a mail-order catalogue and have decided to order a few bits and pieces from there. We are allowed to do this and there is no other way to get clothes.

'All my other gear is either too old or too small,' he explained, poking his stomach. 'It was nearly 30 years ago when I came in, so I have changed a bit since then. Nothing will fit me now.

'When they gave me all my belongings, ready to leave, I had forgotten about all this stuff and much has remained in store ever since. It always accompanies me, though, whenever I move.'

I think Nick was surprised by how well he looked. I had mentioned some of my previous visits, and my letters and calls, and told him about some difficult times. Stephen was pleased to see us and eager to face a new chapter in his life. However, I think he had been deceived slightly by all the talk of an imminent release, and I explained about the long legal battle, the Euro ruling and the probability that it would still take some time to gain his official release.

He mentioned a brief visit from his legal team following the referral and admitted that they too thought he would have to remain in prison until at least the appeal. He said they felt optimistic of getting a bail hearing as soon as possible, but obtaining a quick hearing would be difficult.

Stephen then told Nick about his hopes and ambitions for when he was eventually released – his plans to learn to drive, buy a car, get a job, a house and even a girlfriend, things that had been denied to him since being detained.

Nick and I had been a little nervous about trying to record the conversation, and especially about taking a photograph. We had been there for over an hour and now our time was running out. I could see that the room was plastered with CCTV cameras and warned Nick that it looked impossible to take a photograph without being seen. He was under orders, though, and decided to give it a go.

The first couple of shots went well, but as he adjusted the small device it suddenly flashed, causing a huge stir in the room.

The noise and bedlam in the room stopped and it all went extremely quiet, though not outside the room, where the alarm system had been triggered. Within seconds prison officers were dashing about shouting orders.

A couple of prison officers quickly came across to our table and poor Stephen was led away. We were asked to stand to one side while the other visitors were ushered out and the prisoners were returned to their cells.

Next, a rather furious security chief arrived with a couple more officers who had replayed the source of the flash on CCTV. We faced a barrage of questions and were told the camera would be confiscated. We were warned in no uncertain terms that we would both be banned from any future visits, and we were almost forcibly escorted out. I thought, *Cheers, Nick. Many years of hard work and diplomacy up the spout.*

Nick gave a grin as we finally exited the prison. 'It was a shame losing the camera,' he said, 'but well worth a try.' He was quite nonchalant about the whole episode. I still had the security chief's angry outburst ringing in my ears and was not too pleased to say the least.

After we chatted in the car park, I headed back to Matlock and Nick to London. I pondered that at least he had met Stephen face to face for the first time, and even escaped with a long, secret and recorded exclusive interview. I thought two out of three wasn't bad and celebrated a major scoop.

*   *   *

On 28 November 2000 Prime Minister Tony Blair became involved in proceedings, responding to Patrick McLoughlin's pressure about the timing of the appeal and the question of bail. He said it was a matter for the courts to address.

As December came round, however, it became clear that Stephen might not even be considered for release until after Christmas unless the media pressure was increased.

8 December 2000

Dear Don,

This is just a personal note of thanks for all the support you have given me and my family over the last 12 months, and at times when you have put aside your own problems. I don't know who would have devoted so much time to a campaign as you have, and I should like to extend my note of gratitude to your long-suffering family for their understanding.

I hope that we have at last come to the end of what has seemed a neverending journey. I would like you and your family to enjoy the best Christmas you have ever had, and I hope the coming New Year holds lots of joy and happiness. With warmest best wishes

Stephen Downing

I ran with the emotional *Mercury* headline PLEASE LET MY SON GO, highlighting Nita Downing's plea that he be home soon. With almost constant tears in her eyes, she would ask me when he was coming home.

It was an impossible question to answer. I was trying to secure his release under any possible guise. I had made moves via the Parole Board, European Court and High Court. The most likely method now seemed to be with a bail hearing at the High Court – and this was now the course I was particularly pushing.

The bail terms were confirmed to the Downing family prior to the hearing. The family were to guarantee the ridiculous sum of £5,000, which seemed another totally unnecessary move. The Downings were not well-versed in the protocol around bail – how many of us can say we are? – so there was utter confusion at Bakewell police station when they tried to hand over a bag full of cash, only to be told they just needed to sign a bond guarantee.

A date was finally set for the bail hearing. It would be heard in the High Court in London on 15 December. At least Stephen would be home for Christmas – his first at home with his family in Bakewell for nearly three decades.

*   *   *

Once again, Stephen's bags were packed and he was ready to go. His belongings from nearly three decades of confinement were stuffed into black bin liners and whatever cardboard boxes he could find.

The first sign of trouble came at the court itself when some BBC reporters told me it was a closed hearing. It seemed the press were not allowed to witness this latest débâcle and were refused entry into court. I was furious.

It seemed nothing could be done, but after all these years of fighting I had other ideas. There was a notice posted outside court confirming it was an open hearing, and both the Crown Prosecution Service (CPS) and High Court officials had confirmed the very same thing just the day before, so I believed if it had been listed as being open then it should remain so – what did the authorities have to hide?

The red mist descended, and I suddenly felt extraordinarily brave and confident. I strode through the saloon-type doors into the court and marched towards the bench with a copy of the court notice screwed up in my hand.

I rather cheekily asked the judge what was happening, and I explained that the bail hearing had been listed as open and it should remain open. I said that I had come a long way to listen to the legal argument and dozens of press people were clamouring to know just what was what.

This manner of confrontation was no doubt unheard of, but I had to know the reasons for this U-turn. Stephen's legal team flapped and fussed and tried to push me out. But I was really angry and my patience had been stretched to its limit.

'This is totally unacceptable,' I said to the judge. I waved my paperwork at him again. 'This court should not be closed to the press!' I rarely lost my temper, but this was a ridiculous decision and I wanted to know the reason.

The judge listened carefully. He was embarrassed as he said, 'Give me a few minutes, Mr Hale. I wish to consult with counsel.' He must have recognised my face from the media coverage. I stormed out of court.

The world's press waited outside in the corridor asking question after question. My head was spinning. Some of them had peeked through a half-open door, and one TV presenter told his colleagues that I had just shouted at the judge, which was not quite true, but it gave me a bit of kudos for a few moments as journalists started to shake my hand and pat me on the back.

An usher finally appeared. He gave me a glare in disbelief at what had just happened and called me forward. As I entered the High Court again, an official now confirmed that the media could come in.

There was a massive buzz of excitement and anticipation then as dozens of reporters tried to pack into the small gallery and the ever so tiny press bench. It was a very old-fashioned court and any creak of the door or movement on the benches made it virtually impossible to hear the proceedings.

Stephen's barrister Edward Fitzgerald QC outlined some compelling arguments for the defence and was on his feet for about 20 minutes. This was followed by an immediate and sudden silence. You could have heard a pin drop as we waited. The atmosphere was electric as we awaited with anticipation for a response from the Crown Prosecutor, Julian Bevan.

The theatre in which these events played out resembled an incredible star-studded occasion, yet this was no stage play – it was genuine, real-life drama. Julian Bevan finally rose to his feet, with reporters poised to record his every word.

What he said, however, was quite bizarre, and it created a most unexpected anticlimax to proceedings. He referred to critical sections of Stephen's barrister's claims, but then said he had only had the bail application for about ten days and had not had time to read it.

He also said he was about to go on holiday – that very day, in fact – and so would be unable to form an opinion as to whether the CPS should oppose bail. There was another stunned silence, and then lots of excited chatter. Everyone looked at each other in total disbelief. Journalists checked to clarify his remarks.

We all sat and waited for the judge to lash out. People were repeating his comments – 'not read the paperwork', 'hadn't realised the urgency', 'he was in a rush to go on holiday'? It all seemed so incredibly surreal.

I wondered if the world had gone completely mad. Surely this should have been sorted out much earlier without the need for everyone to attend court. I now realised why the prosecution didn't want the press inside.

We waited for the judge to throw the book at Julian Bevan, who kept fumbling with his notes, as if to keep his head deliberately bowed, and looked for some way out of his predicament.

The judge, however, in a very matter-of-fact motion, merely nodded to the QC and agreed that if Mr Bevan had not had time to read the paperwork and to form an opinion, they must take the view of opposing bail. He was granted a further month to study the file and the application was refused. Goodnight, Vienna!

*　　*　　*

I borrowed a mobile phone and tried to call my wife and the Downing family in Bakewell. Both lines were busy. I could hardly breathe. Exiting the court was like trying to walk against a football crowd.

Questions were being fired at me from all directions. I didn't have the answers. I was hoping someone else could explain. I was told that more media people were waiting outside, and I was then swept along the narrow corridors by the mob, down the stairway and out towards the bright daylight to face the madding crowd.

As I approached the main door there were hundreds of people waiting to hear what I had to say. I thought it was all part of a very vivid dream, and I would soon wake up. I was waved forward and then a barrage of questions started.

Twenty or thirty people were firing questions at me at the same time. They were like a swarm of bees – I could hardly hear what they were asking. I was in complete shock, but I tried to gather my thoughts and reminded myself not to swear or curse in pure frustration at what had just happened.

This was my time to speak out and tell the world's media what I thought – to say what needed to be said.

I asked the British government to act quickly. I wanted someone to urgently intervene. I said I hoped Tony Blair and his family, and the QC Julian Bevan on his holiday island, would remember Stephen Downing while they enjoyed Christmas with their own families. While they would be living a life of luxury, poor Stephen Downing would remain in jail, eating cold turkey on a plastic tray on his own.

The message hit home. My comments were screened and repeated throughout the world. Patrick McLoughlin also spoke and seemed just as furious as I was. He said it was ridiculous, and he was determined to find out what had gone wrong. He stormed off towards Parliament with a pledge to raise the matter that very day at Prime Minister's Question Time.

It was eventually debated in a packed Commons and equally packed gallery, where I watched the proceedings and heard Tony Blair mention my name, some details about the campaign and admit that he shared the MP's concern.

Various TV news teams dragged me first one way, and then the other to give five-minute briefings. The varied broadcasts kept going back and forth to the bleak scene at Littlehey prison, where yet another media pack had been waiting hopefully to see Stephen Downing released.

I somehow managed to grab a cup of lukewarm tea from a paper cup before I was whizzed away by taxi first to Millbank and then on to the BBC headquarters for another marathon round of TV, local radio and interviews, and then onwards again. I trailed up and down stairs, into numerous studios, along endless corridors. I did interviews with people in places as far afield as Pakistan, Hong Kong, Japan and Australia. It was a whirlwind day – and indeed a whirlwind period.

I returned home mentally and physically shattered. I most certainly did not feel like getting up early the next morning to sort out all the main stories for next week's *Mercury*, and to edit the results and league tables from the local darts and dominoes league.

CHAPTER 29

WELCOME HOME

At Littlehey Prison, as Stephen Downing now faced up to his twenty-seventh Christmas behind bars for a crime he did not commit, the prosecutor who had opposed his freedom on bail was now preparing to celebrate and enjoy the festive season in the warmth of the African sun.

Julian Bevan was tracked down by the press to his chambers after the unsuccessful bail hearing. He told the media, 'I am flying out tonight to Kenya. My son is getting married. I have been going for some time.'

He said he had been unable to take in all the details of the case in time for the early-morning hearing, and responded, 'Have you tried to read *War and Peace*? You couldn't have assimilated all the information. It's nine inches high. If a brief is 3 pages, not a problem. It's not 3 pages – it's probably 300 pages.'

A spokesman for the Crown Prosecution Service eventually gave the official explanation: 'A letter addressed to Mr Bevan was sent to his chambers when he was in court, and it was not opened by his clerk. It wasn't until 4.30 p.m. the next day that he received a call from the defence asking to discuss the bail application. He said, "What bail application?" and was told there was to be one at 9.15 the next morning. It was not his fault. Everyone deserves a holiday.'

It seemed to me that Stephen Downing was also long overdue a holiday. He was emotionally shattered and, although his bags were packed, he had to prepare to spend at least another few nights in Littlehey Prison. He told me, 'We're used to setbacks, but this is heartbreaking. I'll be thinking of my family at Christmas – and I'm sure they'll be thinking of me.'

Ray and Nita were in shock. They couldn't believe the outcome of this legal pantomime. The following weekend they travelled the three hours again cross-country to see Stephen in prison, much as they had done for the past three decades.

Ray in particular was very despondent, and explained, 'We've put up with an awful lot over the years, but now we want to know when all this is going to end. We just want to bring him home. I'm 68 now. I can't keep driving hundreds of miles to visit him every fortnight. It's hard to take it after all these years, but we just have to remain positive. I thought we'd be back in Bakewell in our own family home.'

*   *   *

Out of the blue, I was contacted by Granada Television in Manchester and asked if I was available to attend the What the Papers Say TV awards in London just before Christmas. Prizes would be presented by MP and former Tory minister Ann Widdecombe.

The invitation seemed ironic, given how little regard she and her Tory cronies had always shown through Home Office channels to Downing's case. After all, 'there were no innocent people in jail', apparently.

I travelled down to London with Kath and several of my editorial colleagues from the *Mercury*, including Marcus Edwards, firmly in the belief that I was just there for the ride. Many awards came and went, and I was getting fidgety, and even thought about saying to Kath, 'I told you so,' when it came to the very final award, Journalist of the Year.

I could now see all the television cameras, lights and sound booms moving around towards me as the host Clive Anderson read out the nominations.

My name appeared on his autocue. Some of my *Matlock Mercury* stories and controversial headlines now appeared on the large screens scattered about the room. It was an unbelievable feeling as the media attention suddenly focused on my work and my marathon campaign.

It seemed to take him forever to read out some of the dedications. He then confirmed, 'Don Hale waged a lonely and dangerous crusade – without the backing of a Fleet Street organisation ...' and he announced that I was the 2000 Journalist of the Year.

I suddenly felt quite shaky. I had rubber legs. It was unbelievable! It had never been done before. A provincial newspaper had never won a sausage prior to this, with all the plaudits and glory constantly going to the nationals. The atmosphere was incredible. There was a roar from the audience and a standing ovation as I slowly made my way around the packed tables of top journalists. I briefly shook hands with Matthew Parris, *The Times* man and former West Derbyshire MP, on my way up to the podium.

It took several minutes before the applause died down and Anne Widdecombe finally handed me the trophy. She seemed reluctant to let go of my hand as I reminded her that she had once turned Downing down for review. She muttered something back, but like any true politician completely ignored the substance and kept smiling to the cameras.

Later that night Kath and I, together with our team from the *Mercury*, all travelled back together in a taxi to Euston, where we then caught the last train back to Derby. Kath and I had been supplied first-class tickets, while the gang had second-class, but, as we boarded I cheekily asked the train manager if they could join us, as we had just won an award. To my surprise, he knew who I was and what we had achieved, so he waved us all forward to first-class and provided us with free refreshments.

It was a great moment for me personally, and for the paper and the team, but as we headed north on the train it all seemed totally unreal. After all, Stephen was still in jail. And while we would celebrate this night together, tomorrow the campaign would continue. The only award that really mattered was Stephen's freedom.

* * *

Despite all my hopes and efforts for a festive pardon for Stephen, the Christmas deadline came and went.

Back on the mean streets of cold, windswept Bakewell, Stephen Downing's childhood friend Richard Brailsford was enjoying phenomenal success in collecting hundreds upon hundreds of signatures objecting to Downing's bail detention and calling for the government to intervene. The notices also gave fair warning of a town march and rally.

I had arranged with Bakewell Police to hold a short rally on the showground prior to a march through the town. I was offered two local bobbies as escort – just in case – and to ensure public order and safety.

It turned out to be a very bright but cold day with some snow and ice underfoot. One of my escorts that day, a police sergeant, turned out to be the son of my next-door neighbour. A small town indeed.

We had a great turnout considering the conditions, with a few hundred people on site and many more lining the streets. Many participants had travelled from far afield, including a few dozen or more from abroad who had seen the progress of the case on TV.

The huge success of the march surprised the police, who were remarkably understaffed should there have been any problems.

In total we collected over 14,500 signatures within a few days, and as the march went through town we were cheered by residents and fellow supporters. A few days later, by arrangement with Tony Blair, Richard and his children travelled with me by train to London, where we presented the petition at 10 Downing Street.

We agreed to let Richard's youngest James present all the paperwork, and, as he couldn't quite reach the grand door-knocker, we helped him to stretch up while dozens of cameras flashed. It made a wonderful photograph for the papers, keeping the story in the spotlight.

Stephen's mother Nita could hardly believe all the support and publicity after decades of nothing. She kept reminding everyone that Stephen was still in prison, however, and that she wasn't allowed to take anything in for him, despite it being so close to his release.

She told me, 'Stephen has telephoned to tell us he's fine, but he's in prison and, of course, he can't find out what's going on. He's desperate to come home. I know the problems will start when the circus leaves town.'

*　　　*　　　*

Wednesday, 7 February was confirmed as the date for Stephen's new bail hearing at the Court of Appeal. It was brought forward a couple of months due to public pressure, with Tony Blair pledging a special interest.

I was slightly apprehensive about the outcome, as I had not been privy to review Stephen's barrister Edward Fitzgerald's final arguments. I had spoken with Stephen, though, so I knew how he felt. He had no idea about what to expect on the outside, and how the media would hound him.

When I arrived at the High Court the barristers quickly grabbed me. Fitzgerald asked if I would approach the bench to insist on press and public access. I was told to ask for an open hearing.

This time it was an easier request, as both Downing's QC and Crown Prosecutor Julian Bevan QC wanted the press present.

As proceedings commenced, I was pleasantly surprised when Edward Fitzgerald confirmed in his first few sentences that he understood the Crown was not opposing bail. This meant Stephen would be released immediately! After such a long, drawn-out saga, the decision suddenly hit me like a sledgehammer.

Fitzgerald continued setting out the defence case, but I was only half-listening. My mind ran ahead, and some miles down the road, to Stephen at Littlehey, wondering how quickly he could be released.

Fitzgerald reminded the court that at the earlier hearing he had argued there was 'an overwhelming case' that the confession evidence should never have been considered by the jury at Downing's trial.

He said that by applying either the standards of today or those of the time, Stephen's confession should have been totally excluded from the trial. The QC also highlighted a modern-day challenge by experts to the original scene-of-crime forensics analysis.

During the hearing we were also told that Johnson and Younger, two ex-Derbyshire detectives involved with the original police inquiry in 1973, had now provided supporting evidence to the defence during 2000. There was also reference to a plea-bargaining deal for manslaughter at the beginning of the trial, which was rejected by Stephen, as he maintained his innocence.

Fitzgerald said that expert evidence about the bloodstains given at trial had been 'greatly undermined' by a report from a top forensic scientist.

He explained that techniques developed over the past 30-plus years since Wendy Sewell's murder confirmed there was fresh evidence to clarify that small blood spots found on Stephen's clothes may indeed have resulted from Mrs Sewell's exhalations as she lay dying.

He argued that it was only Stephen's refusal to admit his guilt that had kept him in prison for so long.

Although acting for the Crown, Julian Bevan QC was equally critical of Derbyshire police and their actions from 1973.

He conceded, 'I am happy to accept in this case there is a very real possibility that the rights he was entitled to were never brought to his attention. All the indications are they were not.

'Applying present-day standards, the Crown recognises that a failure to inform a prisoner in custody of his rights would be regarded as a serious breach, as, of course, would a failure to caution a suspect at the appropriate moment.'

The court then became exceptionally quiet as we waited for the judge to speak. Mr Justice Pitchford delivered his judgment without any emotion whatsoever, confirming his approval of the bail application, and ordered Downing to be released pending an appeal.

There was a great cheer as the news was announced, and as I left the court I was swept along yet again by a buoyant and enthusiastic mob of journalists. Marcus Edwards, my young reporter, proved invaluable, as we still had to file copy back to the *Mercury* office in time for the next edition.

I was glad to have had a dress rehearsal for meeting the press just a month or so before. It was a daunting and overwhelming experience. This time, though, there was something positive to talk about.

MP Patrick McLoughlin addressed the crowd first, and then I said a few words, followed by the victim's husband David Sewell – who still seemed rather bitter about the campaign and was remarkably still unwilling to accept that the police got it wrong all those years ago.

Prime Minister Tony Blair, however, celebrated the news of Downing's bail success during Question Time in the House of Commons.

He complimented my tireless campaign and the work of the *Matlock Mercury*, and also praised the dedication of the Downing family over the past 27 years.

But I just had one concern now: how and when Downing would be released?

*   *   *

I was in the BBC TV studios late that same afternoon when Stephen finally walked out of prison. Both the presenter and I stopped chatting and watched the proceedings at Littlehey on the TV screen.

My mouth was dry and I could hardly speak. It was just like the closing scene from a TV drama, as the enormous prison doors slowly slid open and Stephen stepped into the glare of the bright sunlight for the first time in many years.

He walked out alone and with dignity in his new catalogue suit. It was a bit like watching a rabbit in the headlights, though.

He looked frightened to death and extremely nervous and unsure. It looked almost like the prison officer had to push him out of the gates.

He only managed a few words of thanks to his family, friends and supporters before he was quickly bundled into a waiting car with a team from the *Mail on Sunday*, including Nick Pryer.

The following day I visited Stephen at home in Bakewell. The press were camped outside – the place was totally besieged.

I had been to their house so many times in the past, but it still came as a huge shock to see Stephen sitting there grinning with a large mug of tea. It was an emotional moment after so many years of effort.

On 15 February the *Mercury*'s front page said WELCOME HOME. I ran an exclusive story of my own, despite all the other media attention, confirming that despite a very busy week Stephen had enjoyed his first ever driving lesson – ironically from a former police officer originally involved in the case.

As the celebrations continued, we were shocked to receive a few more threatening phone calls at the office. We were again advised by the police not to open any suspicious parcels and to warn staff to be extra vigilant.

We had to wait until just a few days before Christmas 2001 to be officially advised of his appeal dates, on 15 and 16 January 2002, with the proviso that the case could be determined within the first day.

CHAPTER 30

FREEDOM

My wife Kath and I arrived early at the Court of Appeal on 15 January 2002. It promised to be a historic occasion, and although it was an hour or more before the scheduled hearing was due to start, we knew the place would be packed to the rafters.

As we approached the main entrance on the Strand we watched in wonder as several hundred media crews from around the world jostled for position. There was an air of nervous anticipation about the place and the cameras flashed when we neared the court entrance.

It had been a long, hard road to reach that day, and I was one of only a few people assembled who really knew just how tough it had been to seek justice. I had survived a rollercoaster series of disappointments, not to mention threats to my life, as our team battled through thick and thin to see justice done.

The corridor to the courtroom was already full of media people, and I could see Stephen waiting by the courtroom door with his parents and his sister Christine. He seemed quite relaxed and smiled. I felt absolutely terrible and was a complete wreck. We shook hands and I wished him good luck.

Finally, the courtroom doors were unlocked and the rugby scrum began. Once again, I was relieved to have been through that same situation twice before during earlier bail hearings, so I knew what to expect.

Kath and I were directed to some seats just below the bench. My *Mercury* colleague Matt Barlow was just in front of me. I could see Edward Fitzgerald and the defence team, and the Crown opponents, taking their places.

Ray, Nita and Christine were crushed between some journalists, and just behind them were Patrick McLoughlin, Matthew Parris and the vicar of Bakewell, Reverend Edmund Urquhart, who had been very supportive in the later stages of the campaign.

I thought it was a surprisingly small court for such an important case and wondered how many other historic decisions had been made in this antiquated room. There was a buzz and chatter as Stephen appeared in the dock, escorted by a security guard. Some people queried the necessity, but I knew that if the appeal failed he could theoretically have been returned to jail to continue his life sentence.

Stephen acknowledged me but showed little emotion. He nodded to his family and was still looking about the court when the three law lords, Lord Justice Pill, sitting with Mrs Justice Hallett and Mr Justice Davis, entered from a door just behind the bench.

The court rose and proceedings commenced.

Edward Fitzgerald QC highlighted the key defence claims once again. The entire scenario of what had happened in the cemetery that day was analysed in infinite detail, with the law lords occasionally seeking points of clarification. Mr Fitzgerald spoke for nearly two hours.

When Julian Bevan QC for the Crown stood up there was a strange movement of expectation and unrest within the court. Everyone wondered what he would say after such a long period of study since the bail hearing.

Within the first few seconds of his declaration, though, it became quite clear there would be no challenge to the appeal.

He spoke slowly and at times almost angrily, admitting, 'The Crown accepts there were substantial and significant procedural breaches.

'Downing should have been cautioned hours before he actually was, and he should have been offered access to a solicitor or relative.'

He also surprisingly confirmed, 'And there may have been deliberate breaches of the Judges' Rules by the police.'

Following his opening remarks there was uproar, and the court quickly adjourned for lunch. It seemed a done deal.

My wife and I grabbed a quick bite to eat and then dashed back to the court to make sure we still had our seats, and to get away from the sheer madness outside. The empty courtroom was calm, peaceful and warm.

Prosecuting QC Julian Bevan continued, and once again made a surprising admission, highlighting a catalogue of serious and damning procedural errors that he said had even prompted the judge at the original trial to raise his concerns that the confession may have been obtained, in the legal phrase, 'by oppression'.

Bevan reported on the original trial, 'He said the judge asked the defence if they were alleging impropriety on the part of the police. "No, sir," the Defence replied at the time.'

So the confession was allowed to stand, the police got away with breaching Judges' Rules and Stephen Downing was found guilty by the jury after just one hour's deliberation.

Bevan said he did not want to accuse Stephen's original defence counsel of ineptitude, but reiterated that he found it difficult to argue that the conviction was safe. Bevan finally sat down at about 3.15 p.m.

Lord Justice Pill said it would be in everybody's best interests if the judgment was made that afternoon. He ordered a short adjournment, and the judges returned just before 4 p.m.

The court rose. It became extremely quiet again, and Stephen sat hunched forward in the dock. He looked like he was straining to hear the outcome. He was fidgeting but stared straight ahead. Kath and I watched him anxiously. We were tense and nervous too.

I noticed Ray across the courtroom. He looked pale and agitated, his head bowed. Nita was sitting, tightly packed, next to him, clutching a small white handkerchief and looked tearful. There was an eerie silence as everyone waited with bated breath.

Lord Justice Pill began his summing up and referred to four main points of contention:

(1) The forensic evidence of the bloodstaining could not be relied upon.
(2) Stephen's confession was not reliable, and it was difficult to understand why it was not challenged at trial.
(3) There was nothing unusual about Stephen's appearance or demeanour at the time of the murder.
(4) Stephen denied making the statements that the police produced.

The judge then reviewed the events of the day, highlighting the anomalies and inconsistencies and explaining how the breaches of the Judge's Rules had occurred. The tension in court was now at fever pitch, and I didn't dare look up at Stephen or around the court. Finally, just before 5 p.m., Lord Justice Pill came to his conclusion.

He confirmed, 'I rule that Mr Downing's initial confessions to the police were unreliable and it follows the conviction is unsafe. We do not address ourselves to the question of whether or not Mr Downing was guilty. The Crown does not seek to uphold the conviction – the conviction is quashed!'

Stephen just stood there looking bewildered, perhaps wondering if he'd heard correctly. The security guard muttered something to him – I think she said he was 'free to go' – but he was still looking around the appeal court for answers. He smiled briefly towards his family in disbelief, as if to ask if it was finally over.

His parents gave him a thumbs-up sign and were clapping with delight, and the court had erupted into joyous celebrations. It was all so hard to believe. Stephen's family hugged each other and the tears flowed freely. Soon, a huddle of friends, supporters, MPs and journalists crowded round the family, offering their best wishes.

Kath and I hugged each other and anyone else that came near.

Everyone seemed hysterically happy, crying, smiling and shaking hands. It was a massive outpouring of relief and emotion. Tears were streaming down my cheeks and Kath too was soon overcome. I could hardly speak, and although to many it might have looked like a foregone conclusion, I had very little faith in the law, knowing as I did what should have happened back in 1973.

It looked like the law lords couldn't get out quick enough, though. They disappeared as speedily as they could behind a set of thick curtains like they were part of a magic act. I was surprised they hadn't installed a trap door for an even quicker getaway, to avoid admitting that an innocent man had been unlawfully detained for 27 years. The Derbyshire police representative left with a sour face, scurrying out of the court, his head bowed.

As the euphoria slowly began to die down, people started to ask, What next? What will happen now? And will the police reopen the case to find the real killer?

After such a drawn-out saga, it seemed something of an anti-climax. It was a vitally important verdict, yet it was delivered in such haste and without any hint of emotion or sympathy.

It was a genuine historic moment, the longest and worst miscarriage of justice in British history – and yet there was no acknowledgement of this fact from the bench, no apology that the system had got it so terribly wrong. They offered no explanation as to why Stephen had spent so many extra wasted years in jail.

*   *   *

Stephen and I shook hands briefly at the entrance, and he thanked me for all my efforts as we walked out together into the blinding illumination of a dozen arc lamps. We were almost immediately swallowed up by a crowd of well-wishers and supporters.

The noise was incredible, with hundreds of people cheering and shouting and reporters firing question after question at us both. Everyone was patting us on the back or grabbing our hands to shake, saying, 'Well done.'

Stephen displayed no anger or animosity, and when asked about his feelings towards the police, he replied, 'I hold no bitterness. They are now a different force altogether. It's all in the past.'

It only seemed to be a few minutes before someone pulled at Stephen's arm, and he was quickly guided towards the pavement where his mother was waiting. They jumped into a waiting black cab, from which they smiled and waved to the watching crowds. Then they sped away, hugging each other. After an ordeal spanning almost three decades, Stephen Downing was finally and officially a free man.

EPILOGUE

Stephen Downing's case was acknowledged as Britain's worst ever miscarriage of justice. It achieved a unique landmark ruling in European and UK law and helped change our perception of human rights.

I was pleased that my many years of hard work finally paid off and justice was belatedly done. The Court of Appeal accepted vital evidence from two former detectives, Johnson and Younger, and from Rodney Jones, who had been in charge of the re-investigation a few years later. Jones identified several officers who had allegedly given false statements, and told of an assault on him and threats made to him by a senior officer.

Another key witness, Jayne Atkins, whom I had interviewed at length but still remained in fear of her life, also gave evidence directly to the CCRC, as did Stephen Martin, the man first mentioned by Crabby some years before, who was interviewed by detective Rodney Jones. Martin's evidence challenged an important alibi and provided further background to the victim's complicated love life. His testimony was welcomed by the CCRC, along with three other Bakewell witnesses I had previously discovered, plus a relative of one of Stephen's co-workers at the time.

I appreciated the efforts of Robert Ervin, the private investigator whose shadow I had often walked in, and how his own enquiries had almost produced the crucial evidence at a first appeal. His dusty paperwork proved beneficial in tying up many loose ends and exposing the inadequacies of the original investigators.

My campaign identified and persuaded at least nine new witnesses to come forward to provide fresh evidence. It also exposed major flaws in a potentially corrupt and biased justice process. It confirmed that Stephen Downing had become a forgotten man, totally lost in a complex system prior to my inter-vention – without any hope of review. I am proud of my small contribution to society, and pleased that, if nothing else, I took the time to stop and listen to a small voice in the dark.

Following Downing's release and the quashing of his convic-tion, many reporters tried to talk to some of the men highlighted within my reports, including several witnesses allegedly seen near the cemetery: Mr Red, Syd Oulsnam, Mr Orange and Mr Blue.

They didn't have much luck, although Nick Pryer from the *Mail on Sunday* did manage a brief talk with Mr Blue, who mysteriously was never interviewed by the police despite claims of allegedly being identified as the running man. He had only previously been challenged by former Central TV reporter Allan Taylor and me.

'I was amazed when Don contacted me the first time,' Mr Blue said to Pryer, 'and I told him everything I know – which is absolutely nothing.'

More recently, when Mr Red was informed that his name kept cropping up in relation to the murder, he simply replied, 'Does it? I don't want to talk about it. I'll just have to leave it at that,' before shutting his door.

*   *   *

More than a year after his conviction was finally quashed Stephen received the first down-payment of a record two-part compensation settlement from the British government.

A few months after the appeal verdict, Derbyshire police ignored a massive national demand for an independent review of the murder and eventually conducted an expensive, half-hearted – and in my opinion totally inadequate – re-investigation called Operation Noble, which failed to address many of the key queries raised during my own enquiries.

I believe the inquiry should only have been conducted by a totally independent outside force, without any expectation of bias or prejudice. I identified several people of interest whose evidence could and should have been properly assessed back in 1973. Many of them were deliberately ignored during the original police investigation. In my opinion, the police were never co-operative, and had no intention of seeking justice, and my own enquiries constantly proved them capable of deception.

During this alleged re-investigation, the police comically introduced their own revised forensic tests – despite failing to challenge the CCRC referral and after being hammered in court by experts and even their own counsel.

They also failed to explain many anomalies about alleged false and fraudulent police statements, and why a senior police officer allegedly viciously attacked and threatened the former detective Rodney Jones, who had been in charge of the 1980s re-investigation, and had deliberately hampered his enquiries.

The police failed to offer any explanation about their initial poor performance and inadequate investigations in 1973, the debacle concerning the numerous scenes of crime errors, witness and timing anomalies, and serious flaws in the presentation of key medical evidence. It seems they were unable to explain why officers rejected fresh and contradictory evidence within days of the attack, and apparently shut down their investigative process once they had obtained an alleged 'confession' from Stephen Downing.

They also ignored, or at least failed to respond to, the severe criticism at the final appeal by their own barrister over alleged 'deliberate' actions that breached the Judges' Rules. The only thing they seemed to establish with any certainty was that many of Wendy's personal effects were later returned to her husband – as apparently much of this detail was not accurately logged in the original evidence files.

I later provided the force with a compelling list of 100 vital questions that demanded a response before they could ever claim to have conducted a genuine review of the case.

Incredibly, during Operation Noble, Stephen's mother Nita was violently attacked and seriously injured at her home by someone who told her, 'Keep your mouth shut!'

This horrific action brought back the memory of similar threats to me and my staff, and the angry warnings made to both Richard Brailsford and to Margaret Beebe and her family.

Speaking live to Sky News at Derbyshire Police HQ, following the press conference at the alleged conclusion of Operation Noble, Derbyshire's Deputy Chief Constable Bob Wood stated: 'Don Hale, the former editor of the *Matlock Mercury*, who campaigned for Mr Downing's release is someone who I greatly admire. I have never criticised him and I think he has done an extraordinary job given the difficult circumstances he has had to work under.'

Detective Superintendent David Gee, who led the allegedly inconclusive and unsuccessful re-investigation, said: 'The work of Don Hale, the author and journalist, was useful. Of course, it had to be useful, because it was a starting point for the investigation in many ways. As you are aware, Mr Hale worked tirelessly on the case over many years, often alone, trying to elicit information from people who may have been unwilling. He's been constructive towards the inquiry and we're happy this helped us at the outset.'

* * *

Further embarrassment for the Derbyshire force was revealed many years later in 2014 when Chris Clark, a former royal protection officer for the Norfolk police, discovered a copy of the original pathology report on Wendy Sewell, which purportedly identified the key officers involved and offered evidence that within days of the victim's death they knew Stephen was innocent, as the forensic and established facts regarding the attack completely contradicted his forced confession.

Following his retirement from the police, Chris Clark has become a notable cold-case detective (someone who investigates historic cases) and believes Wendy Sewell may have been another innocent victim of the Yorkshire Ripper, Peter Sutcliffe. He came across the MO for Wendy's killing while reading about my work on the Downing case, and noted many similarities to the hallmarks of the Ripper.

Chris confirmed: 'Having passed a trained eye over the Pathologist Report, I have reached the following conclusions. Wendy Sewell was originally attacked on the footpath by having a knotted garrote looped over her neck and pulled tight in order to stupefy her. This would explain the massive bruise in the region of her Adam's Apple as well as the bruising to the deep cervical muscles in the back of her neck where the garrote would be twisted in a tourniquet fashion.

'The result of this initial attack would have the effect of her dropping to her knees, where she was then rendered unconscious by repeated blows to the back of the head with the pick axe handle. She was also repeatedly kicked.

'Wendy would have been dragged from the initial site of attack which explains the findings of the bruising found on mouth, nose, cheek, nose and ear all on left side; coupled with bruises found between her left knee and ankle. This is consistent with Wendy having been dragged by her left calf area from the original site of attack to the second area.

'All of this original pathology report was gone through together with three very senior police officers involved in the case present at the post-mortem, and it beggars belief that it was not thought necessary by either the Prosecution or Defence to introduce the asphyxiation method at Stephen Downing's Trial, the later Appeal, or within Operation Noble.'

Chris believes the details may have been kept away from the original trial in 1974, along with other evidence, because it would have destroyed the prosecution case. He added, 'There is a clear pattern that vital evidence was buried at the time and since.'

Chris believes they enhance his claim that the Sewell case, and the similar killings of Jackie Ansell-Lamb and Barbara Mayo, warrant specialist investigation from a totally independent force.

Stephen Downing said, 'The news about the buried pathology report came as a complete shock. I was never asked about any kicking, strangulation or violence regarding the attack. None of these factors were ever mentioned, so it throws a whole new light on this murder and still begs the question as to who really did it.'

The case, however, despite remaining unsolved, is now severely restricted, with many Freedom of Information (FOI) requests made exempt for up to 95 years. Chris Clark confirmed, 'These severe restrictions are most unusual and are normally only related to security issues.'

*　　　*　　　*

Despite it being almost 46 years since the brutal killing of Wendy Sewell, at the time of writing this book, this complex case continues to attract much controversy and heated debate. It remains one of the country's most fascinating and scintillating murder mysteries.

ENJOYED THE BOOK?

Listen to the brand new podcast inspired by the case, featuring new evidence, interviews and insight.

Available wherever you get your podcasts

Follow us

  @reporter_pod